Theology
THAT Sticks

The Life-Changing Power
of Exceptional Hymns

Chris Anderson

Published by Church Works Media, Inc.

Cover Design: Jared Miller and Joe Tyrpak

ISBN:
978-1-7343978-6-4 (Paperback)

First Edition

Printed in the United States of America

For my beloved parents,
Charles and JoEllen Anderson,
with deep gratitude
for teaching me to love Christian music

"Other than the preaching of God's Word, the church has no more powerful teaching tool at her disposal than psalms, hymns, and spiritual songs. Scripture commands the people of God never to cease 'teaching and admonishing one another' with our music (Colossians 3:16; Ephesians 5:19). Chris Anderson has a passion for sound hymnology. He has given the church some powerful, doctrinally rich songs. This volume is a thoughtful compendium of biblical reasons why the teaching of sound doctrine through hymns is so vital to the life and well-being of the church. It is an important work with no parallel that I am aware of, and it meets a pressing need for the church of our generation."

—John MacArthur, Pastor, Grace Community Church of Sun Valley, California, Preacher on *Grace to You* Radio Broadcast, and World-Renowned Author

"If you need help moving beyond worship songs with trite tunes and sloppy theology, Chris Anderson—a seasoned pastor, experienced church musician, and excellent hymn-writer—offers tremendous help. In his clear, wise, winsome, witty, generous, thorough, insightful, practical, thought-provoking, prophetic, Trinity-centered, and church-focused book, he offers numerous examples of the most biblical, beautiful, edifying, Christ-saturated, and God-exalting songs we should sing each Sunday. Moreover, and more importantly, he grounds his observations, examples, insights, and advice directly in what the Bible teaches about congregational singing. A treasure-trove of truths! A gift to the church. A magnificent must-read."

—Douglas Sean O'Donnell, Senior Vice President of Bible Editorial, Crossway Books, and Author of *God's Lyrics*

"If there is one message this generation needs to hear, it is precisely the message of this book, written from the heart of an experienced pastor and gifted hymn-writer. Chris Anderson is in the great line of pastoral hymn-writers that have edified the church through sermon and song across history. His message in this book is simple: It matters what we sing! As churches, our songs should express the full menu of Christian experience, inspire us to worship our great triune God, and, above all, be full of biblical truth. Thanks, Chris, for this timely reminder!"

—Conrad Mbewe, Pastor, Kabwata Baptist Church and Founding Chancellor of African Christian University in Lusaka, Zambia

"I read *Theology That Sticks* both as a pastor and as an adjunct professor of pastoral theology. In both roles, I have found a resource that I will reach for first on the topic of worship. Chris has skillfully culled works on this topic—past and present—and has produced a winsome yet meaty work that is now my favorite. The inclusion of 'Bonus Tracks' in the appendix is now a cheat-sheet for me on each topic as well. Having a pastor, not an academic, write this book is a win for us. It is church history, theology, and hymnody... with the smell of sheep on it."

—Jim Newcomer, Pastor, Calvary Baptist Church of Ypsilanti, Michigan, and Adjunct Professor of Pastoral Theology

"Chris has given the church a thorough, theologically rich resource for recovering the glorious place of song in our worship gatherings. It's a much-needed, practical, and reasoned challenge to remember what, how, and why we are called to sing."

—Steve Green, Award-Winning Christian Recording Artist

"Chris captures so well the urgency of corporate worship. It's an unmistakable message that's pastoral, winsome, and direct: What we sing about God is eternally important."

—Dan Kreider, Music Minister, Grace Immanuel Bible Church, Jupiter, Florida, and Editor of *Sing the Wonders* and *Psalms for the Church*

"*Theology That Sticks* is proof that Chris Anderson loves Christian music and theology. He has filled his book with biblical content about church music that interacts with a broad selection of theologians, musicians, and cultural commentators. Through winsome writing and well-placed questions, Chris helps his readers consider the critical nature of loving both music and theology."

—Will and Christy Galkin, Gospel Grace Church, Salt Lake City, Utah, Plant4theGospel, and Galkin Evangelistic Team

"Christians are a singing people. Our songs both express our devotion and shape us as disciples. Song selection, therefore, is a weighty task. In this warm, accessible, and persuasive book, Chris Anderson offers invaluable guidance on how to choose songs that exalt our triune God, edify His people, and contribute to evangelizing the lost. Packed with a plethora of insightful quotes and loaded with lists of hymns in every category imaginable, this volume is one I wish every pastor, church music leader, and believer would read. It gave me several new practical ideas for my weekly song-leading ministry, and more importantly, it spurred me to long more deeply for the day when all who trust in Christ will join our voices in the heavenly anthem that drowns all music but its own."

—Matt Merker, Author, Hymn-Writer, and Director of Creative Resources and Training for Getty Music

"Hymns are a gift from the Lord to the church. What Christian hasn't had their heart stirred by strong doctrinal lyrics set to music that befits our holy God? Our brother Chris Anderson has reminded us why the church needs worshipful music that is a deep and powerful elixir for our faith. Filled with rich quotes, anecdotes, and biblical truth, the book continuously drew my mind to the great hymns of our faith over and over as I read. Every pastor and worship minister needs to read Chris' helpful case for true worship grounded in the Word. For some it will act as a necessary spiritual alignment, and for others it will reaffirm their commitment to biblical worship in song."

—Richard Bargas, Executive Director, IFCA International

"I have always been amazed at how lyrics of a song will stick in my mind so much easier than memorizing verses. That's one reason this book is so important. Scriptural, historical, theological, and practical, this book helps us all think about what we sing, how we sing it, why we sing it, and so much more. Chris brings clarity to a complicated area, provoking thought on how we can serve others well and worship God faithfully."

—Thomas White, President, Cedarville University

"This book was needed a long time ago! Songs that we sing during our worship services carry in themselves huge power to influence souls. Songs and hymns are ideas, amplified with music. This is why you cannot overestimate the importance of a correct approach to what we sing in our churches. Chris Anderson does an excellent job presenting this issue in colorful detail, with the convincing power of the Word of God. This is why this book will be helpful not just for pastors but for everyone in the church."

—Alexey Kolomiytsev, Pastor, Word of Grace Bible Church, Battle Ground, Washington, and Head of Word of Grace Ministries

"We have used Chris' hymns and writings in our ministry for many years and do it with great joy. We have always appreciated his careful, deep, theological, thought-provoking style. Whether we are leading a congregation in worship, preparing an arrangement with a small group, or recording for a publication, Chris' theologically rich texts have impacted us in a profound way. In a similar way, *Theology That Sticks* will encourage you to think, consider, and evaluate your choices of hymns used in worship with God's people. Let us not casually approach this highly important aspect of our ministry!"

—Matt and Christy Taylor, Recording Artists and Ministry Leaders at Bethany Baptist Church, Brevard, North Carolina, and The Wilds Christian Camp

"The spiritual health of any church can often be diagnosed by the songs it sings. Weak worship songs reflect shallow theology in the pulpit. But strong worship songs reveal sound doctrine in the preaching. Chris Anderson has provided us with a helpful resource in his book, *Theology That Sticks*, to help us navigate these often turbulent waters. Biblically based, doctrinally sound, and pastorally sensitive, this well-studied book on how our theology shapes our doxology is one I am certain that you will want to read."

—Steven J. Lawson, President of OnePassion Ministries, Professor at The Master's Seminary, Teaching Fellow for Ligonier Ministries, and Lead Preacher, Trinity Bible Church of Dallas, Texas

"I've always known Chris Anderson to direct his readers to ponder God's grace—grace displayed in salvation, providence, and artistry. Church music is yet another grace, and I found his articulation on this subject to be one of the most beneficial deliveries for our generation. His anecdotes are witty, his research thorough, and his insights invaluable. His pastor's heart lovingly urges churches to insist on scriptural depth and resist shallow trends. But he doesn't address only church leaders in consideration of their service planning; he writes to every living saint who is given the grace of singing with God's people. Read this book—from start to finish, you'll enjoy every moment."

—Molly Ijames, Composer, Arranger, Pianist, and Publisher at mollychurchmusic.com

"A healthy church is always a worshiping church—a church overflowing with joyful, expressive love and a desire for authentic ministry. To that end, Chris Anderson has done the local church a great service in *Theology That Sticks*. This book should be read by every pastor and worship leader, as well as every church member and worship team member. Chris does a masterful job of articulating the value of singing our theology in gospel-centered, corporate worship; and he equips church leaders and Christians with practical steps to building a deeply theological worship ministry. These pages will help you and your church take worship more seriously, creatively, and biblically."

—Cary Schmidt, Pastor, Emmanuel Baptist Church, Newington, Connecticut, and Author of *Stop Trying: How to Receive—Not Achieve—Your Real Identity*

"Since there are hundreds of outstanding hymns, the church should not be content to sing shallow songs that came out ten minutes ago (or ten decades ago) and that nobody will request to sing on their deathbed. Chris Anderson wisely and engagingly counsels us what to sing."

—Andy Naselli, Associate Professor of Systematic Theology and New Testament, Bethlehem College and Seminary, Minneapolis, Minnesota, and a Pastor, Bethlehem Baptist Church

"In my little corner of Christianity, we're often known more for what we're against than what we're for. Anderson's book gives us something we can really be for. Each chapter is full of helpful principles the believer can thoughtfully apply and be much the better for it."

—Ben Everson, Evangelist and A Cappella Recording Artist

"Few gifts have been more mismanaged and misunderstood by the church than God's good gift of music. What was given by the Lord to teach, unify, and strengthen the body of Christ has all too often proven instead to be divisive, as too many have focused on preference at the expense of purpose. In *Theology That Sticks*, Chris Anderson helps the church view music through a biblical lens and recapture the joy and blessing found in congregational singing. As he shows churches how to select songs that best teach sound doctrine and edify God's people, Chris keeps the focus of this volume on glorifying the Lord rather than catering to man's opinions. This book will instruct the reader in a helpful way and strengthen the local congregation that puts these truths into practice."

—Michael Staton, Pastor, First Baptist Church of Mustang, Oklahoma

"*Theology That Sticks* feels like a little hideout from the worship wars, a rock of biblical common ground for us all, a feeling of rest from conflict. I don't know if Chris set out to do this, but he sure seems to me to have transcended the worship wars. He has listed out in his clear, effusive style a long series of biblical truths that any serious Christian can and must incorporate into worship. He has helpful application sections at the end of each chapter, too, where he talks to musicians as well as to the people in the pew. And he's a diligent collector of pithy wisdom from other Christian voices. During my years as a church music director, my church loved Anderson's richly doctrinal, modern hymns. I'm not at all surprised that he had all this theology sticking in his mind."

—Mark Ward, Editor, *Bible Study Magazine*

"This is one of the best, most balanced books I have ever read on church music. Chris challenges you to think through why you sing and what you sing in church and gives practical tips for each church size. He is passionate that God be glorified and that the same care given to the preaching of God's Word be given to the congregational worship of God through singing. A must-read for any church leader!"

—Jim Tillotson, President of Faith Baptist Bible College, Ankeny, Iowa

"While godly worship is a wonderful end in itself, true worshipers of God eventually discover that worship produces transformative outcomes for the worshipers themselves. Enter *Theology That Sticks*, a thoughtful book bristling with biblical guidance designed to help Christians worship God with theological depth and power, in a way that both expresses and enriches the heart of the worshiper, redounding to God's glory. Chris Anderson's book is a timely arrival for students of Christian worship, be they worship leaders, pastors, or laypersons who desire to grow in worship. I recommend this book and trust it will benefit you as much as it has benefited me."

—Milton Vincent, Pastor of Cornerstone Fellowship Bible Church, Riverside, California, and Author of *A Gospel Primer for Christians: Learning to See the Glories of God's Love*

"Chris Anderson's book *Theology That Sticks* is a compelling, irenic call to examine and improve the church's worship and life. Music matters, particularly the hymns and songs that accurately communicate the truth of the Scriptures by their lyrics and poetic structure. Chris gives practical, positive guidance for the church's hymnology. In a day when 'worship wars' entangle the church, this book flies above the fray for the benefit of all."

—David E. Strope, Interim National Representative, General Association of Regular Baptist Churches

"This book has filled me up with refreshing reminders of Christian essentials needing to be passed on to the next generation. *Theology That Sticks* is flooded with Bible 'whys' for deliberate scrutiny of music choices—at church and at home. As a Christian wife, mother, and music artist myself, I appreciate what this book has done to deepen my commitment to careful theology, which I pray spills over into richer songwriting. Chris' gracious tone, engaging writing style, and sprinkled-in humor made this read not only accessible but also enjoyable. Favorite line describing what we should do with a shabby, shallow, Christian song: 'Drop it like day-old sushi from a truck stop.' Point taken!"

—Heather Schopf, Composer, Forever Be Sure Music

"Great hymns make our theology sing. They give voice to the truth and put the truth in the voices of God's people. I am grateful for the chorus of theologians who are giving such care and attention to the hymnody of the church. This book will be a help to all who want to seriously consider this well-deserved subject."

—Matt Boswell, Hymn-Writer, Pastor of The Trails Church, Celina, Texas, and Assistant Professor of Christian Music and Worship, The Southern Baptist Theological Seminary

CONTENTS

Foreword
What Language Shall I Borrow?   i

PART I
WHAT WE SING MATTERS

Introduction
Sing Great Songs   3

Chapter 1
The Sticking Power of Christian Music   11

PART 2
A HYMN GRID FROM THE
NEW TESTAMENT

Chapter 2
Sing Songs That Are Biblical   25

Chapter 3
Sing Songs That Are Doctrinal   41

Chapter 4
Sing Songs That Are Christian   55

Chapter 5
Sing Songs That Are Trinitarian   69

Chapter 6
Sing Songs That Are Congregational   85

Chapter 7
Sing Songs That Are Unifying   103

PART 3

A HYMN GRID FROM THE PSALMS

Chapter 8
Sing Songs That Are Inspired   121

Chapter 9
Sing Songs That Are Diverse   137

Chapter 10
Sing Songs That Are Emotive   155

Chapter 11
Sing Songs That Are Experiential   171

Chapter 12
Sing Songs That Are Beautiful   187

Chapter 13
Sing Songs That Are Doxological   207

PART 4

ADDITIONAL RESOURCES

Appendix A
"Bonus Tracks": Wise Words on the Theme of Each Chapter   225

Appendix B
Tips for Singing with Understanding   263

Appendix C
Tips for Aspiring Hymn-Writers   265

Appendix D
Tips for Worship Leaders, Musicians, and A/V Techies   269

Appendix E
The Hymns and Poems of Chris Anderson   277

Appendix F
Sample Thematic Service Orders   285

Acknowledgments   291

Bibliography   293

Scripture Index   311

Name Index   317

Hymn Index   323

WHAT LANGUAGE SHALL I BORROW?

R. ALBERT MOHLER, JR.

I have no memory of life without hymns. Born to Christian parents, taken to worship in a faithful gospel church, and surrounded by the singing of hymns, I was never far from the great hymns of the Christian faith. I knew two books of worship. The first was the Bible, the very Word of God. The second was a hymnal, the song book of the church. Before I would read, I had learned to find my way in both the Bible and the hymnal.

In the most private area of my study, I am surrounded by a host of Bibles and hymnals at close hand. I turn to the Bibles constantly, and I turn to the hymnals often. When I was twelve, I was presented with my own personal copy of the hymnal, with my name inscribed in gold letters on the front cover. The inscription inside cited Colossians 3:16, and the apostle Paul's instruction to "let the word of Christ dwell in you richly in all wisdom; teaching and admonishing one another in psalms and hymns and spiritual songs, singing with grace in your hearts to the Lord."

When I was a boy, the Bible and the hymnal sat on the table beside my bed. I was never confused about the difference between the Holy Scriptures, verbally inspired by God, and the hymns, written by believers in order to sing praises to God. But I knew I needed both books.

Elisabeth Elliot once spoke of the night that her husband and four other missionaries went missing, knowing in her heart that they were likely all dead. She was right, and the missionaries had been killed even as they had attempted to share the gospel. In the terror of that long night, Elisabeth Elliot said that she was kept sane by the discipline of singing the great hymns of the Christian faith in her head and in her heart.

In moments of distress, I have felt the same comfort. Somehow, the combination of tune and text enables my heart to be stilled. The words fall together as the familiar tunes carry them along.

I exult in God as Christ's people sing the great hymns of the faith in corporate worship. Something beyond measure and beyond imagination takes place when a congregation of believers unites in the singing of a worthy hymn. Biblical truth settles in our souls, joy emerges in our hearts, and a foretaste of future glory is realized in our midst. How does that happen?

God made human beings in His own image, and we are designed to sing and to be affected by music. Christ's redeemed people are commanded to encourage one another in "psalms and hymns and spiritual songs." We do not merely sing alone; we sing in the glad company of God's redeemed people as we worship God, confess the faith, teach doctrine, counsel hearts, and set Christ's people toward obedience. At times, we comfort one another by reading from God's Word and by singing hymns that give us words when we would otherwise have no words.

We are musical creatures, to be sure, but we are also made to be linguistic creatures, dependent upon language. Our minds crave words, but where will we find the right words? Thankfully, the right words are given to us in the Bible. Insofar as a hymn rightly presents biblical truth, those words of truth are combined with tune and set to meter in such a way that truth marches into our hearts. When Christians sing together, that truth marches into our hearts—together.

A hymn, now cherished for centuries, asks the right question: "What language shall I borrow, to thank Thee, dearest Friend?" That hymn is "O Sacred Head, Now Wounded," which can be traced at least as far back as the sixteenth century. It was translated from Latin by the German hymn master Paul Gerhardt, set to tune by Hans Hassler, and harmonized by Johann Sebastian Bach. My own church sings that glorious hymn in English.

We all borrow language. We must borrow language, and even as the first language we employ comes from the Bible, we also borrow from the hymns of the faith.

In this timely book, Chris Anderson underlines the importance of hymns in the life of the church and the urgency of singing biblical truth and sound doctrine. He exhorts the church to sing "exceptional" hymns. What makes such hymns exceptional? They are exceptionally biblical, doctrinal, congregational, beautiful, and doxological. As this timely book reminds us, there are even more criteria that point to truly exceptional hymns, and all are important.

Exceptional hymns may be old (most are) or new, but you can be sure that the most exceptionally faithful hymns are those to which the believing church turns time and again—in times of joy and in times of grief, in times of triumph and in moments of distress. In this book you will find great instruction and encouragement in the hymns. Read the book. Sing the hymns. Let your heart be glad.

In the light of day and in the shadows of the night, tune your heart to sing God's praise. I thank God for giving us a faith to sing.

March 19, 2022
Louisville, Kentucky

"Christianity is the religion of spiritual song. It inherited a magnificent psalmody, but it has also given birth to an invaluable hymnology, as well as the art of harmony to which modern music owes the greater part of its boundless wealth. Outside Christendom, religious music has hardly shed the primitive, animistic character of rhythmic noise, and children's songs are almost unknown. But the Christian religion found in music a congenial ally, ready to aid its progress in the individual heart, and in the world's history. The thought of God, of Christ and His cross, of the Christian graces, and of immortal life, is entirely consonant with musical expression.

Hebrew psalmody and Christian hymnology have served as wings to bear the Gospel far and wide over the earth.... Reformation and Revival have always owed a great measure of their power to the inspiring and truth-conveying aid of music. It has feathered the gospel arrow for quick flight to the hearts of sinning, sorrowing men."

John Harrington Edwards, *God and Music*

PART I

WHAT WE SING MATTERS

"Oh sing to the Lord a new song; sing to the Lord, all the earth!"
—PSALM 96:1

"Christianity has always had a special love affair with music.
The Scriptures are shot through with music,
as is life in the church."
—MICHAEL REEVES[1]

"Take heed that what you sing with your mouths,
you believe in your hearts,
and what you believe in your hearts
you show forth in your works."
—FOURTH COUNCIL OF CARTHAGE, 4ᵀᴴ CENTURY

---

1.   Michael Reeves, *Delighting in the Trinity: An Introduction to the Christian Faith* (Downers Grove, IL: 2012), 58.

SING GREAT SONGS

"Why don't we sing less and get on with the good stuff?"

That's the question I got one Sunday morning from a well-meaning church member who said she wanted preaching, not music.

I could have been flattered. Instead, I told her what I believe is the truth: that singing *is* the good stuff, or at least part of it. I explained that singing exceptional hymns is life-changing. And I described singing as one of the most important things we do—as churches, as families, and as Christians.

"Why are we singing so many new songs?"

This question came from another person I pastored—one who loved congregational singing. But he wanted to sing familiar songs, not new ones. Frankly, new music worried him.

I told him that I understood his concern and explained that it's not our goal to be either traditional or contemporary. We're not moving left or right. We're just moving *deeper*, intentionally singing songs that celebrate sound doctrine and present it in beautiful, moving ways. Our church wants to feast on the very best Christ-centered songs, regardless of their age or authors. And we're doing this because we believe our church and its members will be the better for it.

Every pastor or worship leader has conversations like these. And I imagine that most Christians ponder questions like, "Why in the world are we singing *this*?!" Although the "worship wars" weary me, meaningful conversations about music thrill me. People care about what we sing? People are taking worship seriously? *Great!*

My goal in this book is to address these and other questions. Specifically, I want to consider what Scripture says about the kinds of songs Christians should sing. And I want to provide a sort of "grid" that helps believers measure songs intentionally and objectively rather than sentimentally or randomly.

Now, decisions to sing some songs and pass over others are already being made. Every church chooses its songs for every Lord's Day. Many Christians select a playlist when they take a road trip, go for a jog, or ask Alexa to play something. So... *How do you do it?* What factors do you consider?

Let's think back to your last worship service with your local church. How many songs did your congregation sing? Four to six, give or take a few? That's not a lot—especially when you consider the tens of thousands of worship songs available to us in the English language. Each time we say yes to one, we say no to all the others. I agree with Arthur E. Gregory's statement, penned over a century ago: "There is no part of public worship which calls for more serious and intelligent consideration than the selection of hymns."[2]

So I write as a pastor for fellow pastors and worship leaders. The songs we choose are vital to the health of our churches. Yet, we too often neglect this essential part of church life. In some churches, congregational singing is merely a "warm-up" for the preaching. In other churches, singing is vastly *more important* than the preaching. Music is often *the* reason people choose to attend a church—or to leave a church. And more times than not, songs are selected because of their popularity, their tune, their energy, and so on. Our singing needs help. Lig Duncan laments, "If there is an area

---

2.   Arthur E. Gregory, *The Hymn-Book of the Modern Church* (London: Charles H. Kelly, 1904), 17.

in special need of reformation in the worship of evangelical churches, it is congregational singing."[3]

I'm grateful that Keith and Kristyn Getty have devoted their lives to addressing this need, not only through their music, but through their teaching and influence. They write,

> Though maybe misunderstood, regularly a bone of contention, and often under-practiced, congregational singing is one of the greatest and most beautiful tools we have been given to declare God's "excellencies," strengthening His church and sharing His glory in the world.[4]

Agreed!

I also write as a dad for my four amazing daughters and for my fellow parents. Moms and dads, you're passing on a spiritual and musical legacy to your children. I thank God that my parents passed on to me a love for the Lord, for the Scriptures, for the lost, for the church, and for Christian music. I want to leave my kids a heritage of great music as well. That's why I've introduced them to Bach and Beethoven, to "Schindler's List" and "Gabriel's Oboe," to Nat King Cole and Phil Collins, and so on. But most importantly, that's why I've tried to surround them with music that points their attention to Christ. It's fine that they have a reasonable familiarity with various aspects of secular music. But it's *essential* to me that my daughters know great Christian music—by heart. I want them to be nourished by the songs of the saints. And, someday, I want them to teach my grandchildren great hymns, gospel songs, praise choruses, spirituals, and performance music.

---

3. Ligon Duncan, endorsement for Keith and Kristyn Getty, *Sing!: How Worship Transforms Your Life, Family, and Church* (Nashville, TN: B&H Publishing Group, 2017).
4. Keith Getty and Kristyn Getty, *Sing!: How Worship Transforms Your Life, Family, and Church* (Nashville, TN: B&H Publishing Group, 2017), 21-22.

Collin Morris, the BBC Head of Religious Broadcasting in the 1980s, said that "hymns plant spiritual time-bombs in the mind."[5] Children learn truth even before they understand it—but it will surely "go off" in the future. And so I ask you, as a fellow parent: Are you filling your home with exceptional Christian music? I'd like to help you do so.

Mainly, I write as a Christian for fellow Christians. Singing is a huge part of the spiritual life of every single believer. Singing in a choir is voluntary; singing in a church—a good, Bible-preaching church—is mandatory. Great Christian music is a means of grace. It helps you grow in your faith, delight in your God, and even combat your sin. The songs we sing shape us. It's important, then, that you carefully choose the songs that will make up the soundtrack of your Christian life. And as I've already noted, you're *already* choosing your life's songs, just maybe not as intentionally as you should. To quote the ancient crusader's counsel to Indiana Jones, "You must choose. But choose wisely." I want to help you do that.

Now, if I were you, I'd be asking, "What gives *this guy* the right to tell people what to sing?" In one sense, nothing. I have no inherent authority. I do care, though. I've thought about Christian music deeply for most of my life, and I want to do some good. So let me introduce myself.

I'm a pastor. I'm promoting missions with Biblical Ministries Worldwide now. But for the last twenty-five years, I've been a pastor. I started Tri-County Bible Church in Madison, Ohio, in 1997, and I pastored Killian Hill Baptist Church in Lilburn, Georgia, for nine years, from 2012 through 2021. The former started with a small core of people, and our musical abilities were limited at first. Over time, TCBC has become a great singing church, by God's grace. KHBC has a deep bench of gifted musicians. My point is, I've listened to a handful of believers sing to a badly tuned piano in a dirty high school auditorium with dirtier words carved into the backs of the seats, and I've listened to a well-rehearsed choir leading an eager body of believers in song. To repurpose Philippians

---

5.   Quoted in Timothy Dudley-Smith, *A Functional Art: Reflections of a Hymn Writer* (Oxford, England: Oxford University Press, 2017), 144.

4:12, "I know how to be brought low, and I know how to abound." And I've loved it all!

I'm also a hymn-writer, publishing over fifty hymns through Church Works Media, in a variety of hymnals, and with several choral music companies.[6] I've written songs like "His Robes for Mine" and "I Run to Christ" with Greg Habegger, "Reformation Hymn" with Bob Kauflin, "You Are Always Good" with Jonathan Hamilton. I've been privileged to collaborate with gifted musicians like Dan Forrest, Molly Ijames, Paul Keew, Paul S. Jones, James Koerts, and Richard Nichols. Each time, my main contribution has been lyrics, not music. As far as those who have most influenced me, my hymn-writing heroes are Isaac Watts, Charles Wesley, Bob Kauflin, Stuart Townend, and Keith and Kristyn Getty.

Ultimately, I'm just a music junkie. I've played trombone in a marching band, pep band, Dixieland band, jazz band, pit band, and several symphonic bands. I started singing in the church choir when I was in elementary school—the lone male in a sea of sopranos. I was privileged to be part of a great college choir, performing pieces like John Rutter's *Requiem* and Felix Mendelssohn's *Elijah* under exceptional conductors.

As a listener, I have very eclectic tastes. I love Bach, and I like Phil Collins. I cut my teeth on music as diverse as Air Supply (I know, I know), Journey, and Run DMC. Thanks to my amazing parents, I grew up with constant exposure to hymns and gospel songs, praise choruses (thanks, Maranatha! and Integrity's Hosanna!), children's songs (from a songbook named Psalty and a pirate named Patch), CCM (Steve Green, Keith Green, and GLAD helped disciple me as a teen), and conservative Christian music (kudos to the Pettit and Galkin teams, The Wilds, and Majesty Music). Like I said: *eclectic.* You don't want to play me in *Name that Tune* or *Encore.*

I share these details to dispel any notion that I'm a musical elitist or a worship watchdog. I still enjoy a wide variety of music. But hymns are my first love, and I want them to be yours as well. You will probably come to some different conclusions from mine, and that's fine. What I really

6.   My hymns and poems are listed in Appendix E.

want to do is to *provoke thought*—to help Christians and churches choose worship songs on purpose, based on biblical principles.

I'm hopeful that the book will be useful for Bible studies, Sunday School classes, and small groups. To that end, I have avoided unnecessarily specialized terminology, and I have included reflection and discussion questions called "Grace Notes" which I hope will prove helpful.

I have also made extensive (perhaps excessive?) use of quotations throughout the book. Many have spoken so well on the subject of worship music—people from different denominations, different sides of the "worship wars," different specialties, and different eras. At times, my rabbit holes had rabbit holes as I chased down biblical texts, hymn histories, and thoughts on Christian aesthetics. I learned a lot, so why not share the jewels I uncovered with those who read this book? My hope is that the many quotations and citations will provide readers with a collection of insights and sources for further study. It was inefficient to include every quotation that caught my eye in the body of the book, so I've shared some "Bonus Tracks" related to each chapter in Appendix A.

In Appendix B I've offered "Tips for Singing with Understanding" as a quick checklist for worshiping more intentionally. I've also included appendices that aim to help those with special ministry aspirations or responsibilities: "Tips for Aspiring Hymn-Writers" (Appendix C) and "Tips for Worship Leaders, Accompanists, and A/V Techies" (Appendix D).

Throughout the book I share bulleted lists of my favorite hymns on specific themes. Think of them as "sticky hymns"—worthwhile songs that have pasted themselves into my memory. I readily admit that the lists are arbitrary and inadequate. You may just skip over them. But I hope they will supply real-life models of the principles I'm discussing. For a more exhaustive and regularly updated list of exceptional hymns on specific themes, I encourage you to make regular use of a resource page from Church Works Media: stickyhymns.com.

Let me give a few more clarifications. First, I'm focusing primarily on hymns, not on performance music by Christian artists. My phone is filled with music that doesn't really sing well in church. There's nothing wrong with that, but that's not where I'm focusing my attention here. Still, most of the principles I present will apply to all Christian music, whether you're singing it in church or listening to it in your car.

Second, I'm focusing on texts much more than tunes. I value tunes, and I'm awed by those who have the musical expertise to write them well. A poor tune can sink a song, just as an excellent tune can prop up feeble lyrics. But it's the *words* that carry most of the meaning. Frankly, many conservative churches that wring their hands over guitars and drums are singing some very shallow lyrics. We can and should do better. Since lyrics are my area of expertise, that's what most of this book will address.

Finally, I've tried to write in an intentionally positive way. Everyone knows that church music is a divisive issue. This sad truth was illustrated to me when I entered "worship" as a search topic on the sermon archive site sermonaudio.com. Most of the sermons I found were calls to arms, not calls to worship. Similarly, several of the books I've read on church music are unhelpfully combative. I appreciate the writers' passion for the subject, but I'd occasionally wince at their "red meat" comments. While addressing some of the weaknesses in the songs we sing is necessary, I want to highlight what is excellent, not just critique what is lacking.

Ironically, this book was written during the COVID pandemic of 2020 and 2021. Many churches didn't meet for months at a time. Some states forbade singing in public services. Most choirs took a long sabbatical. Almost all Christians missed out on at least some services, and one of the things we missed most was singing hymns of praise to God together. My hope is that one result of our frustrating time apart will be that we value assembling and singing together more than ever. We need the church. And we need great church music.

Enough introduction! May you be moved to worship our Savior as you read about the life-changing power of hymns—*theology that sticks*.

"Sing to him, sing praises to him; tell of all his wondrous works!"
—1 CHRONICLES 16:9

"We know by experience that singing has great force and vigor to move and inflame the hearts of men to invoke and praise God with a more vehement and ardent zeal. Care must always be taken that the song be neither light nor frivolous, but that it have weight and majesty."
—JOHN CALVIN[7]

"It is not enough to say music is an expression of identity; it is part of the way identity is formed. In short, we do not simply make music, to some extent music makes us."
—JEREMY S. BEGBIE[8]

7.   John Calvin, preface to *The Genevan Psalter*, 1565.
8.   Jeremy S. Begbie, *Resounding Truth: Christian Wisdom in the World of Music* (Grand Rapids, MI: Baker Academic, 2007), 46.

CHAPTER 1

THE STICKING POWER OF CHRISTIAN MUSIC

I don't like music. I love it.

Music is one of God's great gifts to humanity. Scripture tells us that God sings (Zephaniah 3:17). And because we're made in God's image, we sing too. Part of the *imago Dei*—the image of God in people—is that we're hardwired to love the creativity, artistry, and emotion of music.

Especially in the twenty-first century, music is the soundtrack of everyday life. I'm rarely in the car, the study, or even the dining room without some background music playing. Music makes normal life better. Need convincing? Google the countless sports highlights that become comically awesome when you add Celine Dion's "My Heart Will Go On" to them. Or, conversely, watch the last scene of *Star Wars* with John Williams' brilliant music removed. It's comically awkward and flat. Life is better with music.

THE MARVEL OF MUSIC

Part of the power of music is its staggering breadth. Although we have just twelve basic notes in the Western scale, they are capable of astoundingly diverse sounds, moods, and messages. For an illustration of music's majestic breadth, think of a symphony, where woodwinds, brass, strings, and percussion all join forces for one great purpose. Within each of those groups, you have sounds as distinct as a piccolo and a bassoon, a trumpet and a tuba, a violin and an enormous string bass, a xylophone and timpani. Yet, they merge to make mesmerizing music!

If symphonic music isn't your thing (and I can't imagine why it wouldn't be!), imagine a bluegrass group if you'd like. Look at the diversity of a banjo, a mandolin, a string bass, a harmonica, a violin (er, a *fiddle*), a pair of spoons, and maybe even a washboard. (Thank you, *Hee Haw*, for boyhood lessons.) All of these instruments and household items converge to play a single song—separately, but together. Amazing! Through melody and harmony, rhythm and tempo, musicians are able to contribute widely varying parts to a much greater whole.

That's all grand. But add words? BAM! Everything becomes even *more* powerful. A love song—or a break-up song—can stir deep emotions of devotion or loss. A patriotic song can stir different, even stronger emotions. (American readers: Can you make it through Lee Greenwood's "God Bless the USA" or Epcot's "Golden Dream" without tears? If so, *what is wrong with you?!*)

THE UNIQUE POWER OF SACRED MUSIC

Yes, music is powerful. But there's no music so powerful as music that focuses on the very Source of music—our Creator. Music about God doesn't just tickle the ear or stir the heart; it searches the soul. Powerfully. Deeply. And broadly.

Allen P. Ross captures the power of religious music well:

> The use of music in worship is a natural extension of its force in life. It elevates the singers above their mundane experiences by heightening the tone and expression of their speech and thereby increases the

celebration. It also intensifies the pathos of prayers and laments, serving as a powerfully therapeutic way of dealing with the dark riddles of life.[9]

Sacred music can be *triumphant*, like "Crown Him with Many Crowns." What's better than singing that on Easter Sunday? The text is mirrored and magnified by the tune, moving upward, step by step, until its glorious climax!

Sacred music can be *contemplative*, like "Before the Throne of God Above" or "It Is Well with My Soul." I'll not forget gathering with a group of believers around the bed of our friend Linda as she neared the end of her battle with cancer. She didn't want a sermon—she wanted us to *sing*, so a group of around thirty of her fellow church members met in her home and worshiped with her. Linda barely had the strength to sing along, but she tried. And when, at her request, we sang "It Is Well," she signed it, using every bit of her energy to lift her brittle hands in praise. My teen daughters wept, and we all learned unforgettable life lessons about faith, unconditional praise, and great hymns. Memorized truth—theology that sticks—gave Linda a song to sing in praise and faith as she walked through the valley of the shadow of death. Books don't do that. Jokes don't do that. Even pop songs don't do that. But hymns do.

James Montgomery Boice expressed the power of sacred music with an enthusiasm that he could barely contain: "Music is a gift from God that allows us to express our deepest heart responses to God and his truth in meaningful and memorable ways. It is a case of our hearts joining with our minds to say, 'Yes! Yes! Yes!' to the truths we are embracing."[10]

I love that. I agree. "Yes! Yes! Yes!" And Boice was a *Presbyterian*!

9.   Allen P. Ross, *Recalling the Hope of Glory: Biblical Worship from the Garden to the New Creation* (Grand Rapids: Kregel, 2006), 254.

10. Quoted in Paul S. Jones, *Singing and Making Music: Issues in Church Music Today* (Phillipsburg, NJ: P&R Publishing, 2006), 112.

WE NEED TO SING EXCEPTIONAL MUSIC

Because sacred music has such tremendous power, we need to use songs that are exceptional. Seek the best and leave the rest. Dump the dross. Chuck the chaff. Does that sound too negative? Calvin M. Johansson writes, "The fact is that for two thousand years church music has been carefully screened."[11] It was a good thing for hymns to have to make it through an editorial sieve before getting into hymnals. We live in a world in which people are obsessively careful about what they put into their mouths. Fine. But what about what comes *out* of your mouth? What about what enters your ears, and thereby, your permanent memory?

As I already noted, there are *thousands* of songs available to churches and individuals. Saying yes to one is saying no to every other one. It stands to reason, then, that you should choose what's best. The goal of this book is to help define "what's best"—to provide a biblical and practical grid for selecting *great* songs to sing together as a church and to serenade yourself with on your commute.

It's actually pretty simple. Identify the best songs and sing them. That's it. (I once went off-script when I presented this information at a conference workshop and just said, *"Don't sing dumb stuff!"* Alas, that would have made a great book title.)

Why do I believe this issue is nothing less than urgent for the modern church? That's easy. *We need to sing great hymns because hymns teach people how to think about God.* The songs you sing in church *teach*—for better or for worse. Some teach doctrinal truth. Some teach doctrinal error. Some teach that we value nostalgia. Some teach that we value tradition. Some, I'm convinced, teach that we value carousels and polkas. But they teach, nevertheless. As the Gettys warn, "A good melody with unhelpful words is a powerful and deadly combination."[12]

---

11. Calvin M. Johansson, *Music & Ministry: A Biblical Counterpoint* (Peabody, MA: Hendrickson Publishers, 1984), 154.
12. Getty and Getty, 137.

HYMNS ARE RHYMING, RHYTHMIC THEOLOGY

Now remember, I'm a preacher. I value preaching as a powerful means of communicating divine truth. It's a fatal error for churches to emphasize music over preaching. But let's be honest: Songs often stay with us long after sermons are forgotten. Wait; scratch that. I said *often*. Songs *always* stay with us long after sermons are forgotten. Stop rolling your eyes, pastors. It's true!

Luther, the mighty preacher and the champion of the Reformation, knew this well. He knew and used the power of the preached Word. But He also valued the power of the sung Word. Vilmos Vajta explains: "To [Luther] the way of the gospel led through the ear more than the eye. That is why he valued poetry and music so highly, and the hymns which would sing the gospel into the hearts of the common people."[13] Yes. Hymns "sing the gospel into our hearts."

Another giant from church history demonstrates the sticking power of music. John Wesley preached all over Great Britain and the American colonies during the Great Awakening, taking the gospel to millions of hearers during his itinerant ministry—all before the era of motorcars and microphones. John Wesley is one of the most influential preachers in the history of the English-speaking church.

Now, I'd like you to quote some of your favorite lines from John Wesley's sermons. No googling.

Go ahead. I'll wait.

I'm guessing that those of you who don't have a Ph.D. in church history which included writing a dissertation on the sermons of John Wesley probably came up with precisely nothing.

Now...

13.   Vilmos Vajta, *Luther on Worship* (Philadelphia, PA: Muhlenberg Press, 1958), 185.

John Wesley had a kid brother named Chuck. Well, *Charles*—Charles Wesley.[14] Charles preached sermons, and the world has forgotten them. Ah, but he also *wrote hymns*. So let's run the same test. Quote some of your favorite lines from Charles Wesley's songs. No googling.

I'll give you a moment.

Ok, so maybe you still came up with nothing. But that's because you haven't memorized the *authors* of songs. But many of you will recognize the following lyrics:

And can it be that I should gain / An int'rest in the Savior's blood?
Died He for me, who caused His pain? / For me, who Him to death pursued?
Amazing love! how can it be / That Thou, my God, should die for me?

Arise, my soul, arise, / Shake off thy guilty fears;
The bleeding sacrifice, / In my behalf appears;
Before the throne my Surety stands, / Before the throne my Surety stands,
My name is written on His hands.

He breaks the power of canceled sin, / He sets the prisoner free;
His blood can make the foulest clean; / His blood availed for me.

----

14. Hymnologist Robert Guy McCutchan considered Charles Wesley to be "the greatest writer of hymns the world has ever known." *Hymns in the Lives of Men* (New York: Abingdon-Cokesbury Press, 1945), 21. Church historian Douglas A. Sweeney similarly calls him "the greatest writer of hymns in all of history." *The American Evangelical Story: A History of the Movement* (Grand Rapids, MI: Baker Academic, 2005), 39.

Christ the Lord is risen today, Alleluia! / Sons of men and angels say, Alleluia!

Raise your joys and triumphs high, Alleluia! / Sing, ye heavens, and earth reply, Alleluia!

Christ, by highest heav'n adored, / Christ, the everlasting Lord,
Late in time behold Him come / Offspring of a Virgin's womb:
Veiled in flesh the Godhead see, / Hail the incarnate Deity.
Pleased as man with men to dwell, / Jesus, our Emmanuel.
Hark! The herald angels sing, / "Glory to the newborn King!"

Many of you could sing all the stanzas of all of those songs. So, why do you remember song lyrics more easily than sermons—and perhaps even more than Bible verses? Because they utilize rhyme, rhythm, and meter. And because they are joined to music, which captures your attention all the more—both the left brain and the right, if you will. John Frame writes, "Music... enhances God's word by making it more vivid and memorable, by driving it into our very hearts."[15]

Do you get the point? *Songs teach.* That's why I refer to hymns as *rhyming, rhythmic theology.*[16] We sing what we believe—allegedly, at least. But songs also *stick.*

I grew up in Pueblo, Colorado. The summer days of my childhood were spent outside—all day, every day. My brothers and I would play football in vacant lots, race through fields, and ride our bikes through the

15. John M. Frame, *Worship in Spirit and Truth: A Refreshing Study of the Principles and Practice of Biblical Worship* (Phillipsburg, PA: P&R Publishing, 1996), 113.

16. Douglas Bond writes, "Watts' hymns, not surprisingly, have been called rhymed sermons." *The Poetic Wonder of Isaac Watts* (Orlando, FL: Reformation Trust, 2013), 46. Albert Bailey similarly calls hymns "rhymed theology." *The Gospel in Hymns* (New York: Charles Scribner's Sons, 1950), xx. I also like Alistair Begg's reference to hymns as "biblical theology in memorable melodic form." Foreword to Sinclair Ferguson, *In Christ Alone: Living the Gospel-Centered Life* (Lake Mary, FL: Reformation Trust, 2007), 2.

prairies on the edge of town. Without fail, we'd come home with a collection of burrs and briars all over us. Some would be stuck in our pants and socks. They weren't painful, just annoyingly persistent. Others *did* hurt. They'd especially latch onto our shoelaces, and we'd have to pull them out with all the caution of a brain surgeon. As every kid and parent knows, burrs and briars *stick*.

Hymns are like that. We hear them in church a few times, and they're with us for the rest of our lives. They stick with us because they're creative and evocative, poignant and passionate. In a word, hymns, done well, are *beautiful*. There is power in poetry. And so, Carl Trueman warns us to take hymns seriously:

> Careful attention to the selection of hymns and praise songs is important. People learn from everything that happens in a worship service, not just the sermon. Indeed, there are probably many Christians who imbibe more of their theology, for good or ill, from what they sing than from what they hear taught.[17]

That's significant. The hymns we sing *show* our theology. But they do much more. The hymns we sing *shape* our theology. That's why Luther focused so intently on the music of the church. He knew that catchy melodies and clever rhymes would allow even illiterate Christians to take home sound theology, changing their lives, their homes, and their world.

My contention is that we need to raise the bar. We can't just sing songs because they have a catchy tune or a sick beat. We can't just do low-quality covers of the low-content songs we hear on Christian radio. We need to get serious about the songs we sing.

R. Kent Hughes, a faithful and passionate preacher of the Scriptures, recognizes that songs stick and that they deserve careful attention:

---

17.   Carl R. Trueman, "The Trinity and Prayer" in *The Essential Trinity: New Testament Foundations and Practical Relevance*, ed. Brandon D. Crowe and Carl R. Trueman (Phillipsburg, NJ: P&R Publishing, 2017), 239.

The very act of singing God's Word, or singing scriptural truth about God, is intrinsically edifying because music is so easily remembered.... Because music is so naturally affective, great care must be taken to assure its biblical fidelity. Too often today the church serves up affective sentiments without much care for the discipline of the Word.[18]

There are many churches that would never tolerate doctrinal deviations in their statements of faith. They would revolt if they heard heresy from their pulpits. Rightly so! But many of those same churches tolerate a lot of nonsense and blather in their songs. Apparently heresy gets a pass if it is surrounded by a pipe organ or guitar riffs.

In his exceptional book on biblical worship, Allen P. Ross urges more intentionality:

> Even though churches have hymns and songs as a regular part of their services, praise through music needs constant if not urgent attention. Music must meet the same requirements as other forms of praise: it is to be biblically accurate, spiritually uplifting, honoring to God, and edifying to the congregation.[19]

Our songs must be held to the same standards as our sermons. As we've noted, church members don't memorize their church's statement of faith or their pastor's sermons. But there are many who could belt out pseudo-spiritual songs about rain, rivers, oceans, and the like. (What's the attraction to nebulous quasi-religious songs about water?!) Our songs matter. We need to choose the best songs and do so on purpose.

That brings me to the proposition—the point of this book.

18.   R. Kent Hughes, "Free Church Worship" in *Worship by the Book*, ed. D. A. Carson (Grand Rapids, MI: Zondervan, 2002), 167.

19.   Ross, 441-42.

CHRISTIANS MUST SELECT WORSHIP SONGS INTENTIONALLY, USING A BIBLICAL GRID

In the following chapters we'll learn to look for songs that are *biblical, doctrinal, Christian, Trinitarian, congregational, unifying, inspired, diverse, emotive, beautiful, experiential,* and *doxological.*

Music is amazing. And hymns are moving and memorable theology. They stick. So let's talk about how to choose them on purpose.

GRACE NOTES FOR WORSHIP LEADERS

- Do you consider the choice of congregational hymns to be a pastoral concern, alongside preaching? Or do you pass it off to someone else? Why?
- How much time and thought do you give to the songs you teach your church? Enough?

GRACE NOTES FOR PARENTS AND CHILDREN'S TEACHERS

- Would it be concerning to you if your children knew pop hits verbatim but couldn't sing in church if they didn't have words in front of them?
- How can you make life-changing Christian music more influential in your home?

GRACE NOTES FOR EVERYBODY

- If the concepts in this chapter were new to you, are you willing to make adjustments in order to fill your mind with better music?
- Do you engage attentively and joyfully when your church gathers to worship?
- Will you pray now and ask the Lord to use this book to stir your heart and improve your approach to worship, for your own growth and for God's glory?

PART 2

A HYMN GRID FROM THE NEW TESTAMENT

"Let the word of Christ dwell in you richly, teaching and admonishing one another in all wisdom, singing psalms and hymns and spiritual songs, with thankfulness in your hearts to God."

—COLOSSIANS 3:16

"Any discussion of sacred music must begin here. No matter what else a song may have to commend it, if it is not scriptural, it has no place in the life of the Christian musician. Some churches that would never allow heresy to be preached from the pulpit allow it to be included in the lyrics of songs. Error is no less damaging when it is sung. Falsehood so couched may actually be more damaging because of its subtlety."

—DANNY M. SWEATT[20]

"Music in worship is one of God's best tools for getting the word into our hearts."

—JOHN FRAME[21]

20. Danny M. Sweatt, *Church Music: Sense and Nonsense* (Greenville, SC: Bob Jones University Press, 1981), 7.
21. Frame, *Worship*, 121.

CHAPTER 2

SING SONGS THAT ARE BIBLICAL

His name was Mr. Ingle. I'm not sure he even had a first name. He was just "Mr. Ingle" to everybody in our church. Whenever New Life Bible Church met in downtown Pueblo, Colorado, Mr. Ingle was there—in the second row, often leaning back with his knees propped up against the pew in front of him, crab-like, and usually with an enormous pair of headphones strapped on to help him hear the preaching.

It was the late 1970s, and I was a boy of seven or eight. I couldn't imagine that Mr. Ingle had ever been a boy; he was one of those people whom you imagine was a hundred years old the moment he was born. I remember visiting his downtown apartment once with our pastor—my dad. It wasn't squalid, but it also wasn't tidy, well-lit, or spacious. But it suited Mr. Ingle, and it wasn't far from the bus station where he would walk every day to meet people—the captive audience of travelers and indigents waiting in what really *was* a squalid place. He'd sit with them, start conversations, and give them the gospel. Every single day.

Occasionally our church would allow people to choose a favorite hymn or song. I always thought it was a big deal to be able to choose the song for the entire congregation. So did Mr. Ingle, apparently. Every time, he would raise his hand, wait to be called on, then say one word:

"Satisfied." No one was surprised. It was Mr. Ingle's song, and it's still among my favorites.

> *All my life long I had panted / For a drink from some cool spring,*
> *That I hoped would quench the burning / Of the thirst I felt within.*
>
> *Feeding on the husks around me, / Till my strength was almost gone,*
> *Longed my soul for something better, / Only still to hunger on.*
>
> *Poor I was, and sought for riches, / Something that would satisfy,*
> *But the dust I gathered round me / Only mocked my soul's sad cry.*
>
> *Well of water, ever springing, / Bread of life, so rich and free,*
> *Untold wealth that never faileth, / My Redeemer is to me.*
>
> *Refrain:*
> *Hallelujah! I have found Him / Whom my soul so long has craved!*
> *Jesus satisfies my longings; / Through His blood I now am saved.*

What a song. What a story it tells! What a moving depiction of the sinner's desperate plight. What a glorious refrain, lyrically, emotionally, and musically climaxing on "Hallelujah!" And best of all, Clara Williams' text is absolutely *packed* with Scriptural allusions:

- The first stanza makes me think of the woman at the well, so sad and parched in her soul (John 4:10-15).[22] The picture of "thirst" calls to

---

22. I've written on Jesus' conversation with the woman at the well in my book *The God Who Satisfies: How Jesus Seeks, Saves, and Satisfies Samaritan Women—Like Us* (Church Works Media, 2016). I've also written with Greg Habegger a hymn unpacking the woman's experience: "Come, Lonely Heart."

mind Scripture's many invitations to the thirsty to come to the Lord (Isaiah 55:1-2; Matthew 5:6; John 7:37; Revelation 21:6; 22:17).

- The second stanza is an unmistakable allusion to the parable of the prodigal son, so destitute that he "would fain have filled his belly with the husks that the swine did eat" (Luke 15:16 KJV).

- Stanza three moves from thirst and hunger to abject poverty, to the poor seeking for riches but being mocked by life. Choose your biblical allusion: the "poor in spirit" (Matthew 5:3); the rich man and Lazarus (Luke 16:19-31); the man who would gain the world but lose his soul (Matthew 16:26); the spiritually impoverished church at Laodicea (Revelation 3:17).

- The final stanza has still more Bible shoehorned into it. Jesus offers not a mere trickle of spiritual water, but a gushing, overflowing fountain (John 4:14; John 7:38-39). He offers Himself, the free bread of Life (John 6:35, 48, 51; Matthew 26:26). He gives us true and unfailing spiritual riches (Ephesians 1:7, 18; 2:4, 7; 3:8, 16). Notice the brilliant writing: every need from stanzas one through three—thirst, hunger, and poverty—is met in our Redeemer.

- We're finally ready for the refrain—the solution to all of these long-ings of the soul: "Hallelujah! I have found Him!" What a glorious portrayal of the gospel (though I'm tempted to sing the more precise lyric, "Hallelujah! *He* has found *me*!"). This is the story of every sinner, and we sing this "Hallelujah!" with fellow sinners like the satisfied woman at the well, the forgiven and well-fed prodigal, and everyone else who is soul-satisfied with Jesus.

I love that song. But I've taken the time to unpack it because it teaches us a crucial lesson: *Our songs should be absolutely chock-full of the Word.* Good hymn-writing makes explicit allusions to biblical concepts and language. And good hymn-singing *looks* for those allusions, almost like a treasure hunt. Christian music is all about the Bible.

MUSIC IS A MINISTRY OF THE WORD

The book of Colossians is one of the high-water marks of Scripture. The apostle Paul writes to a local church, urging them to resist false teaching and to cling to the supremacy of Christ. The first two chapters relentlessly exalt the Lord Jesus Christ above everything else: He is our Redeemer and King, the very image and fullness of God, the Creator and Sustainer of all things, the Head of His church, the only One worthy of preeminence, our Savior today and our Hope for eternity. And in response to all of this teaching on the person and work of Christ, God commands us to *sing*:

> Let the word of Christ dwell in you richly, teaching and admonishing one another in all wisdom, singing psalms and hymns and spiritual songs, with thankfulness in your hearts to God. (Colossians 3:16)

That's how valuable our singing is to God. In a book bursting with the glory of the incomparable Christ, God says to sing "the Word of Christ" and the psalms. Bible, Bible, Bible. Our hearts are to be so full, so absolutely *saturated* with Scripture that we can't contain it. The Word *in* us flows *out* of us in teaching and in singing. R. Kent Hughes captures this point beautifully: "The ministry of music is not ministry of a different sort. It is first, last, and always a ministry of the Word of God." [23]

"Let the Word of Christ dwell in you *richly*." The Scriptures are to be lavishly at home in your heart—not as a guest, but as a permanent resident. You must read it. Memorize it. Muse on it. Meditate on it. Marinate in it. That's the secret of all the great hymn-writers. Albert Bailey says that Isaac Watts' mind "was saturated with the words of the Bible." [24] There is no other explanation for his profound, biblically rooted lyrics.

23.   Hughes, 172.
24.   Albert Edwards Bailey, *The Gospel in Hymns* (New York: Charles Scribner's Sons, 1950), 51.

Hymns preach. Paul S. Jones, the long-time minister of music at the historic Tenth Presbyterian Church in Philadelphia, explains the inseparable union of singing and preaching:

> Biblical music-making shares many of the same roles and goals as the teaching or pulpit ministry.... Our thinking is more biblical when we understand that musicians and preachers actually share in the ministry of the Word. Proclamation and interpretation of the Bible, and the edification and encouragement of the saints, with the ultimate goal of giving glory to God—these are also purposes of sacred music delineated in the Word of God and heralded by theologians and musicians throughout the history of the church.[25]

That's a high view of worship music! But is it biblical? I believe it is. I believe it aligns perfectly with Colossians 3:16: *Read the Bible; internalize it; teach it; and sing it.*

THE SCRIPTURES SHOULD INCITE OUR SONGS

All worship—including worship in song—must *begin* with God's revelation. Worship is a conversation, and God speaks first, as R. P. Martin demonstrates: "The distinctive genius of corporate worship is the two-beat rhythm of revelation and response. God speaks; we answer."[26]

Notice how this revelation-and-response theme pervades all of our corporate worship:

- We *read* the Word in our public worship services.
- We *pray* the Word in our public prayers.
- We *preach* the Word in our sermons.

25. Jones, *Singing*, 2-3. He later writes: "Music is not in competition with pastoral work. It *is* pastoral work." 282.
26. R. P. Martin, *The Worship of God: Some Theological, Pastoral, and Practical Reflections* (Grand Rapids, MI: Eerdmans, 1982), 6.

- We *support* the Word with our offerings.
- We *visualize* the Word with the two ordinances, baptism and the Lord's Table.
- We *sing* the Word with our psalms, hymns, and spiritual songs.

Scott Aniol and Ryan Martin address the importance of singing the Word: "If the hymns we sing do not accurately articulate Biblical truth, we have disobeyed our Lord on a most basic level."[27] Singing the Scriptures isn't an optional church-enhancement project. It's an obligation. If we're not doing it well, we're sinning.

One of my favorite books on church ministry is *The Deliberate Church* by Mark Dever and Paul Alexander. The title precisely encapsulates the book: everything we do in ministry should be on purpose, a careful application of Bible principles. Commenting on Ephesians 5:19 (the twin of Colossians 3:16), they discuss deliberate music ministry:

> The whole Ephesian church was commanded to build one another up and praise God through song. Part of pastoral leadership, then, is to facilitate that kind of edifying worship.... Jesus uses His Word to build up or edify the church. So it makes sense that we only sing songs that use His Word both accurately and generously. The more accurately applied scriptural theology, phrases, and allusions, the better—because the Word builds the church, and music helps us remember that Word, which we seem to so quickly forget.[28]

THE SCRIPTURES SHOULD SATURATE OUR SONGS

Worship music is serious business. Singing Bible-saturated songs requires intellectual rigor. It takes concentration. Daniel Block pulls no punches

27. Scott Aniol and Ryan J. Martin, preface to *Hymns of the Living God*, ed. Scott Aniol and Ryan J. Martin (Fort Worth, TX: Religious Affections Ministries, 2017), III.
28. Mark Dever and Paul Alexander, *The Deliberate Church: Building Your Ministry on the Gospel* (Wheaton, IL: Crossway Books, 2005), 84.

in calling the church to attention: "In contrast to the vacuous, repetitious, and mindless music of the world, truly worshipful music is filled with Scripture, the story of redemption, sound doctrine, and the glory of Christ."[29]

All worship music should be *about* the Bible and *from* the Bible. But I especially appreciate songs which artfully make use of the Bible itself. John Frame notes that "it is a good thing for God's people to get [the Bible's] words, phrasings, and cadences into their hearts. Helping Christians to do so is one (though not the only) legitimate goal of church music."[30]

Luther recognized that a Word-filled congregation sings. He wrote, "Let God speak directly to His people through the Scriptures, and let His people respond with grateful songs of praise."[31]

Luther's *Ninety-Five Theses* changed the world. But of equal importance were two audacious gifts he made to the German people: He gave them *the Bible* in their own tongue, and he gave them *hymns* in their own tongue—then used those hymns in congregational singing, "so that God might speak directly to them in his Word, and that they might directly answer him in their songs."[32]

This is a gloriously combustible combination. A Word-filled life results in Word-filled speech and Word-filled songs. Colossians 3:16 describes a delightful, Word-filled cycle: We think on the Word, we speak the Word, and we sing the Word—causing us to think on the Word yet again!

Intentionally singing the Scriptures is a hallmark of Protestant Christianity. We believe in the inspiration, authority, and sufficiency of Scripture—the Reformation doctrine of *sola scriptura*. We believe that the Bible is "our only rule of faith and practice." The Bible is our standard—a

29. Daniel I. Block, *For the Glory of God: Recovering a Biblical Theology of Worship* (Grand Rapids, MI: Baker Academic, 2014), 233.

30. John M. Frame, *Contemporary Worship Music: A Biblical Defense* (Phillipsburg, PA: P&R Publishing, 1997), 33.

31. Attributed to Martin Luther by Kenneth W. Osbeck, *Devotional Warm-Ups for the Church Choir: Preparing to Lead Others in Worship* (Grand Rapids, MI: Kregel Ministry, 2016).

32. Martin Luther, quoted in David R. Breed, *The History and Use of Hymns and Hymn-Tunes* (New York: Fleming H. Revell Company, 1903), 39.

God-ordained authority that dictates how we worship, including the kind of songs we sing in praise to God.

THE SCRIPTURES ARE THE MEASURING ROD OF OUR SONGS

The sequence of the Colossians 3:16 argument makes all the difference in the world. The Word comes first, and the *result* is Word-filled music. We don't start with our own ideas, sentimental poems, or well-meaning philosophies. We start with the Bible. Hymnologists Harry Eskew and Hugh McElrath riff on this:

> Scripture is the basic raw material from which hymns are produced. A hymn cannot be useful unless and until it relates closely to the revealed truth about God and his mighty acts as written in the Scriptures. Therefore the effectiveness of any hymn is measurable in large part by the extent to which it functions as a vehicle for scriptural truth.[33]

David R. Breed makes the same basic points in his study of hymns, published in 1903. He speaks so passionately and persuasively about "the indispensable qualities of a true hymn" that I'll risk redundancy so that you might hear him:

> It must be Scriptural, both in sentiment and expression. Beyond all question this is chief. The hymn must be absolutely true to Scripture. Nor is it enough that its thought is not a violation of Scripture truth; the very form in which that thought is cast must be just as true to the Scripture as the thought itself. Otherwise we cannot be safeguarded in the offering of divine praise.[34]

---

33. Harry Eskew and Hugh T. McElrath, *Sing with Understanding: An Introduction to Christian Hymnody* (Nashville, TN: Broadman Press, 1980), 45.
34. Breed, 89.

Note not only Breed's very high bar—a hymn "must be absolutely true to Scripture"—but also the need for the church to be "*safeguarded.*" That's an interesting posture—the idea that the church must be *defended from error* in our worship. Is that so? I believe it is.

Pastor David Doran argues that because psalms, hymns, and spiritual songs are a means of instruction—"teaching and admonishing," per Colossians 3:16—those songs should be held to the same standard as preaching. He specifically argues that our songs should be subject to the command of 1 Thessalonians 5:21 to "test all things" and "hold fast to that which is good."[35] Singers should follow the example of the Berean Christians, weighing their songs to be sure they align with the Scriptures (Acts 17:11).

Listen to this: Scripture is so concerned with sound doctrine that nearly every New Testament book includes a warning against false teaching and false teachers. Of the twenty-seven books in the New Testament, only Philemon lacks a warning against false teaching—and even Philemon was sent alongside the heresy-hunting book of Colossians. Confronting error is a biblical duty, and since our songs teach, we need to inspect them to be sure they are communicating the truth.

They say that "a lie can get halfway around the world before the truth gets its pants on." That's especially true if the lie is carried along by a catchy tune. As the reprobate Voltaire quipped, "Anything too stupid to be spoken is sung." Take a look at the words of many nominally Christian songs and you'll see that he has a point. But it shouldn't be that way. False teaching isn't benign just because it's sung rather than spoken. We should be as conscientious about the content of biblical singing as we are about biblical preaching.

---

35. David Doran, "Three Qualities of God-Honoring Worship Songs," *Sermon Audio*, July 29, 2007, https://www.sermonaudio.com/sermoninfo.asp?SID=820711246. In the sermon, Doran gives three criteria for our song choices: We should insist on songs that are *accurate*, *appropriate*, and *accessible*.

WE NEED TO SING OVERTLY BIBLICAL SONGS

My goal as a hymn-writer is that those who hear my lyrics will recognize the biblical passages behind them. I work hard to fill my hymns not with general Bible-friendly ideas, but with clear biblical quotations and allusions. I take seriously the half-joking advice of Douglas Sean O'Donnell, who challenges songwriters to open their Bibles and "plagiarize."[36]

What does writing a Bible-saturated text look like? Well, in my hymns it varies, but one that is especially filled with biblical allusions is "My Jesus, Fair":

My Jesus, fair, was pierced by thorns, / By thorns grown from the fall.
Thus He who gave the curse was torn / To end that curse for all.

My Jesus, meek, was scorned by men, / By men in blasphemy.
"Father, forgive their senseless sin!" / He prayed, for them, for me.

My Jesus, kind, was torn by nails, / By nails of cruel men.
And to His cross, as grace prevailed, / God pinned my wretched sin.

My Jesus, pure, was crushed by God, / By God, in judgment just.
The Father grieved, yet turned His rod / On Christ, made sin for us.

My Jesus, strong, shall come to reign, / To reign in majesty—
The Lamb arose, and death is slain. / Lord, come in victory!

Refrain:
O love divine, O matchless grace— / That God should die for men!
With joyful grief I lift my praise,
Abhorring all my sin, / Adoring only Him.

---

36. Douglas Sean O'Donnell, *God's Lyrics: Rediscovering Worship through Old Testament Songs* (Phillipsburg, NJ: P&R Publishing, 2010), 176.

Ideally, the biblical allusions should be readily apparent to those who know their Bibles. But let me connect the dots on a few of the lines:

- In stanza 1, I write of Jesus being "pierced by thorns, / by thorns grown from the fall." I want those short phrases to drive the minds of singers to the thorns of Matthew 27:29 and then back to the thorns from Genesis 3:18. I want them to have an "Aha!" moment: "He who gave the curse was torn to end that curse for all" (Galatians 2:13).
- Stanza 2 has Jesus praying for those who crucified Him: "'Father, forgive their senseless sin!' / He prayed, for them, for me." It's a clear allusion to Luke 23:34, but the unexpected language, "senseless sin," should highlight the folly of what sinners have done—sinners including *me*, not just those who were on Golgotha that day.
- I write in stanza 3, "And to His cross, as grace prevailed, / God pinned my wretched sin." Besides the literal nailing of Jesus to the cross, I hope singers will make the connection to Colossians 2:14 and the nailing of our sin debt to the cross.

That's enough to provide an example of what I'm thinking as I write. Now, let me take off my hymn-writer hat and put on my pastor hat. I want the hymns I choose for corporate worship to be overt in their allusions to Scripture as well. There are countless masterful examples of this. Let me cite a few of my favorites.

Whenever I sing Charles Wesley's lyric, "No condemnation now I dread," I can't help thinking of Romans 8:1. Every time! *There is therefore now no condemnation for those who are in Christ Jesus.* Wesley's lyrics are filled with references like that—like his using Peter's rescue from prison in Acts 12:6-11 as an illustration of his own salvation later in "And Can It Be."

What about modern hymns? Do they have clear biblical allusions? The ones worth singing do!

Stuart Townend's and Keith Getty's hymn "The Power of the Cross" is loaded with Scripture, beginning with "the dawn of the darkest day."

Aside from the lovely alliteration (repeated initial consonant sounds; here, the *d* sound), the allusion to the day of Christ's crucifixion as "the darkest day" refers not only to the most infamous day in human history, but to the eclipse-like darkness as Christ hung on the cross (Luke 23:44). There was literal darkness, but there was also great spiritual darkness (Luke 22:53). And their hymn tells us so in one pregnant phrase.

Overt biblical language continues throughout the hymn, as in stanza three:

> *Now the daylight flees; / Now the ground beneath*
> *Quakes as its Maker bows His head.*
> *Curtain torn in two, / Dead are raised to life;*
> *"Finished!" the vict'ry cry.*[37]

Recognize all that? The song reminds us of the miracles that accompanied Jesus' death in Matthew 27: the eclipse (v. 45), the earthquake (v. 51), the tearing of the veil (v. 51), and the resurrections that accompanied Jesus' death (vv. 52-53). When is the last time you sang fairly obscure biblical details like *that* in a hymn? When we finally sing (or nearly shout) the line, "'Finished!' the vict'ry cry," our minds involuntarily go to John 19:30. Even the repeated refrain, "Christ became sin for us," is an unmistakable reference to 2 Corinthians 5:21. That's biblical and beautiful writing. Don't settle for less.

A WORD TO WORSHIP LEADERS: HELP CONNECT THE DOTS

One final word about singing overtly biblical songs. A skillful worship leader will at times "connect the dots" for the congregation. This can be

---

37. Lyrics from "The Power of the Cross" by Keith Getty and Stuart Townend. © 2005 Thankyou Music (PRS) (adm. worldwide at CapitolCMGPublishing.com excluding the UK & Europe which is adm. at IntegratedRights.com). All rights reserved. Used by permission.

overdone, of course; I've heard song-leaders preach a veritable sermon by way of an introduction. Usually a few sentences will suffice, and they should be prepared ahead of time rather than on the fly. But help people sing with understanding (1 Corinthians 14:15). Point out the biblical basis of a few lines of a song, like I did above. Define the word "prostrate" for your people when you sing "All Hail the Power of Jesus' Name." (Be careful: Do angels even *have* prostates?!) Don't omit the word "Ebenezer" from "Come Thou Fount of Every Blessing," but do explain its significance from 1 Samuel 7:12.

Not every song needs to be dissected every Sunday. It can get wearisome listening to the worship leader wax eloquent when we'd rather be singing. But a concise comment can vastly improve the congregation's understanding and focus the congregation's attention:

- "Notice how this song gives praise to the Father in verse 1, the Son in verse 2, and the Spirit in verse 3. Let's sing praise to our Triune God together."
- "Have you noticed how 'In Christ Alone' covers every part of Jesus' earthly life, from His birth to His death to His resurrection? Think on our Savior as we sing."
- "When we sing 'the Father's wrath completely satisfied,' we're singing about the doctrine of propitiation. Jesus *absorbed the wrath* of the Father in total, on our behalf. There's none left for us. Amazing! Marvel at Jesus' love for you as you sing."

The point is, help people think. And rejoice that as you share these insights, you're teaching the congregation to approach *other* hymns this way on their own. Every hymn-sing will become a spiritual treasure hunt, with people looking for the Bible verses behind the lyrics. And that's wonderful!

Sing the Scriptures. It honors the Lord. It builds Christians up in the faith. And it impresses the Word on our hearts with inimitable force, as our friend Martin Luther has said:

We have put this music to the living and holy Word of God in order to sing, praise and honor it. We want the beautiful art of music to be properly used to serve her dear Creator and his Christians. He is thereby praised and honored and we are made better and stronger in faith when his holy Word is impressed on our hearts by sweet music.[38]

GRACE NOTES FOR WORSHIP LEADERS

- Have you ever eliminated a song from your church's repertoire because it lacked biblical support for the text? Which song, and what was the reasoning?
- Do you read through hymns before the service and prepare brief explanations of important concepts or difficult words? Can you start this week?

GRACE NOTES FOR PARENTS AND CHILDREN'S TEACHERS

- We all enjoy hearing kids mangle difficult words, like "Be Thou exhausted" (instead of "Be Thou exalted") or "Jesus, name of the ballgame" (instead of "Jesus, name above all names"). Have your kids done something similar?
- Do you take time to explain the meaning of songs to your children rather than just hope they "get it"?

38. Martin Luther, preface to *The Burial Hymns*, 1542.

GRACE NOTES FOR EVERYBODY

- Is there a line of a hymn that you have never understood? If so, what is it?
- Do you engage your mind when you sing hymns, hunting for biblical allusions? If not, start this Sunday, or even when you listen to Christian music in your home today. You're going to gain so much more from well-written songs!

"I will sing praise with my spirit, but I will sing with my mind also."

—I CORINTHIANS 14:15

"It has been truly said that if you want to survey the full substance of the church's faith you should go to its hymns."

—J. I. PACKER[39]

"Our songs are the public manifesto of what we believe."

—KEITH AND KRISTYN GETTY[40]

39. J. I. Packer, foreword to *From Heaven He Came and Sought Her: Definite Atonement in Historical, Biblical, Theological, and Pastoral Perspective*, ed. David Gibson and Jonathan Gibson (Wheaton, IL: Crossway, 2013), 13.

40. Getty and Getty, 87.

CHAPTER 3

SING SONGS THAT ARE DOCTRINAL

Think back on your last Sunday worship service. Did you recite a creed—say, the *Westminster Confession of Faith*, the *Second London Baptist Confession of Faith*, the *Apostles' Creed*, or the like? (What I'm really asking is, are you a Presbyterian, for whom the answer is *yes*, or are you a non-Presbyterian, for whom the answer is probably *no*? I'm joking. Kind of.)

Well, if you said *no*, let me correct you. You *did* recite a doctrinal statement. Several, in fact. You just *sang* them. Our hymns are our creeds. Which is kind of terrifying, to be honest, depending on what you sang.

Harry Eskew and Hugh McElrath explain why theologically astute hymns are so important, especially for those of us who don't make regular use of creeds in our worship services:

> The recitation of creeds and confessions of faith makes up an important part of public worship of many Christians; but in those worshiping groups where this is not the normal practice, the hymn stands as an alternate means of objectifying belief corporately. Replete with the lyric expression of universal doctrine which has been distilled

from the church's twenty centuries of experience, the hymnal is truly a book of "grass-roots theology."[41]

"Grass-roots theology." Yeah. Sometimes with weeds.

Let me suggest another analogy. Religious songs are both a thermometer and a thermostat. As a thermometer, they measure the fervor of a church and a life. They *show* what we believe and celebrate. But they do more. They also *shape* what we believe and celebrate. As a thermostat, they actually play a part in *setting* our spiritual temperature, not just *telling* it.

As we noted earlier, hymns are *rhyming, rhythmic theology*. For better or for worse, the songs you sing in your church, play as background music while you eat, and belt out in your car indoctrinate you. As William S. Smith puts it, "Hymns... carry theological freight."[42]

Martin Luther knew that hymns are pocket-sized creeds. He was determined to put theology to music so that it would be prized and remembered. He sought out poets to do it skillfully, and he leaned into the work himself. Paul Westermeyer explains Luther's fixation on music as a means of communicating the Scriptures:

> Luther was not simply fond of music. Luther thought music has a theological reason for being: it is a gift of God, which comes from the "sphere of miraculous audible things," just like the Word of God.... It almost seems as if Luther sees music in its own right as a parallel to preaching.... But the weight falls on its association with the Word and words that carry the Word.[43]

James Montgomery Boice knew that hymns are creeds. Under his watch at Tenth Presbyterian Church in Philadelphia, "hymns (yes, *hymns!*)

---

41.   Eskew and McElrath, 59.
42.   William S. Smith, *Joyful Noise: A Guide to Music in the Church for Pastors and Musicians* (Franklin, TN: Providence House Publishers, 2007), 35.
43.   Paul Westermeyer, *Te Deum: The Church and Music* (Minneapolis: Augsburg Fortress, 1998), 144-46.

were sung and learned because of their power to teach doctrine (yes, *doctrine!*)."[44] This was true even in children's classes. *Especially* in children's classes. What a novel idea—teaching our kids doctrinal hymns they will remember for the rest of their lives!

Sinclair Ferguson knows that hymns are creeds. He describes hymns as "potent shapers of evangelical piety"—maybe even more than Christian writings.[45] That's an astounding comment from a respected Christian preacher and author.

Most importantly, the apostle Paul knew that hymns are creeds. In Colossians 3:16, Scripture tells us that the church's songs are one of the ways we "teach and admonish one another in all wisdom."

As we noted in chapter 2, songs must be biblical. But they must also be instructional. Indeed, they already are. All songs teach. Not all songs teach well.

What is it that we're looking for, then? I'm going to suggest seven simple principles regarding Christian songs and the doctrinal "freight" they carry.

SING SONGS THAT ARE DOCTRINALLY ACCURATE

As we will see in chapter 12, hymns should be beautiful. They should have poignant texts and stirring, memorable melodies. But if a song's doctrine is inaccurate, nothing else matters. Drop it like day-old sushi from a truck stop. Insist on absolute biblical fidelity. "Close enough for a song" is not a legitimate category. We need to have zero tolerance for doctrinal deviations, even in our songs.

I've mentioned that my parents gave me a love for Christian music. They gave me an ear for it. But they also gave me a *mind* for it—a mental filter to discern what a song teaches. I remember listening to the radio in

---

44. Shared by Dr. Boice's friend Sinclair B. Ferguson, *Some Pastors and Teachers: Reflecting a Biblical Vision of What Every Minister Is Called to Be* (Carlisle, PA: Banner of Truth, 2017), 614.

45. Ibid., 467.

the car with my dad one December during my teen years. The radio was tuned to a local Christian station. As we listened to a newer Christmas song, Dad suddenly interrupted the singer: "Did you hear that, Chris? That song just said that Jesus 'laid aside His deity and entered our humanity.' That's not true! Jesus didn't 'lay aside His deity.' He never stopped being God." The lesson took, and I'm passing it on nearly four decades later. Lyrics matter. Don't tolerate falsehood, no matter how catchy or popular the song may be.

SING SONGS THAT ARE DOCTRINALLY RICH

I would acknowledge that few songs I've sung in church were doctrinally wrong. I'm glad for that. But many—old and new—have been doctrinally *light*. Os Guinness laments that "much contemporary Christian music is vapid, shallow, and theologically flimsy."[46] Ouch! But he's not wrong.

Now, conservative churches and Christians should be careful not to congratulate themselves too quickly. I've been in churches that wouldn't sing songs played on the local Christian radio station, but which majored on songs that were mostly sentimental. I've sung plenty of downright silly songs in conservative churches. I've heard right-wing churches that blistered CCM for using "7-11 songs"[47] even as they themselves sang "Cheer Up, Ye Saints of God" and whistled "Are We Down-Hearted?"

I get that we need to be balanced. Not every song needs to be a theological treatise. Children's songs—some, not all—can be fun.[48] And I'm okay with "Precious Lord, Take My Hand" at times as an expression of

46.   Os Guinness, endorsement for Keith and Kristyn Getty, *Sing!: How Worship Transforms Your Life, Family, and Church* (Nashville, TN: B&H Publishing Group, 2017).

47.   "7-11 songs" are a sarcastic description of songs with only 7 words which are repeated 11 times. Clever. But here's an assignment: Count the number of times the word "Hallelujah!" is repeated in Handel's masterpiece "The Hallelujah Chorus." I've yet to encounter anyone willing to cast it aside as meaningless.

48.   Not all children's songs are created equal. Rather than singing silly songs, consider the doctrinal meat in songs like "Stop and Let Me Tell You," "One Way," "Good News!" and "S-A-L-V-A-T-I-O-N" from Children's Evangelism Fellowship (CEF), as well as gospel-centered

our dependence on our Savior. But we do need to be careful that the levity or sentimentality of our songs isn't giving a wrong impression about our great God—or even taking His name in vain.

Now, compare the songs above to the remarkably succinct and insightful lyrics Matt Merker added to the old hymn text "He Will Hold Me Fast":

For my life He bled and died, Christ will hold me fast;
Justice has been satisfied, He will hold me fast;
Raised with Him to endless life, He will hold me fast;
Till our faith is turned to sight when He comes at last.[49]

Now *that* is a doctrinal text. It's dense. It covers Christ's vicarious atonement (line 1) and propitiation (line 2), our resurrection and union with Christ (line 3), and Jesus' return and our glorification (line 4). Books are written on those themes, and yet Matt dug down deep into them in four brief, easily understood lines. Just gorgeous.

That's the kind of song we should sing. Not only true, but *rich*.

SING SONGS THAT COVER ALL THE MAJOR DOCTRINES OF THE BIBLE

Since singing is part of the overall teaching ministry of the church, it's the job of church leaders to ensure that we're singing "the whole counsel of God" (Acts 20:27). Singing songs about justification is my personal delight. But there's so much more doctrine in the Bible to celebrate! Matt Merker writes, "Make sure that over time your congregation learns songs

children's songs from Patch the Pirate, Sovereign Grace, and Steve Green's *Hide 'Em in Your Heart* recordings. And hymns! Teach children hymns!

49. Lyrics from "He Will Hold Me Fast" by Matthew Merker (new music and lyrics) and Ada Habershon (public domain lyrics), 1861-1918. © 2016 Getty Music Publishing / Matthew Merker Music (BMI) (both admin. by Music Services). All rights reserved. Used by permission.

that cover all the main headings of systematic theology."[50] Sound intimidating? It doesn't need to be. Here's a quick sample:

SING ABOUT THE SCRIPTURES (BIBLIOLOGY)

- "How Firm a Foundation" (traditional)
- "Speak, O Lord" (Townend and Getty)
- "Thy Word" (Grant and Smith)
- "God's Sufficient Word" (Anderson and Anglea)
- "God Has Spoken" (Anderson and Habegger)

SING ABOUT GOD (THEOLOGY PROPER)

(See chapter 13 for a list of hymns on the attributes of God.)

SING ABOUT JESUS' PERSON AND WORK (CHRISTOLOGY)

(See chapter 4 for a list of hymns on the person and work of Christ.)

SING ABOUT THE HOLY SPIRIT (PNEUMATOLOGY)

(See chapter 5 for a list of hymns on the Holy Spirit.)

SING ABOUT OUR SALVATION (SOTERIOLOGY)

- "Jesus, Thy Blood and Righteousness" (von Zinzendorf)
- "How Sweet and Awesome Is the Place" (Watts / traditional Irish melody)
- "And Can It Be" (Wesley and Campbell)
- "Rock of Ages" (Toplady and Hastings)

50.　Matt Merker, *Corporate Worship: How the Church Gathers as God's People* (Wheaton, IL: Crossway, 2021), 139.

- "The Solid Rock" (Mote and Bradbury)
- "Jesus Paid It All" (Hall and Grape)
- "Complete in Thee" (Wolfe, Gray, and Nyce)
- "His Mercy Is More" (Boswell and Papa)
- "The Gospel Song" (Jones and Kauflin)
- "Jesus, Thank You" (Sczebel)
- "Thank You Jesus for the Blood" (Gayle)
- "Reformation Hymn" (Anderson and Kauflin)
- "His Robes for Mine" (Anderson and Habegger)

SING ABOUT THE CHURCH AND ITS MISSION (ECCLESIOLOGY)

- "The Church's One Foundation" (Stone and Wesley)
- "O Church, Arise" (Townend and Getty)
- "By Faith" (Townend and Getty)
- "Soldiers of Christ, Arise" (Watts and Elvey)
- "O Zion, Haste" (Thomson and Walch)
- "Facing a Task Unfinished" (Houghton and Wesley / Getty, Getty, Cash, and de Barra)
- "For the Cause" (Townend, Getty, and Getty)
- "Thou Whose Almighty Word" (Marriott and de Giardini)
- "For the Sake of His Name" (Anderson and Habegger)

SING ABOUT CHRIST'S RETURN (ESCHATOLOGY)

- "Look, Ye Saints! The Sight Is Glorious" (Kelly and Monk)
- "Lo, He Comes in Clouds Descending" (Wesley and Hughes)
- "Christ Returneth" (Turner and McGranahan)
- "There Is a Higher Throne" (Getty and Getty)
- "Christ Our Hope in Life and Death" (Getty, Boswell, J. Kauflin, Merker, and Papa)
- "Come Quickly, Lord" (Anderson and Habegger)

MEMORIZE HYMN LYRICS

You've been there. You're singing a hymn in church using a screen rather than a hymnal. And the words don't get displayed in time, either because there's a technology glitch or an A/V-guy glitch. The singing just craters. People don't know the words. Or you're at a retreat, around a campfire. People want to sing, but there are no lyrics in sight. Sure, you could google hymns and use your phones. But what if there's no Wi-Fi or cell service?

It saddens me that Christians don't know hymn lyrics by heart. I get it, in a sense. I've lived in Atlanta for nine years and I still use my phone's map program to get around, even locally. But when I'm on my deathbed, or awake on a sleepless night, or even imprisoned for my faith, it's not a map I'll need. I need Scripture, hidden in my heart (Psalm 119:11). And I want the lyrics of hymns.

I'm grateful that I have the lyrics to most stanzas of many hymns memorized. Part of it is the result of being raised by Christian parents who loved Christian music. Part of it is just being a "word nerd." But maybe this is something you need to work at. Maybe you need to listen to more hymns on your commute or in your home. One way or another, you should try to memorize hymns. The struggle of even lifelong Christians to sing hymns from memory is one evidence that we're not thinking about what we're singing. Work at that.

THINK WHEN YOU SING

Years ago, I read what a well-known Bible teacher said to someone who asked him how to get more out of her Bible reading: "Think." The one-word answer made me smile, but it's an accurate appraisal of the problem for most of us.

The same answer would greatly enhance our singing as well.

Think. Paul called for worship that is both spiritual and thoughtful in 1 Corinthians 14:15: "I will sing praise with my spirit, but I will sing with my mind also." The modern church needs such a conviction. Paul S. Jones believes that mental laziness is one reason hymns are disappearing from congregational worship: "It is because [hymns] require thought, and we do not want to think."[51]

Sing with your mind! Don't just mindlessly repeat familiar phrases. Engage your brain. Look for biblical allusions. Investigate which doctrines are being addressed and whether they're being taught in an accurate and insightful way. Ask yourself why a particular word was used and what it contributes to the song's meaning. Notice the progression from one stanza to another, or how a refrain or bridge builds on the message of the stanzas.

LOOK FOR LOGICAL PROGRESSION WITHIN A SONG

This is really a continuation of the previous point. Part of thinking through a song is thinking through its progression from one stanza to the next. Hopefully the song you're singing *does* progress and isn't just a random list of sentences—or worse, phrases that the author didn't even bother turning into sentences. The best hymns move deeper into an idea with each stanza, or move chronologically from Christ's first coming to His second. But they *move*, and they *climax*.

I remember hearing pastor and author John Piper dress down a Sonny and Cher love song, which he hilariously sang (with a twang), then critiqued:

My case is that good poetry or good songs will usually have sound argument. If a song has a bad argument, it ruins the song, including the emotional impact. For example, Sonny and Cher had a song back in 1966 which had a line that went, "I'd live for you, I'd die for you, I'd even climb the mountain high for you." What's wrong with that argument? The word "even" implies that climbing mountains is

51. Paul S. Jones, "Hymnody in a Post-Hymnody World" in *Give Praise to God: A Vision for Reforming Worship*, ed. Philip Graham Ryken, Derek W. H. Thomas, and J. Ligon Duncan III (Phillipsburg, NJ: P&R Publishing, 2003), 251.

more drastic or sacrificial than dying, which is false. The logic of the poem is contradictory and so the song is poor, and its total impact is weakened.[52]

Maybe it's just because I'm an amateur poet, but Piper's point stuck. It was funny, and it was true. What's *not* funny is how few people think or care enough to notice if Christian songs do similar, nonsensical things.

I've urged worship leaders to choose hymns on purpose. But do more. Choose the *stanzas* of your hymns on purpose—and when possible, sing them all, or all that your hymnal includes. Why? Because great hymns tell a story, and omitting a stanza might be leaving a big hole in the song. Asking the congregation to "sing out on verses 1, 2, and 4," merely out of habit, is lazy. (I'm looking at you, Baptists.) Verse three might very well be the highlight of the hymn! When I'm in a congregation that's singing "It Is Well with My Soul" and the worship leader omits the verse about my sins being nailed to the cross, it's all I can do not to charge the platform.

It can be even worse. Comically so. Let me illustrate. I had the privilege of taking study tours with a small group of pastors in 2006 (to Greece), 2008 (to Turkey), and 2010 (to Israel). When pastors get together, we sing—loudly, with harmony, and from memory. It was delightful. However, on one occasion we were in a bunker in Northern Israel, hearing about the Six-Day War. My friend suggested that we sing Luther's classic hymn, "A Mighty Fortress Is Our God." Great! We were in a refuge, of sorts, so it made perfect sense. The trouble is, we sang just one verse, and as a result, we essentially offered praise to the Devil:

> *For still our ancient foe / Doth seek to work us woe;*
> *His craft and power are great, / And armed with cruel hate;*
> *On earth is not his equal.*

52.   John Piper, "Delighting in the Law of God," *Desiring God*, July 21, 1980, https://www.desiringgod.org/messages/delighting-in-the-law-of-god.

As my friends prepared to leave, I begged them to sing at least one more verse, lest lightning strike. I wanted us to get us to *Jesus*—"the Man of God's own choosing... Lord Sabaoth... that Word above all earthly powers"! The point is, choose hymn stanzas on purpose. And generally, choose them all. Enjoy the logical progression of the whole song.

STRETCH, HUMBLY—AND STOOP, HUMBLY

If anything should humble us, it's singing praises to our incomparable God. Isaac Watts was right to call us "worms" in comparison to the Most High God. We need to proceed with humility, neither congratulating ourselves for giving attention to these important matters nor looking down on those who aren't giving much thought to these things yet.

My friend and professor Michael Barrett used to challenge seminary students to "be easily blessed" by the preaching we heard. Yes, we were learning important principles of Bible interpretation during our class time. But we needed to sit under the preaching of the Word as *disciples*, not *critics*. In the same way, you need to value great hymns. You need to stretch yourself and those under your influence to learn even better hymns. But you need to do so with humility and grace, not a cantankerous, divisive spirit. And endeavor to enjoy the truths in the songs you're singing, even if you'd prefer better songs.

I love singing theological songs like "Arise My Soul, Arise" and "Before the Throne of God Above." I want meat, not peanuts. But there is good reason to choose some simpler songs for each service, as well. *Stretch* people to learn and think as they worship with weighty songs. But also *stoop*. Be mindful of children in the congregation. Empathize with new believers. Think about how to serve those who struggle to follow a lot of complicated theological concepts.

My friend Nick taught me this. Nick found our church in Madison, Ohio, because of our singing. We had no building for the first twelve years of Tri-County Bible Church's existence. We met in the local high school on Sunday mornings, but on Sunday nights we met in a community center. Nick—an illiterate addict and unbeliever when I met him—heard our singing one Sunday evening and came to check it out. Eventually he came to Christ, and one of our members discipled him. He became an important part of our church family.

One day I stood next to Nick during a worship service. We sang a deep, theological hymn, something like "Jesus, Thy Blood and Righteousness." I belted out the beautiful truths we were singing. I was loving it. But Nick was quiet. He couldn't read. He didn't know the song. He listened, but couldn't comprehend much. Lyrics go by fast!

Then we sang "God Is So Good." It's simple. It's repetitive. But it's sound. And suddenly Nick was *singing*! "God is so good, God is so good, God is so good, He's so good to me." He continued, easily joining in with "He loves me so," "He died for me," and "He's coming soon." It was beautiful to hear him. He was finally able to participate. He finally *belonged*.

Worshiping with Nick rebuked me, and it taught me something. Yes, we need to help people grow to appreciate deep theology in our music. But there's also something beautiful about simplicity. It reminds me of how William Tyndale desired that a common plowboy might be able to read and understand the Scriptures. In a similar way, Bible truth, presented *clearly*, is one of the marks of a great hymn. Ken Boer writes, "Don't force your people to work through a fog of unnecessarily hard language or complex music to see Jesus."[53] We want our simplest members to understand and grow with us.

John Frame writes, "There is a place in the Christian life to ponder complexities. But there is also a place in the lives of even the most mature Christians to ponder the profundity of the simple."[54] So sing "Jesus, Thy Blood and Righteousness." Then follow it up with "Jesus Loves Me." Enjoy

53. Ken Boer, "The Worship Leader and the Gospel" in *Doxology and Theology: How the Gospel Forms Worship Leaders*, ed. Matt Boswell, (Nashville, TN: B&H Publishing Group, 2013), 195. Luther urged those writing German hymns in his day, "I would like you to avoid new-fangled, fancied words and to use expressions simple and common for people to understand, yet pure and fitting." *Luther's Works*, 53:221.
54. Frame, *Contemporary*, 27.

them both. After all, the ocean is deep enough to drown the most experienced swimmer but also shallow enough at its shores for a child to safely frolic in it.

But whatever else you do, sing doctrinal hymns. For, as hymnologist Esther Rothenbusch soberly warns, "It is dangerously likely that whatever elements of our theology we do not sing, we will ultimately lose."[55]

GRACE NOTES FOR WORSHIP LEADERS

- Are you including doctrinal hymns in your church's repertoire? From all the major doctrines of Scripture?
- Do you intentionally have some "low-hanging fruit" for children and new Christians?

GRACE NOTES FOR PARENTS AND CHILDREN'S TEACHERS

- Are your children learning hymns in addition to children's songs like "Zacchaeus," "The Lord's Army," and "Deep and Wide"?
- Do you have a list of songs you want your children to memorize and master while they are under your care?

GRACE NOTES FOR EVERYBODY

- Do you value songs that make you think doctrinally?
- Do you demonstrate humility when you encounter songs that are less doctrinal?

---

55. Esther Rothenbusch, "The *SBJT* Forum: The Current State of Worship" in *The Southern Baptist Journal of Theology* 2, no. 4 (1998): 61.

"And they sang a new song, saying, 'Worthy are you to take the scroll and to open its seals, for you were slain, and by your blood you ransomed people for God from every tribe and language and people and nation.'"
—REVELATION 5:9

"Christian worship is new-covenant worship; it is gospel-inspired worship; it is Christ-centered worship; it is cross-focused worship."
—D. A. CARSON[56]

"If most of our songs could be sung by Buddhists, Muslims, or Hindus, it's time to change our repertoire."
—BOB KAUFLIN[57]

56.   D. A. Carson, "Worship under the Word," in *Worship by the Book*, ed. D. A. Carson (Grand Rapids, MI: Zondervan, 2002), 37.
57.   Bob Kauflin, *Worship Matters: Leading Others to Encounter the Greatness of God* (Wheaton, IL: Crossway, 2008), 62.

CHAPTER 4

SING SONGS THAT ARE CHRISTIAN

You're watching a movie. Someone significant has died. There's a funeral. The mourners are wearing black. All the cars are black. It's raining, obviously. And the umbrellas are black. The priest recites a portion of Psalm 23. Then, on cue, the bagpipes play a mournful but triumphant song. And what's the song?

"Amazing Grace." Of course.

This is fiction. But it's also reality. "Amazing Grace" is likely the most recognizable hymn in the world. One reason is that both the text and the tune are stunningly beautiful.

But another reason is that its theology is fairly general. It's theistic, but it's not overtly evangelical in its lyrics.[58] That's not to say that it's a bad hymn or that we shouldn't sing it. It's masterful! It gives comfort to God's people in life's darkest seasons. But those who are born again sing it with Christian theology that we *assume* based on its biblical allusions and our knowledge of author John Newton's faith. To others, it's just a comforting

---

58. See Mark A. Noll and Edith L. Blumhofer's introduction and D. Bruce Hindmarsh's article "'Amazing Grace: The History of a Hymn and Cultural Icon" in *Sing Them Over Again to Me: Hymns and Hymnbooks in America*, ed. Mark A. Noll and Edith L. Blumhofer (Tuscaloosa, AL: The University of Alabama Press, 2006), xi, 3, 16. Bob Kauflin notes the lack of explicit gospel content in the hymn, as well: *Worship Matters*, 78.

spiritual song that (thankfully) doesn't mention Jesus by name—and so it's at home in movies, in secular concerts, and so on. I'm glad that people hear it in those settings! But there are countless songs that are so overtly Christian that they're unwelcome in the public arena.

EXHIBIT A: "IN CHRIST ALONE"

Should we sing "Amazing Grace"? Yes! With bagpipes! But it should probably be immediately followed in a worship service by a song that makes it unmistakably clear—in the lyrics themselves—that the saving grace of God comes to us *only through the Lord Jesus Christ.*[59] Consider now the very Christ-specific lyrics of Townend's and Getty's text "In Christ Alone":

> *In Christ alone my hope is found, / He is my light, my strength, my song;*
> *This Cornerstone, this solid Ground / Firm through the fiercest drought and storm.*
> *What heights of love, what depths of peace, / When fears are stilled, when strivings cease;*
> *My Comforter, my All in All, / Here in the love of Christ I stand.*
>
> *In Christ alone! – who took on flesh, / Fullness of God in helpless babe.*
> *This gift of love and righteousness, / Scorned by the ones He came to save*
> *Till on that cross as Jesus died, / The wrath of God was satisfied,*
> *For every sin on Him was laid / Here in the death of Christ I live.*
>
> *There in the ground His body lay, / Light of the world by darkness slain:*
> *Then bursting forth in glorious day / Up from the grave He rose again.*
> *And as He stands in victory / Sin's curse has lost its grip on me,*

---

59.   While I'm not always a fan of adding bridges and refrains to classic hymns, the adaptation which Chris Tomlin and Louie Giglio give the hymn in "Amazing Grace (My Chains Are Gone)" roots the song in the saving work of Christ: "My God, My Savior has ransomed me."

*For I am His and He is mine— / Bought with the precious blood
of Christ.*

*No guilt in life, no fear in death, / This is the power of Christ in me;
From life's first cry to final breath, / Jesus commands my destiny.
No power of hell, no scheme of man, / Can ever pluck me from His hand.
Till He returns or calls me home / Here in the power of Christ I'll stand.*[60]

That glorious hymn takes us from Christ's incarnation, to Christ's vicarious
and penal atonement, to Christ's resurrection, to Christ's return—and to
the effect of His work on believers, from every possible angle. As a result,
you probably won't often hear it in blockbuster movies.

SING "THE WORD OF CHRIST"

"In Christ Alone" stands up well to Sinclair Ferguson's standard for
sturdy hymns:

> Worship is theology set to music. The praises of Christ are christolo-
> gy in song since we praise him for who he is and for what he has done.
> Praise is therefore energized and expanded by an increased vision of
> his accomplishments, and correspondingly limited whenever it fails
> to show forth the totality of his work.[61]

The thrust of this chapter is that our songs—or most of them—should
be distinctly *Christian*. To compare hymns to the Bibles of my youth, we
want to sing "red-letter" songs that point us directly to the person and
work of Jesus Christ. Once again, Colossians 3:16 gets us there:

---

60. Lyrics from "In Christ Alone" by Keith Getty and Stuart Townend. © 2002 Thankyou
     Music (PRS) (adm. worldwide at CapitolCMGPublishing.com excluding the UK & Europe
     which is adm. at IntegratedRights.com). All rights reserved. Used by permission.
61. Ferguson, *Some Pastors*, 428.

Let the word of Christ dwell in you richly, teaching and admonishing one another in all wisdom, singing psalms and hymns and spiritual songs, with thankfulness in your hearts to God.

In this theme verse for the singing church, the Bible is called "the Word of Christ." Only Colossians 3:16 and Romans 10:17 use that specific title for the Scriptures. It's a big deal. The Bible—the basis of our "songs, hymns, and spiritual songs"—is called "the Word of *Christ*." Our entire lives (including our worship) are to be lived "in the name of the Lord Jesus" (Colossians 3:17). And even our thanks to the Father is to be offered "through him [Jesus]" (Colossians 3:17). *So, our hymns are to be overtly Christian.* The Bible isn't just a book about religion or general theism. Rather, it is a distinctly *Christ-centered* book. Christianity is a *Christ-centered* religion. And Christian singing should be *Christ-centered* singing.

SING SONGS THAT UNBELIEVERS CAN'T

There are some excellent songs that don't mention Jesus by name. I'm not an iconoclast; I'm not calling for us to burn or even discard them. "Great Is Thy Faithfulness" is a great hymn, though it doesn't mention Jesus. It's beautiful. Sing it. Make good use of "I Sing the Mighty Power of God," "For the Beauty of the Earth," "Praise, My Soul, the King of Heaven," "Like a River Glorious," and "10,000 Reasons." But songs that don't mention Jesus Christ explicitly should be the exception in our services, not the rule, and we should surround them with more explicitly Christian songs. Theologian Daniel Block insists, "Evangelicals must recover the centrality of Christ and the cross in their music."[62] Respected church musician Edmund S. Lorenz concurs: "Christian hymns should be genuinely Christocentric. A Christian hymn should express some definite

---

62. Block, 237.

recognition of God as manifested in Jesus Christ.... This is the very heart of the Christian hymn."[63]

Put it this way: I want to sing songs a Jew, a Mormon, or a theological liberal would be unable to sing. I'm not belittling those people. I'm just saying that our hymns should be so overtly Christian that only Christians can honestly sing them. That's how explicitly gospel-centered I want to be with the doctrine of the hymns I write, as well as the hymns I sing.

Let's look back at "In Christ Alone" as a test case. Several years back the theologically liberal Presbyterian Church (USA) wanted to include the song in its hymnal—but only if Stuart Townend and Keith Getty would alter one line on the meaning of Christ's death: "Till on the cross as Jesus died / The wrath of God was satisfied." The PC (USA) rejects the notion that God is a God of wrath and that Christ's death was a propitiation of that wrath in the place of sinners. Instead, they wanted to change the line to say this: "Till on the cross as Jesus died / The love of God was magnified." That's a true statement. It works—it has the right number of syllables, the right accentuation, and so on. Townend and Getty could have written it that way. But they didn't. And—thankfully—they refused to change it, even though it cost them income and exposure.[64]

That's what I mean about the songs we sing. They should be so Christian that those who reject the Bible's teaching about Jesus' person and work are offended by them. That's not the goal—but it can be a pretty good test of a song's doctrine.

63.   Edmund S. Lorenz, *The Singing Church: The Hymns It Wrote and Sang* (Nashville, TN: Cokesbury Press, 1938), 31.

64.   Collin Hansen, "Keith Getty on What Makes 'In Christ Alone' Accepted and Contested," *The Gospel Coalition*, December 9, 2013. https://www.thegospelcoalition.org/article/keith-getty-on-what-makes-in-christ-alone-beloved-and-contested. I had a similar experience with a hymn called "God's Sufficient Word," with music composed by Peter Anglea. One of the words the song uses to describe the Bible is *inerrant*. When Peter and I went to publish the song, the word proved to be an obstacle. A major (and relatively conservative) choral music publisher said that the word would hurt sales since many churches don't believe in inerrancy. They'd publish the song, but only if we would replace the word *inerrant* with *sufficient* (which the song already uses). We refused. If orthodoxy limits opportunity, so be it.

SING OF THE PERSON AND WORK OF CHRIST

Why this insistence on singing about Jesus? Why not sing about every member of the Trinity? Our worship should be Trinitarian, as we'll see in the next chapter. But it is fitting that it be uniquely *Christ*-ian, as well. That's the emphasis of the New Testament Scriptures:

- It is Jesus Whom the Father sent to be the Savior of the world (1 John 4:10, 14).
- It is Jesus Who reveals to us the unseen God (John 1:18; 14:7-11).
- It is Jesus Who took on our flesh to bridge the gap between God and humanity by becoming Immanuel—God with us, as one of us (Matthew 1:23; John 1:14).
- It is Jesus Who fulfilled all righteousness, keeping the Law on our behalf (Matthew 3:15; Philippians 3:8-9).
- It is Jesus Who was made to be sin for us and Who died as our Propitiation, entirely absorbing and exhausting the wrath of God against us (2 Corinthians 5:21; 1 John 2:1-2).
- It is Jesus Who conquered death and was raised for our justification (Romans 4:25).
- It is Jesus Who is seated at the Father's right hand, interceding for us even now (Hebrews 7:25).
- It is Jesus Whom the Holy Spirit glorifies (John 14:26; 15:26; 16:13-14).
- It is Jesus Whose name is the only name that can save (Acts 4:12).
- It is Jesus Who gives us access to God—both at the moment of our conversion and every day of our Christian lives (John 14:6; Ephesians 3:12; Hebrews 10:19-20).
- It is Jesus—crucified—Who is the core of our message to the world (1 Corinthians 2:1-5; 15:3-4).
- It is Jesus Whose return to fix this broken world is our blessed hope (Titus 2:13).

- It is Jesus Who will have His enemies as His footstool and all things brought under His dominion (Psalm 110:1; Acts 2:34-36; Ephesians 1:22).
- It is Jesus Who humbled Himself through the incarnation and crucifixion, Whom the Father has honored with a name above all names, and to Whom every knee will bow and Whom every tongue will confess as Lord (Philippians 2:5-11).
- It is Jesus Who will judge the living and the dead (2 Timothy 4:1).
- It is Jesus Who will make all things new (Revelation 21-22).
- Perhaps most conclusively, it is Jesus Who is the subject of the inspired hymns recorded throughout the New Testament: Philippians 2:6-11; Colossians 1:15-20; 1 Timothy 3:16; Hebrews 1:3; and Revelation 5:9-13.

Jesus Christ is the focal point of God's salvation plan, and He is the focal point of Christian worship. Bryan Chapell urges us not to be bashful about the Christ-centeredness of our worship:

> Keeping the ministry of the Son at the center of our worship is not an abandonment of the glory of the Father or the Spirit, but is rather faithfulness to the gospel they make Scripture's focus.... In short, we don't need to worry that the Father will get his feelings hurt if we glorify the Son, or that the Spirit will sulk in a corner if we magnify the Christ of his anointing.[65]

WHAT SINGING OF CHRIST LOOKS LIKE

Okay, so it's not exactly a secret that we should sing a lot about Jesus. But how? Which songs should we prioritize? Well, compared to other doctrinal themes, there are seemingly countless songs that exalt Christ and

---

65. Bryan Chapell, *Christ-Centered Worship: Letting the Gospel Shape Our Practice* (Grand Rapids, MI: Baker Academic, 2009), 114-15.

focus on different elements of His person and work. We just need to look a little, discern between good and great, and *think*! Below are some of my favorite Christ-saturated hymns, including both old and new songs.

SING ABOUT THE BIRTH OF CHRIST

Don't just sing sentimental songs. Sing songs that overtly teach biblical doctrine and cause people to marvel at the incarnation.

- "Hark! the Herald Angels Sing" (Wesley, Whitfield, and Mendelssohn)
- "O Come, All Ye Faithful" (Wade / traditional Latin hymn)
- "Come, Thou Long Expected Jesus" (Wesley and Prichard)
- "O Come, O Come, Immanuel" (Neale and Helmore / traditional Latin hymn)
- "You Who Were Rich Beyond All Splendor" (Houghton / traditional French carol)
- "All Praise to Thee, for Thou, O King Divine" (Tucker and Williams)
- "Of the Father's Love Begotten" (Prudentius / DIVINUM MYSTERIUM)
- "Joy Has Dawned" (Townend and Getty)
- "From the Squalor of a Borrowed Stable" (Townend)

SING ABOUT THE LIFE OF CHRIST

This category is more challenging, and songs here sometimes exalt Christ our *Example* to the neglect of Christ our *Savior*. Still, we have four Gospels which captivate us with Jesus' words and works—and we should put them to music. Keep in mind that a key part of Jesus' earthly work was fulfilling all righteousness on our behalf (Matthew 3:15), living a vicarious life before He died a vicarious death.

- "Our Great Savior" (Chapman and Prichard)
- "Jesus, the Very Thought of Thee" (Bernard of Clairvaux and Dykes)
- "Fairest Lord Jesus" (Silesian folk melody)
- "Jesus, Strong and Kind" (Thompson, Robinson, Farren, and Buchanan)
- "Turn Your Eyes" (Romanacce, Winebarger, Stiff, and Trout)
- "Come, Lonely Heart" (Anderson and Habegger)
- "The Love of Christ" (Anderson and Nichols)

SING ABOUT THE DEATH OF CHRIST

There are so many great songs to choose from here, so choose wisely. Look especially for songs that tell not only the *what* of the crucifixion but the *why*.

- "When I Survey the Wondrous Cross" (Watts and Mason or GIFT OF LOVE)
- "Hallelujah, What a Savior" (Bliss)
- "Stricken, Smitten, and Afflicted" (Kelly / O MEIN JESU, ICH MUSS STERBEN)
- "O Sacred Head, Now Wounded" (Gerhardt and Hassler/Bach)
- "Alas! and Did My Savior Bleed?" (Watts and Wilson)
- "Here Is Love" (Reese and Lowry)
- "Lamb of Glory" (Nelson and McHugh)
- "There Is a Redeemer" (Green)
- "The Power of the Cross" (Townend and Getty)
- "Come Behold the Wondrous Mystery" (Boswell, Bleecker, and Papa)
- "I Will Glory in My Redeemer" (Cook and Cook)
- "Jesus, Thank You" (Sczebel)

- "Jesus Saves" (Cottrell and Moffitt)
- "My Jesus, Fair" (Anderson and Habegger)
- "His Robes for Mine" (Anderson and Habegger)

SING ABOUT THE RESURRECTION OF CHRIST

There are relatively few songs about Jesus' resurrection compared to the crucifixion. Sing them. And aspiring hymn-writers, write some more.

- "Christ the Lord Is Risen Today" (Wesley / in *Lyra Davidica*)
- "Hail the Day That Sees Him Rise" (Wesley and Cotterill)
- "Crown Him with Many Crowns" (Bridges, Thring, and Elvey)
- "Christ Arose" (Lowry)
- "See What a Morning [Resurrection Hymn]" (Townend and Getty)
- "Christ Is Risen, He Is Risen Indeed!" (Getty, Getty, and Cash)
- "Mercy Tree" (Neale and Nordhoff)
- "Living Hope" (Wickham)
- "O Lord, My Rock and My Redeemer" (Stiff)

SING ABOUT THE ASCENSION AND INTERCESSION OF CHRIST

This is an underappreciated doctrine, but while the sacrificial work of Jesus is finished, the priestly, mediatorial, and intercessory work of Jesus continues. Sing about it!

- "Arise My Soul, Arise" (Wesley and Edson)
- "Before the Throne of God Above" (Bancroft and Cook)
- "A Debtor to Mercy Alone" (Toplady and Kauflin)
- "The Blood of Jesus Speaks for Me" (Moffitt and Cottrell)
- "Yet Not I But through Christ in Me" (Farren, Robinson, and Thompson)
- "I Run to Christ" (Anderson and Habegger)

SING ABOUT THE RETURN AND REIGN OF CHRIST

Often this doctrine appears in a concluding verse of a great hymn on another theme, as with the final stanzas of "How Great Thou Art" or "It Is Well with My Soul." But there are several hymns that focus on Jesus' return.

- "All Hail the Power of Jesus' Name" (Perronet and Holden or Ellor)
- "Jesus Shall Reign" (Watts and Hatton)
- "Rejoice, the Lord Is King" (Wesley and Darwall)
- "Look, Ye Saints! The Sight Is Glorious" (Kelly and Monk)
- "Lo, He Comes in Clouds Descending" (Wesley and Hughes)
- "Christ Returneth" (Turner and McGranahan)
- "Joy to the World" (Watts and Handel—and no, including this song here isn't an error)
- "There Is a Higher Throne" (Getty and Getty)
- "One Day [When We All Get to Heaven]" (Hewitt and Redman)
- "Come Quickly, Lord" (Anderson and Habegger)

SING ABOUT THE ENTIRE SCOPE OF JESUS' LIFE AND WORK

A few hymns follow Christ from the humble cradle to the empty grave and into eternity.

- "In Christ Alone" (Townend and Getty)
- "One Day / Glorious Day" (Chapman and either Marsh or Hall and Bleecker)
- "Praise Our Savior, Jesus Christ" (Anderson and Jones)

Martin Luther said, "God has preached the gospel through music."[66] Yes—not just general truth, but *the gospel*—the person and work of Jesus

---

66. Martin Luther, *Table Talk*, ed. Theodore G. Tappert, *Luther's Works* (Philadelphia, PA: Fortress Press, 1967), 54:129.

Christ. If we want to sing songs inspired by the Scriptures, we must sing of Christ.

GRACE NOTES FOR WORSHIP LEADERS

- Do you read through hymn texts to verify that you're singing predominantly Christian hymns rather than general theistic hymns?
- What overtly Christ-centered songs would you add to the lists in this chapter?
- What are some songs that perhaps you should sing less, or even not at all?

GRACE NOTES FOR PARENTS AND CHILDREN'S TEACHERS

- Are you intentionally teaching children songs—including adult hymns—which will help them understand the saving work of Jesus?
- Which of the songs your children sing are true, but perhaps rather light or moralistic?

GRACE NOTES FOR EVERYBODY

- What are some of your favorite hymns that accurately teach overt truths about Jesus and His saving work?
- Which of the songs you sing are so Christian that an Orthodox Jew couldn't sing them?

*"The grace of the Lord Jesus Christ and the love of God
and the fellowship of the Holy Spirit be with you all."*
—2 CORINTHIANS 13:14

*"God-centered worship is Trinitarian worship. Our worship should
be clearly directed to God as Father, Son, and Holy Spirit."*
—JOHN FRAME[67]

*"God is triune; there are within the Godhead three persons, the
Father, the Son, and the Holy Spirit; and the work of salvation
is one in which all three act together, the Father purposing
redemption, the Son securing it and the Spirit applying it."*
—J. I. PACKER[68]

67. Frame, *Worship*, 7.
68. J. I. Packer, *Knowing God* (Downers Grove, IL: InterVarsity Press, 1973), 20.

CHAPTER 5

SING SONGS THAT ARE TRINITARIAN

In the fall of 1990 I became a student at Bob Jones University. To say it was a culture shock would be an understatement. I had attended public schools all my life. The only time prayer was allowed was when we sang Bon Jovi's "Living on a Prayer" on the band bus after a football game. (Yes, the band bus. Don't start.) As for the music at my church, it was full of the gospel, but it wasn't anything "high church."

Yet, there I was, in Greenville, South Carolina, sporting a suit and tie, seated in a huge auditorium, singing the "Gloria Patri" with thousands of other students, all accompanied by a pipe organ that seemed to vibrate the entire campus:

> *Glory be to the Father, and to the Son, and to the Holy Ghost.*
> *As it was in the beginning, 'tis now, and ever shall be;*
> *World without end! Amen! Amen!*

What was *that*? Actually, it was one of the oldest hymns of the Christian church, composed way back in the fourth century. The Council of Nicaea (AD 325), which defined and defended the deity and humanity of Christ and the eternal existence of the Trinity, gave birth to Trinitarian hymns intended to combat stubborn heresies that denied the Trinity.[69] Little did college-freshman Chris realize that I was affirming biblical orthodoxy from nearly 2000 years of church history. That's beautiful. We should sing the "Gloria Patri" more often!

I've stated already that our songs should be distinctly Christian. But some of them should also be boldly Trinitarian. We worship one God Who exists in three distinct Persons. This is an essential doctrine of the Christian faith. And yet, the doctrine of the Trinity isn't really something most Christians celebrate.

Robert Letham writes, "To the vast majority of Protestants the Trinity is little more than an abstruse mathematical conundrum."[70] He's not wrong. The doctrine of the Trinity confuses us. If we're honest, sometimes it even embarrasses us: we have to believe it, and so we do, but we can't make sense of it. How can one be three? How can three be one?

It shouldn't surprise or trouble us that we can't fully comprehend God. We aren't His peers, and the fact that He's so great that we can't mentally "master" Him is actually a good thing. But the doctrine of the Trinity ought to be a *glorious* truth to us, not a conundrum. It tells us about the Godhead's delight in mutual love and fellowship for eternity past. It tells us of a God Who planned together as the Triune Community to create us. It tells us of a God Who similarly planned to save us—the Father designing salvation, the Son accomplishing it, and the Spirit applying it. We're accustomed to saying and singing that "Jesus saves." And so He does. But the Father also saves. The Spirit also saves. As Brian Rosner writes, "Salvation is the narrative of the saving Trinity's acting on behalf of human beings."[71] "The saving Trinity"—I love that. Our Triune God col-

---

69.   Robert Letham notes that the heretic Arius, who denied the deity of Christ, "attracted a large following, drawn by a range of choruses he composed." *The Holy Trinity* (Phillipsburg, NJ: P&R Publishing, 2019), 110. Once again we see that error as well as truth is spread through hymns.

70.   Letham, *The Holy Trinity*, 254. Also see pages 241 and 290.

71.   Brian S. Rosner, "Paul and the Trinity," in *The Essential Trinity*, ed. Brandon D. Crowe and Carl Trueman (Phillipsburg, NJ: P&R Publishing, 2016), 122.

laborated to achieve our redemption. And through the gospel They—the three Persons of the Godhead—have pulled us into Their perfect loving relationship. They—each One of Them—are to be praised.

As Michael Reeves explains in his profound book *Delighting in the Trinity*, were there no Trinity, there would be no love—only a self-absorbed autocrat to be feared rather than a gracious, loving, joyful God to be adored.[72] The doctrine of the Trinity isn't the fine print of the Christian faith; it is in bold on the title page. And it's a doctrine we should celebrate in our songs.

So far in this book we've rooted our criteria for excellent hymns in Colossians 3:16-17. I'd like to look at those verses again, this time alongside a parallel passage, Ephesians 5:18-20. Read both texts, and this time keep an eye out for Trinitarian teaching.

> Let the word of Christ dwell in you richly, teaching and admonishing one another in all wisdom, singing psalms and hymns and spiritual songs, with thankfulness in your hearts to God. And whatever you do, in word or deed, do everything in the name of the Lord Jesus, giving thanks to God the Father through him. (Colossians 3:16-17)

> And do not get drunk with wine, for that is debauchery, but be filled with the Spirit, addressing one another in psalms and hymns and spiritual songs, singing and making melody to the Lord with your heart, giving thanks always and for everything to God the Father in the name of our Lord Jesus Christ. (Ephesians 5:18-20)

The essential New Testament texts that command us to sing give honor to the Father, Son, and Spirit. Let's unpack that a bit.

---

72. Michael Reeves, *Delighting in the Trinity: An Introduction to the Christian Faith* (Downers Grove, IL: InterVarsity Press, 2012), 9, 14-18, 39-42.

Our worship is to include *God the Father*. Most notably, we are to *give Him thanks*:

- We sing "with thankfulness... to God" (Colossians 3:16).
- In everything we do, we "[give] thanks to God the Father" (Colossians 3:17).
- Our worship in song leads us to "[give] thanks always and for everything to God the Father" (Ephesians 5:20).

Our worship is to include *God the Son*. We worship *Him*, and we *approach the Father through Him*:

- As we noted in chapter 4, it is the "word of Christ" in us that launches our teaching and singing (Colossians 3:16).
- All of our worship—in fact, *"whatever* [we] do, in word or deed"— we do "in the name of the Lord Jesus" (Colossians 3:17).
- When we approach God the Father, we always do so "through him [Jesus]" (Colossians 3:17). Jesus is our only means of access into the Father's presence *every* day, not just on the day we were saved (John 14:6; Hebrews 10:19-20).
- Our "singing and making melody" is "to the *Lord*"—the New Testament's constant designation for Jesus (Ephesians 5:19).
- Our thanksgiving to the Father is given "in the name of our Lord Jesus Christ" (Ephesians 5:20).

Our worship is also to include *God the Spirit*. He is as active in our salvation and as worthy of our songs as the Father and the Son:

- The "word of Christ" dwelling in us and causing our songs is the Spirit-inspired Word (Colossians 3:16; 2 Peter 1:21).
- We sing praises to God because we are "filled with" or "under the influence of" the Spirit (Ephesians 5:18). Being full of Christ's Word

(Colossians 3:16) and being filled with the Holy Spirit (Ephesians 5:18) are synonymous concepts.

- The songs we sing include "*spiritual* songs" (Colossians 3:16 and Ephesians 5:19).
- Our praise and thanksgiving are offered "in" and "with" our hearts—what we offer is not merely words but the overflow of lives that have been Spirit-regenerated and are now Spirit-controlled (Colossians 3:16 and Ephesians 5:19).

Worshiping the Spirit is the sticking point for some. Giving praise to God the Father and God the Son doesn't raise eyebrows. But some Christians get nervous about worshiping the Holy Spirit. In fact, I was once rebuked for writing a prayer to the Holy Spirit in the third stanza of my hymn "A Triune Prayer." Such skittishness about praying to and praising the Holy Spirit is wrongheaded. In fact, I think it flirts with heterodoxy. Yes, we give honor to the Lord Jesus Christ, our Redeemer. But our neglect of the Spirit (and even of the Father at times) can almost be a functional Unitarianism—as though only the Son were God. We worship one God Who exists in three Persons. While it is true that the Spirit directs our attention to the Son and the Father, the Spirit Himself *is God*: eternal with the Father and Son, equal with the Father and Son, and deserving of our adoration and praise as surely as the Father and the Son.

Think of worship—specifically *Whom* we worship—in this way:

- When Peter wanted to honor Moses and Elijah alongside Jesus during His transfiguration, God the Father rebuked him: "This is my beloved Son, with whom I am well pleased; listen to him" (Matthew 17:5).
- When Cornelius fell at the feet of Peter and wanted to worship him in Caesarea, Peter stopped him: "Stand up; I too am a man" (Acts 10:26).
- When the idolaters from Lystra mistook Paul and Barnabas for Hermes and Zeus and tried to make sacrifices to them, the apostles

tore their clothes and rushed out to stop them: "Men, why are you doing these things? We also are men, of like nature with you" (Acts 14:15). Paul would rather have been stoned than worshiped—and he *was* stoned (v. 19)!

- When John fell at the feet of the glorious angel during his heavenly vision, the angel rebuked him: "You must not do that! I am a fellow servant with you and your brothers.... Worship God" (Revelation 19:10).
- When John fell at the feet of the glorious angel—again—when he was granted a vision of the new heaven and new earth, the angel again rebuked him: "You must not do that! I am a fellow servant with you and your brothers....Worship God" (Revelation 22:9).

But when a Christian bows to worship the Holy Spirit, there will be no rebuke, no tearing of garments, no correction. For the command to "worship God" is absolutely obeyed when we worship God the Spirit. Indeed, the three Members of the Godhead are so united that to adore One is to adore Them All. There is no rivalry or jealousy within the Trinity—only perfect harmony and mutual affection. As Charles Hodge unapologetically writes, "[The Holy Spirit] is therefore presented in the Scriptures as the proper object of worship."[73]

The *Westminster Confession of Faith* states, "Religious worship is to be given to God, the Father, Son, and Holy Ghost" (21.2). Yes. Just so.

Scott Aniol and Ryan Martin make a similar statement in the preface to *Hymns to the Living God*: "We sing to God. We sing to the Father, thrice holy and forever blessed. We sing to our Savior, Jesus Christ, who shed His blood for us. We sing to that Holy Spirit whom God has given to us to dwell in our hearts, making us God's holy temple."[74] Beautiful!

The "Gloria Patri" is right: "Glory be to the Father, and to the Son, and to the Holy Ghost."

73. Charles Hodge, *Systematic Theology* (Peabody, MA: Hendrickson Publishers, 2001), 1:528.
74. Aniol and Martin, i.

The traditional Doxology is right: "Praise Father, Son, and Holy Ghost."

Gospel songwriter Margaret J. Harris was right:

Glory, glory to the Father!
Glory, glory to the Son!
Glory, glory to the Spirit!
Glory to the Three in One!

So, that's settled. Now, what does singing Trinitarian songs look like in practice?

WE SHOULD SING SONGS TO EACH MEMBER OF THE TRINITY

Just as a single sermon cannot cover the entire Bible, no single song can address all that we believe. Every song won't be a Trinitarian song. But we should still be intentional about worshiping the Father, the Son, and the Spirit. First, we should make use of excellent hymns which honor Them individually:

SING PRAISE TO THE FATHER

- "I Sing the Mighty Power of God" (Watts and Württemberg)
- "This Is My Father's World" (Babcock and Sheppard)
- "How Deep the Father's Love for Us" (Townend)
- "Praise, My Soul, the King of Heaven"[75] (Lyte)
- "Almighty Father" (Williams and Harlan)

---

75. Greg Habegger prefers to sing the text of "Praise, My Soul, the King of Heaven" to the tune HYFRYDOL (commonly associated with "Our Great Savior"). Similarly, he sings "I Will Sing the Wondrous Story" to the tune HYFRYDOL or NETTLETON (commonly associated with "Come, Thou Fount of Every Blessing") rather than to its common (and rather bouncy) tune.

- "Only a Holy God" (Farren, Robinson, Smith, and Thompson)
- "God Is For Us" (Farren, Ferguson, Tranter, Reeves, Robinson, Tealy and Thompson)
- "Praise Ye Jehovah" (Jones and Gustafson)
- "The Father Looks on Me" (Anderson and Holden)

SING PRAISE TO THE SON

- "Crown Him with Many Crowns" (Bridges, Thring, and Elvey)
- "Our Great Savior" (Chapman and Prichard)
- "Jesus, the Very Thought of Thee" (Bernard of Clairvaux and Dykes)
- "Fairest Lord Jesus" (Silesian folk melody)
- "In Christ Alone" (Townend and Getty)
- "Jesus, Strong and Kind" (Thompson, Robinson, Farren, and Buchanan)
- *(See chapter 4 for a fuller list of hymns on the person and work of Christ.)*

SING PRAISE TO THE SPIRIT

- "Spirit of God, Descend upon My Heart" (Croly and Atkinson)
- "Come, Holy Spirit, Heavenly Dove"[76] (Watts and Dykes)
- "The Comforter Has Come" (Bottome and Kirkpatrick)
- "Breathe on Me, Breath of God" (Hatch and Jackson)
- "Spirit of the Living God" (Iverson)
- "Holy Spirit, Living Breath of God" (Townend and Getty)

The lists above are far from exhaustive. Perhaps for that reason, they conceal the fact that there is a troubling lack of hymns about the Holy Spirit. Here's an illustration of that point: The table of contents in *Hymns*

---

76. This relatively obscure text by Isaac Watts sings well to ST. AGNES (commonly associated with "Jesus, the Very Thought of Thee").

of Grace, the excellent new hymnal from The Master's Seminary, has 93 hymns on God the Father and 222 on God the Son, but only 7 on God the Spirit.[77] Similarly, the Southern Baptist Convention's *Baptist Hymnal* contains 126 hymns on the Father, 200 on the Son, and only 9 on the Spirit.[78] There is a gaping hole in English hymnody when it comes to the person of the Holy Spirit.

Carl Trueman gives the following charge to those who select—and write—hymns:

> Not all hymns are explicitly trinitarian but we should take time to make sure that those which are trinitarian are used regularly and to good effect. Those with the gift of writing hymns and praise songs should consciously strive to make them trinitarian, both as exercises in doxology and as examples of pedagogy.[79]

Robert Letham, one of the foremost Trinitarian theologians of our time, similarly calls for more Trinitarian hymns:

> There is a need to refocus Western hymnody. We need more Trinitarian hymns. There was an outpouring of such hymns following the Trinitarian crisis [in the fourth and fifth centuries], but by the high Middle Ages, this had slowed to a trickle, eventually to dry up altogether.[80]

I have felt the same burden, and I have labored over several Trinitarian hymns, including "Holy, Mighty, Worthy," "A Triune Prayer," and "I Am with You." I have not, however, written a satisfactory hymn on the Holy

77. *Hymns of Grace*, ed. Philip Webb (Los Angeles, CA: The Master's Seminary Press, 2015).

78. *Baptist Hymnal*, ed. Mike Harland (Nashville, TN: LifeWay Worship, 2008).

79. Trueman, "Trinity," 239.

80. Letham, *The Holy Trinity*, 509. He issues a similar call in "The Trinity and Worship" in *The Essential Trinity: New Testament Foundations and Practical Relevance*, ed. Brandon D. Crowe and Carl R. Trueman (Phillipsburg, NJ: P&R Publishing, 2017), 279, 283.

Spirit, although I have tried. It's a challenging task, but the need is certainly there. Perhaps someone reading this book will be part of the solution.

A few years ago I had the opportunity to collaborate with Dan Forrest, a renowned choral composer, a devoted Christian, and a personal friend. Our aim was to write a Trinitarian anthem, modeled after the *Apostles' Creed*, but with expressions of delight and wonder in addition to faith: "We believe... We praise... We rejoice... We know... We adore... We yield... We affirm... We believe, and we rejoice!" The result of our efforts is the hymn and choral anthem "We Believe," one example of what Trinitarian hymnody can look like.

> *We believe in God Supreme– / Ever present, never seen;*
> *God Most High, who reigns above; / Father nigh, whose name is Love.*
> *We whose prayers to God ascend / Praise creation's Source and End.*
>
> *We rejoice in Jesus Christ– / God's own Son, our Sacrifice;*
> *Very God, yet virgin born; / Sinless, yet for sinners torn.*
> *We whom Jesus died to win / Know He lives to come again.*
>
> *We adore the Spirit free– / Author of our unity.*
> *Giver of the sacred Word, / Wellspring of the second birth.*
> *We whom He indwells and fills / Yield our hearts and minds and wills.*
>
> *We, the Church, affirm our faith / In the Triune God of grace;*
> *Kingdoms fall and ages change– / Faithful, changeless, God remains!*
> *One in Christ, we lift one voice! / We believe, and we rejoice!*[81]

---

81.   Lyrics from "We Believe" by Chris Anderson and Dan Forrest. © 2015 Beckenhorst Press, Inc. All rights reserved. Used by permission of Beckenhorst Press, Inc.

WE SHOULD SING SONGS TO THE THREE-IN-ONE

While it is appropriate to sing hymns to the individual Persons of the Trinity, we should delight to sing songs of praise to the complete Godhead, as well—Father, Son, and Spirit. Often hymns will devote a stanza to each Member of the Godhead. When a song does so, it is essential not to omit a stanza during public use. Other times, the hymn simply mentions the different roles of the Father, Son, and Spirit. Still other hymns use refrains—or the 21st century concept of bridges—to overtly worship the Three-in-One.

SING PRAISE TO THE TRINITY

- "Holy, Holy, Holy" (Heber and Dykes)[82]
- "The Doxology" (Ken and Bourgeois)
- "Praise Ye the Triune God!" (Charles and Flemming)
- "Come, Thou Almighty King" (unknown / Giardini)
- "Arise My Soul, Arise" (Wesley and Edson)
- "Eternal Father, Strong to Save" (Whiting and Dykes)
- "There Is a Redeemer" (Green)
- "We Are Heirs of God Almighty" (Townend)
- "Is He Worthy?" (Peterson and Shive)
- "All Creatures of Our God and King" (final stanza – St. Francis of Assisi)

---

82. Sing the first line in your head. Did you notice that the three repetitions of the word "holy" use the three tones of a musical triad? John B. Dykes' masterful tune (appropriately called NICAEA) actually gives a musical tip-of-the-hat to the Trinity with this musical symbol. Brilliant. This was pointed out to me by Paul S. Jones in *Singing*, 73. Jeremy Begbie similarly uses the three-note chord as an illustration of the Trinity, arguing that an aural illustration is more meaningful and less problematic than the visual illustrations that are almost always inadequate and misleading. Jeremy Begbie, "Through Music: Sound Mix" in *Beholding the Glory: Incarnation through the Arts*, ed. Jeremy Begbie (Grand Rapids, MI: Baker Academic, 2001), 147-49.

- "The Lord Is My Salvation" (bridge – Getty, Getty, Nockels, and Myrin)
- "Our Triune God" (Henson and Taylor)
- "You Are the Lord" (Hoskinson)

SING IN THE POWER OF THE SPIRIT

We cannot do less than sing orthodox Bible doctrine, including hymns on the Trinity. But we must do more. That is, merely reciting the words of excellent hymns isn't worship. Indeed, if the heart isn't engaged, mere recitation may make us guilty of taking the Lord's name in vain.

Worship must be *spiritual*, not just physical or oral.

We noted earlier that both Colossians 3:16-17 and Ephesians 5:18-20 require that worship come from our hearts. Yes, singing involves our vocal cords, our diaphragms, even our eyes and ears and minds. But worship is first and foremost a *spiritual* exercise. Calvin, commenting on Ephesians 5:19, writes, "Let your praises be not merely on the tongue, as hypocrites do, but from the heart."[83]

Harry Eskew and Hugh McElrath call for from-the-heart worship in even more urgent terms:

> Here is the crux of the matter of the hymn as theology. No matter how precise and correct the theological teaching of a hymn may be, its doctrine remains frozen in moribund wording and lifeless musical notation until its meaning is devoutly embraced by the one who sings it.[84]

It's all too easy to sit through a song service mumbling words with our lips while our minds and hearts are a thousand miles away. It takes intentional,

---

83. John Calvin, *Calvin's Commentaries*, trans. William Pringle (Grand Rapids: Baker Books, 1999), 21:316.
84. Eskew and McElrath, 71.

diligent effort to focus on the service. But we must, for it is the height of irreverence to let our minds wander when we are supposed to be hearing from God and responding with worship.

To battle such carelessness, John Wesley published ten "Directions for Singing" in the 1761 edition of *Select Hymns*, an early Methodist hymnal. The seventh direction reads as follows:

> Above all, sing spiritually. Have an eye to God in every word you sing. Aim at pleasing him more than yourself, or any other creature. In order to do this attend strictly to the sense of what you sing, and see that your heart is not carried away with the sound, but offered to God continually.[85]

Very good. Focus. Concentrate. Clear your mental clutter. Engage.

But still, you need more than good intentions and sincerity. *You need divine assistance.* Your worship is acceptable only because Jesus makes it so—not because of your devotion (Hebrews 13:15). You need grace—even to be grateful for the grace you've already received. With that idea in mind, my family formed a habit of praying together as we drive to church on Sunday morning. When we'd reach a certain curve in the road, we'd pray together for Sunday School teachers, ushers, musicians, nursery workers, pastors, and ourselves. You should try the same. Before the service even begins, pray that the Spirit of God will tether your heart to Himself, clear your mind of distractions, and help you to worship God aright.

How convicting is it that we need divine enablement even to worship correctly? And yet, how encouraging is it that God grants that help, that we might commune with Him and exalt Him? Every part of the Christian experience—from commencement to culmination—is by God's grace and for God's glory.

Because I love the church, and because the purpose of the church is to bring glory to our Triune God (Ephesians 1:6, 12, 14; 3:20-21), my

---

85.　John Wesley, "Directions for Singing" in *Select Hymns*, 1761.

favorite stanza of any hymn I've written is the climactic verse of "Holy, Mighty, Worthy." United to Greg Habegger's stately tune, it gives voice to the adoration of the church for the many graces we have received, exalting the Father, Son, and the Spirit. *Soli Deo gloria*—all glory to God!

> *"Glory, glory, glory!" We, Thy church, adore Thee,*
> *Called by grace to bring Thee praise; trophies of Thy pow'r to save!*
> *None shall share Thy glory! All shall bow before Thee.*
> *Father, Son, and Spirit: One! "Glory, glory, glory!"*

GRACE NOTES FOR WORSHIP LEADERS

- Do you intentionally include Trinitarian hymns in your service orders? How often?
- Most of our songs focus on the person and work of Jesus—with good reason. But how can you help your church to be grateful to the Father and the Spirit as well?

GRACE NOTES FOR PARENTS AND CHILDREN'S TEACHERS

- The Trinity is a complex doctrine for adults, not to mention for children. But it's an essential part of our faith, and kids need to learn it early and be reminded of it often. What are some Bible stories and children's books that can help you explain the doctrine of the Trinity? (Beware of illustrations and similes, which almost always depict the Trinity in an inaccurate way!)
- Of the songs listed in this chapter, which seem ideal to teach children about the Trinity?

GRACE NOTES FOR EVERYBODY

- How aware are you of the grace extended to you by the Father and the Spirit, as well as the Son?
- How often do you give praise to the Father and the Spirit, both in your personal prayers and in the songs you sing?
- If you haven't already done so, plan to read Michael Reeves' excellent book, *Delighting in the Trinity*—soon!

"Praise the LORD! Sing to the LORD a new song, his praise in the assembly of the godly!"
—PSALM 149:1

"Music and notes, which are wonderful gifts and creations of God, do help gain a better understanding of the text, especially when sung by a congregation and sung earnestly."
—MARTIN LUTHER[86]

"Congregational singing is the primary musical expression in worship."
—FRANKLIN SEGLER[87]

86. Walter Buzin, *Luther on Music* (St. Paul, MN: North Central, 1958), 14, quoting Martin Luther, "Treatise on the Last Words of David" in *Luther's Works*, ed. Jeroslav Pelikan (St. Louis, MO: Concordia Publishing), vol. 15.
87. Franklin M. Segler, *Christian Worship: Its Theology and Practice* (Nashville, TN: Broadman Press, 1967), 102.

CHAPTER 6

SING SONGS THAT ARE CONGREGATIONAL

What does great church music sound like?

Some love a mighty pipe organ. Some prefer a praise band. But again, *what does great church music sound like?*

There's only one right answer: Great church music sounds like the congregation. It sounds like *human voices* blended together in praise to God. In an insightful article titled "The Most Important Instrument on Sunday Morning," Bob Kauflin explains how Scripture prioritizes the human voice over musical instruments:

> Psalm 150 notwithstanding, Scriptures that reference using voices to praise God far outweigh those that reference using instruments—about 7 to 1. That's not conclusive, but it certainly points us in a direction.[88]

88. Bob Kauflin, "The Most Important Instrument on Sunday Morning," *Desiring God*, March 8, 2020, https://www.desiringgod.org/articles/the-most-important-instrument-on-sunday-morning.

God delights to hear His people sing, and so should we.

Many of my most memorable worship experiences have been times of *a cappella* singing. One such time—my favorite—was during the first Getty *Sing!* conference. We worshiped to big, energetic music throughout the conference, and it was wonderful. But then Joni Eareckson Tada took the stage. She literally *took* it—an enormous stage with nobody on it but a woman in a small wheelchair. And we were transfixed. As she so often does, she shared her testimony, then occasionally just broke into a song. No notice. No piano. No band. No lyrics projected onto a screen. Just her voice. And by the time she finished the first phrase of a hymn, the entire auditorium, packed with people, was singing with her, from memory, with harmonies and without accompaniment. We were especially mindful of the *meaning* of the songs because Joni's powerful testimony made us appreciate the lyrics as never before. It was unforgettably glorious.

What could be better? Well, singing with my own local church. I enjoy that shock and awe of conference singing. But it's rare and somewhat artificial. No singing in the world is more important than singing with your own church, and no singing in the church is as important as the singing of the *whole* church. Prepared music sung by a soloist, ensemble, or choir is fine. We'll get to that in a minute. Prepared music is valuable. But congregational singing is *invaluable*. Listen to the Gettys (who are exceptional performers) on the importance of congregational singing:

> While we may have church choirs within our churches made up of voices who have expertise and ability, the congregation of a church is the ultimate choir, and it is without auditions—everyone can be in it and should be in it.[89]

89.　Getty and Getty, 3.

THE SILENT, SONGLESS CONGREGATION

God wants His people to sing. Scripture mentions music over 600 times, from cover to cover. The Old Testament—especially in the Psalms— abounds with both songs and commands to sing. The New Testament refers to music less, in part because the topic was already covered so thoroughly in the Hebrew Scriptures.[90] But the New Testament once again commands us to sing (Colossians 3:16; Ephesians 5:19; James 5:13). How important is it to God that His people sing? *The command to sing is the most frequent command in the Bible.* Here are just a few examples of Scripture's "Sing!" imperatives:

- "Sing to the LORD, for he has triumphed gloriously; the horse and his rider he has thrown into the sea." (Exodus 15:21)
- "Sing to him, sing praises to him; tell of all his wondrous works!... Sing to the LORD, all the earth! Tell of his salvation from day to day." (1 Chronicles 16:9, 23)
- "Sing praises to the LORD, who sits enthroned in Zion! Tell among the peoples his deeds!" (Psalm 9:11)
- "Sing praises to God, Sing praises! Sing praises to our King, Sing praises! For God is the King of all the earth; sing praises with a psalm!" (Psalm 47:6-7)

I suppose that last one makes the point rather well.

And yet, the ideal of God's people singing His praises together has not always been met. For centuries, the saints of God were songless and silent. First, songs were sung in Latin and so were unintelligible to congregations. Second, songs were sung by clergy and choirs, not the laity.

---

90. "The New Testament does not go into a detailed description of praise and music and musical instruments for the early church; it did not have to because all of that was so much a part of the Israelites' worship of God. The writers simply assume that such praise should continue and will continue in glory." Ross, 261.

Abraham Kuyper describes how congregational singing was all but extinguished during the Middle Ages:

> At first nearly all congregational psalm singing, and then nearly all congregational singing, was lost. Choirs replaced congregational singing.... Also, the songs they sang often left much to be desired. The sound, the tone of voice, and the artistic element became most important, and the content of the song of secondary importance. Singing became an artistic exhibition and ceased to be an expression of thanksgiving and adoration of God by the believers.[91]

Thankfully, this error was corrected—along with other doctrinal and practical deviations—during the Protestant Reformation. The Reformers' emphasis on Bible doctrine (including the priesthood of the believer) resulted in giving worship back to the laity—by giving them the Word of God in their own language, by directing them to God directly rather than by way of priests, and by involving them in congregational singing, again in their own language.[92] Congregational singing was a huge part of the Reformation.

Luther, in particular, championed congregational singing in Germany. The hymnals printed by Luther and other Germans during his lifetime

---

91.   Abraham Kuyper, *Our Worship*, ed. Harry Boonstra, trans. Harry Boonstra, Henry Baron, Gerrit Sheeres, and Leonard Sweetman (Grand Rapids: Wm. B. Eerdmans Publishing Company, 2009), 40. Fred Coleman's language when describing the medieval church and sacred music is also significant: "The clergy of the medieval and monastic eras 'stole' congregational singing from 'the people in the pews' and restricted hymn singing to choirs of priests." Preface to *Hymns Modern and Ancient*, ed. Fred R. Coleman (Milwaukee, WI: Heart Publications, 2011).

92.   Luther championed the singing of hymns; Calvin allowed only psalms; Zwingli prohibited congregational singing altogether. So, the Reformers' approach to congregational singing wasn't homogeneous. William S. Smith notes that the two most famous pre-Reformers, John Wycliffe and John Hus (both of whom died a century before Luther posted his *Ninety-Five Theses*) encouraged congregational singing. Where the gospel goes, congregational singing follows. William S. Smith, *Joyful Noise*, 58.

often had in their titles the German phrase "fur die layen"—*for the laity.*[93] One title page from a hymnal published in 1526 describes its contents along with a joyful exclamation which indicates its significance: "Spiritual hymns and psalms, as are now (God be praised) sung in the churches."[94]

We, like the Reformers, believe that every believer can and must sing. To exalt elite performers over the congregation actually rolls back the Reformation. And yet, there is a trend in much of evangelicalism to turn the congregation back into an audience and to turn worshipers back into observers. The staging, atmosphere, complexity, and volume of the musical portions of many worship services are marginalizing the congregation.

Throughout my pastoral ministry I have preached the importance of "every-member ministry." Congregational singing is for everybody, not just the praise band or the choir. The Gettys agree: "Listening to each other mumbling quietly along as a band performs brilliantly on the stage in a church building is not the same as singing together as a congregation."[95]

Amen. God intends for you not merely to listen, but to sing!

"ADDRESSING ONE ANOTHER…"

Most of the Bible's commands to sing appear in the Psalms. But our twin texts on singing in the church—Colossians 3:16-17 and Ephesians 5:18-20—speak clearly about how our singing ministers to one another. Singing is primarily directed to God. But there is mutual edification that takes place during hymn-singing as well. The reciprocal pronouns—the "one anothers" (for non-word-nerds)—make this clear:

---

93. Robin A. Leaver, *The Whole Church Sings: Congregational Singing in Luther's Wittenberg* (Grand Rapids, MI: Wm B. Eerdmans Publishing Co., 2017), 111, 141.
94. Ibid., 133.
95. Getty and Getty, 72-73. Matt Merker suggests that churches turn *down* the volume of the accompaniment and turn *up* the congregational lighting, both of which will help avoid a "concert" feel and encourage congregational involvement. *Corporate*, 142, 149. See Appendix D in this book for more tips for those leading, accompanying, or running tech in worship services.

Let the word of Christ dwell in you richly, teaching and admonishing one another in all wisdom, singing psalms and hymns and spiritual songs. (Colossians 3:16)

Be filled with the Spirit, addressing one another in psalms and hymns and spiritual songs. (Ephesians 5:19)

Colossians could be read to say that we teach each other and *then* sing, although most Bible interpreters see the singing as part of the teaching. But Ephesians 5:19 is unmistakably clear: We "*[address] one another* in psalms and hymns and spiritual songs." Hendriksen comments, "The point to note is that by means of these psalms, hymns, and spiritual songs, Spirit-filled believers must *speak to each other*."[96]

Both the books of Colossians and Ephesians were written to local churches—not the Christian public at large. I'm grateful for Bible conferences and Christian recording artists. But the local church is essential, and its singing is essential. The Scriptures tell local churches that God intends for *every* Christian to sing to his or her brothers and sisters in Christ—*in the meetings of the local assembly.*

There are those—chiefly men, in my experience—who stand through a song service and scarcely mumble the words to the songs. They reason that music isn't "their thing." But worshiping God in song is to be *everybody's* thing. Even if your voice leaves much to be desired, your church and its members need you and your singing whenever they assemble. Sing— loud and proud! Doing so should be a delight, but it's also a duty.

So, how can we cultivate better congregational singing?

VALUE CONGREGATIONAL SINGING

Let me talk to pastors for a minute. Everybody else is welcome to eavesdrop.

---

96. William Hendriksen, *New Testament Commentary: Exposition of Ephesians* (Grand Rapids, MI: Baker Academic, 1967), 240.

Great congregational singing begins with pastors. If we don't love to sing, neither will the congregation. Pastors must demonstrate—from their preaching to their commentary to their eager participation—that congregational singing is an essential element of church life. For my part, I love to include germane hymn lyrics in my sermon—and to *sing* them, not recite them. Do whatever you can to highlight the importance of congregational singing.

Please hear me, pastors. You're a *member* of the church, not just the leader. Don't be the guy who comes in halfway through the song service or who works on his sermon notes on the front row or on the platform while everybody else sings. It doesn't make you look focused; it makes you look unprepared and disengaged. Franklin Segler writes, "It is probably true that the level of church music can rise no higher than the minister's estimation of its importance in the life of the church."[97] Every single member of the church should show up ready to lean in and sing out—especially the pastor!

Besides demonstrating that you *love* congregational singing with your church, make time for it. Don't use it merely as a "warm-up" to preaching, a chance to move people to or from the stage, or the like.[98] Make it clear to God and to your people that worship is a priority, not an appetizer. Even Spurgeon, the Prince of Preachers, warned against minimizing the importance of any part of the worship service:

I have heard prayer and singing, now and then called "the preliminary services," as if they were but a preface to the sermon; this is rare I hope among us—if it were common it would be to our deep disgrace. I endeavor invariably to take all the service myself for my own sake, and I think also for the people's.[99]

---

97. Segler, 105.
98. I confess that I once said, "We'll give the choir the opportunity to 'get down' while we sing the next hymn." I meant, "descend from the choir loft and be seated," but hilarity ensued.
99. Charles H. Spurgeon, *Lectures to My Students* (Albany, OR: AGES Software, 1996), 1:67.

Now, for the rest of the church...

You need to value congregational singing, too. Don't arrive late. Don't whisper, sort through your purse, or scroll on your phone during the songs. Sing! Encourage your kids to sing out with you. Show them how. God requires this of you—and honestly, singing is one of the easiest commands of God to fulfill.

I often notice that shared joys are multiplied, just as shared sorrows are diminished. We are incurably social people—even the introverts among us. (Ish. To a degree.) It's more enjoyable to see the Grand Canyon, hear a great symphony, or read a great book *with someone*. Sharing what we're experiencing with others increases our enjoyment. That's certainly true with music. If I hear a great song, I want my family to hear it, too.

The church—and congregational singing in particular—celebrates this hunger for community and shared experiences. It's *us* singing, *together*. I'm fine with a singer closing her eyes and lifting her hands. I'll do it myself—though as a Baptist my hands can extend only slightly above my rib cage. But too much "singing-with-your-eyes-closed" can be unhelpfully isolating. It's important to remember that you're part of a *church* that's singing; you're not just an individual singing in a crowd.

MORE FOR LEADERS: CHOOSE SONGS THAT SING WELL!

Nothing kills congregational singing more quickly than singing the wrong songs. Those who choose the songs—a group that hopefully includes a pastor—need to choose only songs that are "singable." Avoid even popular songs that aren't.

Hear this, friends: The fact that a song sounds good on Christian radio doesn't mean it's going to sing well with a congregation. I'm grateful for stirring performance music. But some hit songs are about as easy to sing congregationally as Handel's *Messiah* or *The Holy City*. That's just not what they were made for, and trying to sing them together in a worship service will be painful. As usual, Matt Merker speaks with clarity:

"Ideal congregational songs have beautiful, expressive melodies that are nevertheless easy to learn for people from various generations, cultures, and tastes."[100]

The rule of thumb I share with Greg Habegger when we collaborate to compose a hymn is that if we don't remember and sing a tune well after two or three hearings, it's not a great hymn tune.[101] A tune needs to "stick" without being childishly predictable—and that's no easy task. Beyond being memorable, the tune should avoid complicated rhythms, odd chords, and drastic tonal "jumps" or "dips." And it's generally ideal for the song's range to stay between C and C on the musical scale, perhaps with a very brief venture up to a D.

I'm all for introducing new songs. But dose them. It's so deflating to go through a song service and recognize almost none of the songs. I recommend that you teach only one new song per service, and sing it in consecutive services for a month to learn it well. But be sure to reward the congregation's efforts by following the new song with a song that's in the church's wheelhouse. Give them a song they love, and let them belt it!

WHAT ABOUT PREPARED OR PERFORMANCE MUSIC?

Most of this book has focused on congregational singing. But what about choirs? What about soloists? What about what many churches call "special music"?

Historically, it's been a mixed bag. Martin Luther championed congregational singing but still used choirs. John Calvin sang only Psalms, congregationally, and he prohibited choirs. To those who have grown up singing in church choirs, that may seem odd. However, many churches today have done away with choirs—at times due to lack of interest or in order to pursue a more contemporary sound, but at other times as a

---

100. Merker, *Corporate*, 139.

101. Hymnologist Erik Routley concurs: "A good hymn tune is one that can be sung by ear after two or three hearings." *Rejoice in the Lord: A Hymn Companion to the Scriptures* (Grand Rapids, MI: Wm. B. Eerdmans Publishing Company, 1985), 9.

concrete way to emphasize the importance of congregational singing. For example, Capitol Hill Baptist Church is one of the best singing churches I've ever attended, and they have no choir, on purpose.[102]

What does Scripture say about prepared small-group or solo music? I think the Bible advocates having gifted musicians serve the congregation in song, as long as congregational singing remains the priority. There's no question that professional musicians were responsible to aid in temple worship in the Old Testament (1 Chronicles 15-16). Allen P. Ross describes the ministry of such singers in ancient Israel, highlighting both the skill they exercised and their role in promoting congregational singing:

> Choirs were used in Israel for the singing of psalms, hymns, and other anthems. These were made up of qualified people who gave their lives to such ministry.... The choir was a type of "firstfruits" of praise—the best (in voices) that the people of God could offer to God; but it was also the inspiration for the worship and praise of the people, for they, following the pattern of the choir, were also instructed to sing praises to God. This is an essential ingredient of worship.[103]

Now, what about the New Testament? There's a paucity of information on the topic. However, 1 Corinthians 14:26 does describe individual believers coming to the gathering of the church with a song prepared. This is something clearly distinct from congregational singing, and I believe it supports the concept of gifted musicians ministering to the entire assembly in song.

---

102. Mark Dever and Paul Alexander warn that performance music can foster "passive observation" rather than active participation. Dever and Alexander, 116-17. I'm sympathetic to their concerns, but I still maintain that choirs, ensembles, and soloists can be used in ways that complement congregational singing and don't compete with it.

103. Ross, 438-39. Interestingly, and germane to our chapter 2 discussion comparing music ministry to preaching and pastoring, the temple singers were *Levites*, part of the priestly tribe in Israel.

For my part, I think it makes sense for those who are uniquely gifted to have an opportunity to use their talents in ministry, provided that the goal is clearly the glory of God and the edification of the entire church, not the glory of the musician. Congregational songs are musically simple by design. But why not provide an opportunity for gifted composers and musicians to adorn the truth of the Scriptures through more complex and moving pieces of music—to make music "skillfully" (Psalm 33:3)? Should this level of artistry really be relegated to academia, concert halls, or community arts associations, and lost to the church? Does the church—hardly a harbor for artists in modern times as it is—really want to marginalize them even more by removing opportunities for them to use their gifts for the glory of God and the good of the church? I don't think so. I agree with John Frame, who sees value in both congregational singing and prepared music: "It is good to sing; it is also good to meditate while others are singing."[104]

Charles King, who led the music ministry of College Church in Wheaton, Illinois, regularly challenged his choir to be worship leaders, not performers. He wrote to his choir, "Making music in corporate worship is never for ourselves, but always to draw others into the joyous understanding of what we have learned and sing."[105] The music director, choir, and soloist must echo the ambition of John the Baptist: "He must increase, but I must decrease" (John 3:30).

Here are some ideas for fostering a ministry vs. performance mindset.

- Include the prepared song in the overall theme of the service, which will generally require (1) planning significantly ahead and (2) asking

104. Frame, *Worship*, 129. John MacArthur likewise advocates the intentional use of performance music: "It should be our goal to encourage the proper components in worship. The hymns and special music, as well as pastoral prayer and sermon, must articulate truth. Yet they should also stir the emotions and activate the will." "Frequently Asked Questions About Expository Preaching" in *Preaching: How to Preach Biblically*, ed. Richard L. Mayhue and Robert L. Thomas (Nashville, TN: Thomas Nelson, 2005), 281.

105. Charles King, "Appendix D: When Music Equals Worship" in *Worship by the Book*, ed. D. A. Carson (Grand Rapids, MI: Zondervan, 2002), 192.

soloists to sing a song that fits the theme rather than one of their choosing (which might avoid some awkward situations anyway).

- Project the lyrics of the song onto the screen or print them in the bulletin so that the congregation is encouraged to focus on the words of the song and not just the abilities of the singers or instrumentalists.

- Use the prepared music to promote congregational singing. I love it when we've done this at the churches I've pastored. Use a soloist or choir to introduce a new song to the congregation, then sing it congregationally as a "hymn of the month." Even better, look for choral arrangements which either bring the congregation in on the final stanza or which can easily be adapted for congregational use.[106] *I love this!*

- Be sure the response to the song gives glory to God rather than the performer. For many churches, the right response is an "Amen" at the conclusion. For others, it's clapping. I'm fine with either or neither. Frankly, I don't understand why applause triggers some people, especially because clapping in our culture often just indicates agreement, like during the State of the Union Address. My counsel on this sometimes-thorny issue is two-fold: (1) whatever you practice as a church, go out of your way to give glory to God alone (Psalm 115:1) even as you express gratitude to musicians, and (2) don't make this a test of biblical fidelity; it isn't that important.

William S. Smith does a good job of summarizing how musicians can best aid congregational singing:

> The primary role of a choir (and all other musicians in a service) is to help the congregation sing. The choir may help the congregation sing

---

106. Some examples of choral arrangements that can be easily used for the whole congregation are Heather Sorenson's arrangement of "10,000 Reasons" and Benjamin Harlan's arrangement of "Almighty Father."

by its vocal support of the song of the congregation, and by its modeling singing both in its choral and its congregational song. Such modeling is audible and, if the choir is in front of the congregation, visible.[107]

VIDEO KILLED THE RADIO STAR

We live in strange times. For the first time in history, music has become something we primarily *hear* rather than something we *make*. Prior to the invention of phonographs, 8-tracks, CDs, and Spotify, music had to be performed live, and often in community. As much as I enjoy having an almost infinite number of songs available to me on my cell phone, the technology of the last one hundred years has changed the way we encounter music. And not entirely for the better.

I'm reminded of the annoyingly catchy song the Buggles sang in 1980: "Video Killed the Radio Star." It's true. Each technological leap makes the previous medium obsolete. Sadly, recorded music has tried to kill congregational singing. Kevin Mungons and Douglas Yeo, who give a blow-by-blow description of how entertainment music eclipsed congregational singing in their exceptional biography of Homer Rodeheaver, provide this succinct summary: "The new technology turned music producers into music consumers."[108] Rodeheaver himself used the radio to plug his products, but he later lamented that congregational singing was part of the collateral damage: "We appreciate the radio but must admit that it has taken from the young and old much of the initiative and desire for individual participation."[109]

---

107. William S. Smith, 64.

108. Kevin Mungons and Douglas Yeo, *Homer Rodeheaver and the Rise of the Gospel Music Industry* (Urbana, IL: University of Illinois Press, 2021), 164.

109. Ibid., 128. Walter Isaacson, in his fascinating book *The Innovators*, tells how the transistor radio further isolated listeners: "The radio was no longer a living-room appliance to be shared; it was a personal device that allowed you to listen to your own music where and when you wanted—even if it was music that your parents wanted to ban." *The Innovators: How a Group of Hackers, Geniuses, and Geeks Created the Digital Revolution* (New York: Simon & Schuster, 2014), 151.

The solution isn't banning recorded music, obviously. How blessed we are to have centuries of music so readily available to us! But churches must make a conscious decision that our worship services will not become spectator events, especially when it comes to our music.

Congregational singing isn't a quaint reminder of a bygone era. It's a gift from God. It's good for the soul. It's good for the church. And it's commanded by God throughout the Scriptures. Vibrant, engaged congregational singing *is* special music!

ENCOURAGE HYMN-SINGING AT HOME

One more quick thought. Singing at home is a great way to minister to your own soul, train children and teens, and "practice" for public worship. Scott Aniol and Ryan Martin urge private worship with hymns: "Every Christian should have a hymnal (or several) at home for personal and family worship. Hymns ought to be contemplated, understood, and sung to the Lord outside church gatherings."[110] Family singing can be as elaborate as gathering around the piano or as simple as substituting a song of praise for the usual pre-meal prayer. (Try it!) I've always loved it—as a child, and now as a parent—when my family has sung together in the car. Even if your family isn't extremely musical, download favorites and make a playlist for singing along at home or on the road. One way or another, sing together.

Think of it this way: Violins are great. So are cellos, trumpets, and timpani. But it's glorious to be part of an amazing *orchestra*. The ideal is for the various instrumentalists to practice at home, grow in their abilities, then put it all together when they gather. In the same way, private worship is beautiful. Sing songs at home. Then eagerly anticipate gathering with the entire "orchestra" of your local church.

One challenge for many young people (and adults) is that most of the music they listen to during the week is performed by soloists. Although

110. Aniol and Martin, iv.

we can certainly sing along in the safety of the car or shower, that singing doesn't help us learn to love congregational singing. A great way to address this need is to make good use of recordings that focus on hymns sung by congregations—not soloists. My favorites are the three recordings in *The Majesty and Glory* series (the original, then Christmas, then the Resurrection) by Tom Fettke. The "T4G Live" recordings led by Bob Kauflin have a more authentic, non-studio sound since they feature a conference congregation. And the simple, acoustic hymn recordings of Fernando Ortega are very worshipful and will help people learn and appreciate great hymns. There are plenty of other recordings as well, including albums from Church Works Media. The point is, expose yourself and your family to great hymns and great hymn-singing!

GRACE NOTES FOR WORSHIP LEADERS

- How can you ensure that congregational singing is prioritized in your church?
- Which songs does your congregation sing best? Why?
- Which songs does your congregation struggle with or not seem to enjoy? Why?

GRACE NOTES FOR PARENTS AND CHILDREN'S TEACHERS

- Are you teaching your children great hymns at home?
- Do you ever listen to recordings of great hymns with your children? If not, are you ready to begin?

GRACE NOTES FOR EVERYBODY

- Do you "lean in" and "sing out" during your church's congregational singing, thinking through the words and participating with enthusiasm?
- How could you better prepare for and benefit from congregational singing this coming Lord's Day?

"Behold, how good and pleasant it is when brothers dwell in unity!"
—PSALM 133:1

"Our weary hearts long to hear the gospel reverberate around us in surround sound. We hear the voices of our fellow church members, and remember that we're not in this alone. God has welcomed us into his family."
—MATT MERKER[111]

"I regard with deep satisfaction the growing taste for hymn singing and praise, as an essential part of Christian worship.... Nothing is so likely to heal 'our unhappy divisions,' and to make us of 'one mind,' as an increased spirit of praise as well as prayer."
—J. C. RYLE[112]

111. Merker, *Corporate*, 136.
112. Quoted in Eric Russell, *J. C. Ryle: That Man of Granite with the Heart of a Child* (Fearn, Scotland: Christian Focus, 2001), 90.

CHAPTER 7

SING SONGS THAT ARE UNIFYING

"Our hymns have brought all of us closer together in a spirit of Christian unity." So says Franklin Segler.[113]

I love that statement. But Segler must have attended churches distinctly different from mine. Music is one of the more divisive issues facing the church in my lifetime. As Robert A. Cook describes it, discussion about church music "has too often gotten down to the level of a shouting match between the purists who hold that old is good, and the faddists who feel that the latest is the greatest."[114]

Yeah, that's more like the churches I've experienced.

But it need not be so. It *should* not be so.

UNITY IS A REALITY, NOT JUST A GOAL

Christians often talk about how the church needs to be unified. What they mean, I think, is that we should get along and stop our in-fighting. I agree.

---

113. Segler, 96.
114. Robert A. Cook, "That New Religious Music," *Moody Monthly*, April 1977, 40. I tracked down this article in the Moody archives, just certain that the original must have said "old is *gold*" and "the latest is the greatest." But alas, that's not what it says, and I'm low-grade mourning the missed rhyming opportunity.

Fighting with other orthodox, gospel-loving Christians makes about as much sense as the United States sending soldiers to Europe in 1942 to attack *Britain*. Ridiculous? Of course. They were our allies—despite some differences like accents, July 4, and football. But there was a real and evil enemy to be fought. The same is true today. I wish Christians would stop wasting spiritual bullets on each other and instead fight the secularism all around us, labor to bring the lost to Christ, and earnestly "contend for the faith that was once for all delivered to the saints" (Jude 3)—not endlessly quarrel over turf.

And yet, there's a sense in which church unity isn't a *goal*; it's a reality. There *is* one body (1 Corinthians 12:20; Ephesians 4:4-6). Christ already *has* united people from different backgrounds and ethnicities into "one new man," the church (Ephesians 2:15). The gospel already *has* abolished our pre-salvation distinctions (Galatians 3:27-28). We already *have* been joined to Christ and to one another through the baptism of the Spirit (1 Corinthians 12:13). The objective reality is that Christ's church is already spiritually united because of His great work. We just need to stop messing that very real unity up. Ephesians 4:3 doesn't tell us to *create* unity—just to work hard to *maintain* it.

Still, we know that there's a big gap between the unity that exists as a spiritual reality and the schism we see in the church as a daily struggle. Scripture regularly calls on Christians to stop picking at each other, almost the way my dad used to tell me and my brothers to stop fighting before he had to pull the car over and settle it. The Bible calls us to unite around the gospel—though never at the *expense* of the gospel—again and again and again:

- "By this all people will know that you are my disciples, if you have love for one another." (John 13:35)
- "Each one of you says, 'I follow Paul,' or 'I follow Apollos,' or 'I follow Cephas,' or 'I follow Christ.' Is Christ divided? Was Paul crucified for you? Or were you baptized in the name of Paul?" (1 Corinthians 1:12-13)

- "Why not rather suffer wrong? Why not rather be defrauded? But you yourselves wrong and defraud—even your own brothers!" (1 Corinthians 6:7-8)
- "But if you bite and devour one another, watch out that you are not consumed by one another." (Galatians 5:15)
- "Do nothing from selfish ambition or conceit, but in humility count others more significant than yourselves. Let each of you look not only to his own interests, but also to the interests of others." (Philippians 2:3-4)
- "I entreat Euodia and I entreat Syntyche to agree in the Lord." (Philippians 4:2)
- "As for a person who stirs up division, after warning him once and then twice, have nothing more to do with him, knowing that such a person is warped and sinful; he is self-condemned." (Titus 3:10-11)
- "Clothe yourselves, all of you, with humility toward one another, for 'God opposes the proud but gives grace to the humble.'" (1 Peter 5:5)
- "Beloved, let us love one another, for love is from God, and whoever loves has been born of God and knows God. Anyone who does not love does not know God, because God is love." (1 John 4:7-8)

Jesus calls us to unity—not occasionally, but constantly. So, let's be clear about this important follow-up point: Music doesn't cause disunity. It reveals it. The church has dealt with controversies from the time it was founded. Read Acts and the grumbling about biased care for widows (Acts 6:1), the controversy over how to treat Gentile converts (Acts 15:1-35), the discord over how and whether to restore a failed apprentice (Acts 15:36-41), and so on.[115] Music is a symptom, not the main problem. Pride is the main problem. Rivalry is the main problem. *Sin* is the main problem.

---

115.   It's instructive that Paul and Barnabas won a major battle together in defense of the gospel—only to split immediately afterwards over what to do with John Mark. How often do we stand with each other on major doctrinal issues, then snipe at and split from each other over preferences? God, help us.

"THE MIDDLE WALL OF PARTITION"

What divides us is sin, not music. And that's good news, because if sin is the problem, then the gospel is the answer. Not music—the gospel. Not compromise—the gospel.

I live in one of the most diverse counties in the United States. The whole world lives here. The number of nationalities and ethnicities is staggering. And it's beautiful. One of my great passions is to demonstrate how the gospel dissolves divisions, even cultural and ethnic divisions. "Grace trumps race." The church I pastored doesn't yet look as diverse as the local Walmart, but it's getting there. I believed and preached that if we reach our community, we'll reflect our community. And it's happening. As I'm writing this book, the church's most recent members are a Romanian man married to a Mexican woman, along with their children; a Hispanic grad student married to an Asian grad student; an Indian family; a black family; a white man married to a Filipino lady; a white man married to an Australian Asian lady, and their children; a white family; a Hispanic family. That's just the way our community is. And the gospel has united all of those people and more into a single church.

When I taught our church's orientation class, I repeatedly emphasized that what unites our church isn't shared political views, common educational choices, similar backgrounds, or musical preferences. What unites us—per the Scriptures—is the gospel of Jesus Christ. Nothing else can do what the gospel can do. The world can push political correctness, but—as the racial tensions in our nation regularly reveal—they've just papered over serious problems. They haven't resolved them. They can't. Only the gospel can.

Paul describes the amazing unity the gospel produces in Ephesians 2:11-21. He was addressing people who were once strangers to each other—*enemies*, even. They were divided by culture, ethnicity, and background. The dividing line was Jew versus Gentile in Paul's context; it is diversity of different types in our context. And yet, miraculously, those former enemies were brought together into "one new man" in the church

(v. 15). The wall of partition that kept Gentiles from approaching God in the Jerusalem temple (and, in fact, threatened them with death if they trespassed beyond it), was demolished by Christ. Just as the veil which separated us from God was torn when Jesus died (Matthew 27:51), so also the wall that separated us from each other was demolished (v. 14). We have been reconciled to God through Christ and thereby reconciled to Christians as well (v. 16). Our spiritual alienation has been turned to access through Jesus (vv. 17-18). We're no longer strangers but family members (v. 19). We're now part of God's great building project called the church—all of us, without distinction (vv. 20-22). That's something that should amaze us. Thrill us! Change and motivate us!

And of course, that's doctrinal truth that we should delight to sing about together. Read these lyrics from Kristyn and Keith Getty's hymn "Beneath the Cross" with fresh eyes:

> *Beneath the cross of Jesus / His family is my own—*
> *Once strangers chasing selfish dreams, / Now one through grace alone.*
> *How could I now dishonor / The ones that You have loved?*
> *Beneath the cross of Jesus / See the children called by God.*[116]

Do you see how the work of Christ not only accomplishes spiritual unity but also motivates practical, day-to-day unity? If reconciling us to Himself and to each other was worth the blood of Christ, are we really willing to disrupt that unity over music? Or influence? Or preferences? Notice the rhetorical question the Gettys pose: "How could I now dishonor / The ones that You have loved?" How, indeed.

Music doesn't divide us—sin does. And music doesn't unite us—the gospel does. But music can display and grow and celebrate that unity. Music should be a great *unifying* force in the local church, not a source

---

116. Lyrics from "Beneath the Cross" by Kristyn Lennox Getty and Keith Getty. © 2006 Thank-you Music (PRS) (adm. worldwide at CapitolCMGPublishing.com excluding the UK & Europe which is adm. at IntegratedRights.com). All rights reserved. Used by permission.

of tension and schism. And this can happen! As Paul S. Jones writes, "Engaging in church music ought to be a uniting, compelling, involving activity—not a divisive, troubling one."[117]

Awesome. But how?

UNITY FOSTERS MUSIC AND MUSIC FOSTERS UNITY

As usual, let's look back at Colossians 3. We've focused again and again on the command to sing in Colossians 3:16. Now let's zoom out a bit and take a look at the larger context. In Colossians 3, before the church is commanded to *sing* together, the church is commanded to *live* together and relate to one another peacefully.

> Put on then, as God's chosen ones, holy and beloved, compassionate hearts, kindness, humility, meekness, and patience, bearing with one another and, if one has a complaint against another, forgiving each other; as the Lord has forgiven you, so you also must forgive. And above all these put on love, which binds everything together in perfect harmony. And let the peace of Christ rule in your hearts, to which indeed you were called in one body. And be thankful. (Colossians 3:12-15)

Did you catch all that? Look at all the calls to unity that precede the call to worship:

- Christians are to embody Christ-like virtues: compassion, kindness, humility, meekness, and patience (v. 12). Notice that these virtues are all social and ethical, demonstrated in relationships with others.

117. Jones, *Singing*, xi.

It won't do to say you're a growing Christian who just doesn't get along with other believers.

- When people annoy us, we are to respond with forbearance (v. 13a); when they sin against us, we are to respond with forgiveness (v. 13b). Applying *just this verse* would resolve most church and family conflict.
- Above all, we are to put on love—the chief Christian virtue—and thus to live in harmony (an ironic word in context, v. 14).
- Finally, we are to live in peace, recalling that we have been united together into one body (v. 15). We are to let *peace* rule—not conflict.

Verse after verse calls us to unity... and *then* we are to sing the Word of Christ (v. 16)... *together*! And not only together, but *to and for each other*! Church music thrives when there is harmony—spiritual harmony, not just musical.

Remember, Colossians 3:16 and Ephesians 5:19 teach that singing together is part of our mutual instruction. It's one way in which we serve each other and remind each other of biblical truth. Matt Merker describes the unifying encouragement that happens as we sing truth together as a local church:

> The church member enduring persecution from his earthly family needs to hear his spiritual brothers and sisters sing, "Jesus, I my cross have taken, all to leave and follow Thee." The Christian burdened by shame needs to hear us exult, "My sin, not in part, but the whole, has been nailed to the cross, and I bear it no more!" Our weary hearts long to hear the gospel reverberate around us in surround sound. We hear the voices of our fellow church members, and remember that we're not in this alone. God has welcomed us into his family.[118]

118. Merker, *Corporate*, 136.

Congregational singing is a beautiful expression of church unity. Singing songs together is an oral and aural symbol of unity amid diversity. People with high voices and low sing together. We harmonize. Sometimes, if the song allows it, we sing antiphonally—some of us answering or repeating others, as we do when we sing "It Is Well with My Soul" or "Is He Worthy?" or the bridge in "Behold Our God" or the fun countermelodies of "Wonderful Grace of Jesus."

It's remarkable, really. And whether or not you know it, *you're already doing this.* The very science of singing requires it. You listen to each other—to pitch, to rhythm, to volume. You adjust your tempo to stay with the whole congregation, even when the song slows at its conclusion. Unless you're completely silent or an incurable monotone, the singing of those around you affects how you sing, without your even realizing it. Songs virtually *force* people to vocally align with one another in a vibrant picture of the unity that should be the norm for Christ's church. Through congregational singing, dozens, hundreds, and even thousands of Christians are able to sing truths we hold in common and do so *together*! I can't imagine a more vivid depiction of unity. Mark Dever and Paul Alexander write, "Congregational singing is an expression of the unity and harmony of the gathered congregation."[119]

Remember, Ephesians 5:19 doesn't only command us to sing together, but to "*[address]* one another in psalms and hymns and spiritual songs." Although it might feel awkward, we're commanded to sing *to* each other! That means the joyful lady in the choir who smiles and makes intentional eye contact with as many people as she can isn't socially awkward. She's just obeying Scripture. And that means you should take notice of the people around you, even giving them an occasional smile or nod of affirmation as you sing. Celebrate the fact that we are praising our Savior and affirming what we believe *together*!

In the churches I've pastored we would conclude our communion services by joining hands and singing together. Did that *make* us united?

---

119.   Dever and Alexander, 118.

I wish it were so easy. But it was a great visual and audible picture of the spiritual ideal we were working toward.

"BLEST BE THE TIE THAT BINDS"

We are united by the gospel—not shared backstories, standards, or preferences. So the members of the same church prefer different styles and eras of music. *So what?* Diversity of experiences and preferences within biblical orthodoxy is part of the beauty of the body of Christ. A church in which everyone agrees on every issue—including music—is kind of a frightening specter. Lockstep agreement may mean that you're not reaching people different from you, that you've aligned on extrabiblical preferences, or that there's an unhealthy pressure to conform within the church. Diverse opinions give you a chance to demonstrate that the gospel really works!

Honestly, a big part of the solution to our in-fighting about things like music is just to humble ourselves. To stand down. To exercise forbearance. To submit to one another. In musical parlance, *to blend.*

If you've ever been in a choir, you've learned the importance of blending. The best choirs don't necessarily have the best singers. In fact, sometimes a great soloist can be a liability to a choir, especially if she is unwilling to "fit in." The choir I was part of during college had some exceptional musicians with *huge* voices—and I certainly wasn't one of them! I envied those talents. But getting the operatic soprano or tenor to blend in could be a challenge at times. It's not a new problem, as John Wesley's instructions to singers make comically clear:

> Sing modestly. Do not bawl, so as to be heard above or distinct from the rest of the congregation, that you may not destroy the harmony; but strive to unite your voices together, so as to make one clear melodious sound.[120]

---

120. John Wesley, "Directions for Singing" in *Select Hymns*, 1761.

That's good counsel for singing, whether in a choir or in a congregation. But it's *great* counsel *for life*. Don't make it all about you. Don't "bawl." Don't try to stick out. Don't destroy harmony. Unite with others to make "one clear melodious sound" for the glory of God. Even if every song isn't your favorite.

CONGREGATIONAL SINGING IS MULTI-GENERATIONAL

One of the beauties of Christ's church is how it brings together people who would otherwise have nothing to do with one another. The same church should be home to members from a wide variety of backgrounds, educational levels, and incomes. And it should be home to members from a wide spectrum of ages. Look around your church on Sunday and marvel that children, teens, and octogenarians are uniting their voices in song. We may take it for granted (perhaps because we've seen it all our lives), but it's a remarkable and beautiful thing. The significance of the young and old singing together isn't lost on William S. Smith: "In a society in which musical preferences tend to divide along generational lines, is there any activity that is more intergenerational than congregational singing?"[121]

It has always been so for the people of God. Psalm 148:12-13 extends a call to worship that cuts across generational lines: "Young men and maidens together, old men and children! Let them praise the name of the Lord."

Congregational singing is a *de facto* revolution against the individualism of our age. It's a revolt against age-ism. It's one way to resist the temptation for younger moms to hang with younger moms, retirees with retirees, teens with teens, and so on. Congregational singing brings us beautifully together.

121. William S. Smith, 40.

UNITY EMBRACES DIFFERENCE AND
EXTENDS DEFERENCE

We sometimes confuse unity with unanimity. It's been said that "you don't have to be my twin to be my brother." In reality, you won't *love* every song your church sings—and that's probably a good thing! It reveals that your church is serving the tastes of its broad membership, not merely catering to those who want traditional music, contemporary music, or whatever. Music gives people a chance to "outdo one another in showing honor" (Romans 12:10) and to "submit to one another" (Ephesians 5:21). That's one reason why I cringe when I see churches that have a "traditional service" and a "contemporary service." I much prefer a blended selection of excellent songs, both for the reasons discussed throughout this book and in order to teach people to love each other by worshiping together. John Frame concurs: "Maintaining unity among the diversity of the church's membership requires that we defer to one another in love, being willing to sing one another's music rather than insisting on the music we most enjoy."[122]

Deference is a word and concept we need to become more familiar with. Deference allows *differences* without letting them become *divisions*. It's giving someone space to have another opinion, and even being willing to go along with that person's preference at times—to "put up with it," as we say, even if it's not something you would choose. There's something very healthy about that. It takes maturity to not always have to get your own way. *Within the parameters of orthodoxy and orthopraxy, made explicit for the church by its doctrinal statement, Christians should appreciate difference and practice deference.*

That's a different concept for me, I confess. I can show love to other members by singing songs they enjoy, even if the songs aren't my favorites. And they can do the same for me. So, stretching myself regarding the songs my church sings—provided they are biblically accurate, of course—can

122. Frame, *Contemporary*, 28.

actually be an opportunity to (a) love others, (b) promote unity, and (c) grow in my humility and selflessness. Matt Merker is one of the few people I've heard highlight the potential *upside* of divergent musical preferences in this way:

> Since one of the main purposes of corporate singing is to build others up, music gives us a wonderful opportunity to "count others more significant than [ourselves]" (Phil. 2:3).... Remember: for every song that resonates with you musically, there are probably church members who are laying down their preferences for your sake![123]

Every church will have its own unique sound. That's beautiful. My challenge to you is to selflessly promote unity rather than division regarding music, and to be willing for your church's sound to *expand*. Let me explain. I mentioned that I pastored in a remarkably diverse area. As more diversity manifests itself in the church, should the church not reflect that in its songs? Should members from Jamaica, Ghana, Mexico, Romania, Peru, Australia, the Philippines, India, Haiti, and elsewhere just learn America's Christian songs without also teaching us some of theirs? Should teens not learn older songs that have been a lifelong blessing to seniors? Should seniors not learn the best new songs from the Gettys or Sovereign Grace or CityAlight? Should members who prefer high-church music not be open to some Bible-saturated southern gospel? (I confess, that was slightly hard to type. *I'm* stretching, too.) And can Gaither-lovers not learn to appreciate a Craig Courtney anthem? Should we not *all* stretch, *all* learn something new, *all* show love and deference? *Why not?!* I agree with John Frame: "It is a good idea... for all of us to learn to appreciate music that doesn't immediately appeal to us. In that way we serve one another, and we also grow by learning to praise God in new ways."[124]

123. Merker, *Corporate*, 144–45.
124. Frame, *Worship*, 141.

Capitol Hill Baptist Church has done this on purpose. Based on their diverse body, they made the intentional decision to learn several hymns that are part of the rich African-American hymn heritage. Why? Matt Merker explains:

> The goal was not only to show hospitality to black members and visitors, but also to edify all our members by celebrating the richness of the African-American hymn tradition, recognizing God's abundant grace in the men and women who penned these songs.[125]

I love that. It's not pandering. It's not political correctness. It's allowing the church's musical culture to be shaped by the *entire* church family. That means that a church's musical culture will inevitably change and stretch as new members from different cultures join. The alternative is to welcome people on the condition that they're willing to adapt to "how we do things around here." But I think such a self-defending posture is ironically self-defeating.

I can't improve on what Mark Dever and Paul Alexander have written on the unifying effect of church music, and so I'll gladly give them this chapter's last word:

> Singing the gospel together, as a whole church, forges unity around distinctively Christian doctrine and practice. Our congregational songs function like devotional creeds. They give us language and opportunity to mutually encourage each other in the Word and call each other out to praise our common Savior. One of the most important functions of congregational singing is that it highlights the *corporate* nature of the church and the mutual ministry that builds us up in unity. One reason we come together on Sundays is to remind ourselves

---

125. Merker, *Corporate*, 146. Kevin DeYoung similarly argues for intentionally singing songs from different cultures on occasion. "Ten Principles for Church Song," *The Founders Journal* 90 (Fall 2012), 19.

that we are not alone in our confession of Jesus Christ and our conviction of the spiritual truths we hold so dearly. What a blessing it is to hear the whole church singing together with all our hearts![126]

GRACE NOTES FOR WORSHIP LEADERS

- Has music been a source of division in your church? According to the truths presented in this chapter, how can you use music to foster unity in the future?
- What is the "glue" that keeps your church together? Shared history? Politics? Home schooling? Music? How can you make it clear that you are united by "gospel glue"?

GRACE NOTES FOR PARENTS AND CHILDREN'S TEACHERS

- When you speak about your church's music or preaching in front of your children, are you careful not to do so with a critical spirit, mindful that they're listening and learning from you?
- How might your family use the gift of music to be a blessing, perhaps to an older member of your church?

GRACE NOTES FOR EVERYBODY

- Are you willing to defer to others in your church who enjoy different styles of music?
- Can you engage in your church's song service this coming Lord's Day with the intent to be more aware of and more encouraging to those around you? Can you make it your goal to help a fellow believer by singing truth to them?

126. Dever and Alexander, 116.

PART 3

A HYMN GRID
FROM THE PSALMS

"For God is the King of all the earth; sing praises with a psalm!"
—PSALM 47:7

"Above all [Luther] prized the hymns of Scripture. The Holy Spirit was for him the greatest poet and singer of praise to the Lord."
—VILMOS VAJTA[127]

"The Psalms give voice to our hearts. The wide range of human feeling is here given concrete expression. We are given language to address God with thanks and praise, but also with our feelings of desolation or despair or overwhelming guilt because of our sin."
—DANE ORTLUND[128]

127. Vajta, 161.
128. Dane C. Ortlund, *In the Lord I Take Refuge: 150 Daily Devotions through the Psalms* (Wheaton, IL: Crossway, 2021), 7.

CHAPTER 8

SING SONGS THAT ARE INSPIRED

"Things would have been so much simpler if God had anticipated the 'worship wars' and just inspired a hymnal."

I shared this wish with my friend Kevin Bauder between sessions at a conference on worship. We laughed together. Because God *has* inspired a hymnal. We just don't bother to use it. Although we're used to *reading* the 150 psalms, they were made to be *sung*. As Johann Gottfried von Herder noted over 200 years ago, "The Psalter is the hymn-book for all times."[129]

The Psalms have been precious to God's people for 3500 years. Martin Luther—the catalyst of the Reformation, preacher of Paul's epistles, and unofficial "Father of Congregational Singing"—loved the Psalter. His study of books like Romans and Galatians changed his life, and then changed the world. And yet, Luther called the Psalms his favorite book of the Scriptures. The seven psalms of confession were the subject of his first printed book. And Psalm 46 is the source of his unforgettable hymn, "A Mighty Fortress Is Our God." Luther found the gospel in the Psalms, and indeed, the content of the entire Bible within this one book:

---

129. Quoted in William S. Plumer, *Psalms: A Critical and Expository Commentary with Doctrinal and Practical Remarks* (Carlisle, PA: The Banner of Truth Trust, 2016), 8.

[The Psalter] should be precious to us if only because it most clearly promises the death and resurrection of Christ, and describes His kingdom, and the nature and standing of all Christian people. It could well be entitled a "little Bible" since it contains, set out in the briefest and most beautiful form, all that is to be found in the whole Bible.[130]

The Psalms have a vital role to play in churches today. But what is that role precisely? I like a description by my favorite seminary professor, Dr. Michael Barrett: He refers to the Psalms as both "a handbook and a hymnbook" for the church.[131] As a *hymnbook*, the Psalms give the church songs to sing and pray; as a *handbook*, the Psalms teach the church how to think and feel. But I would add one more descriptor, as well. As a *sketchbook*, the Psalms point the church to Jesus Christ.

THE PSALMS ARE A HANDBOOK

The Psalms are a handbook for worship, and indeed, for all of life. The Psalms teach us how to *think* and how to *feel*. Arno C. Gaebelein notes how the 150 psalms contain "descriptions of every possible kind of human experience."[132] This is an echo of the words of John Calvin.

Calvin calls the Psalms "an anatomy of all the parts of the soul":

There is not an emotion of which anyone can be conscious that is not here represented as in a mirror. Or rather, the Holy Spirit has here drawn to the life all the griefs, sorrows, fears, doubts, hopes, cares,

130. Martin Luther, *Martin Luther: Selections from His Writing*, ed. John Dillenberger (New York: Anchor Books, 1962), 38.
131. Michael P. V. Barrett, *The Beauty of Holiness: A Guide to Biblical Worship* (Greenville, SC: Ambassador International, 2006), 175.
132. Arno C. Gaebelein, *The Book of Psalms: A Devotional and Prophetic Commentary* (Neptune, NJ: Loizeaux Brothers, 1965), 9.

perplexities, in short, all the distracting emotions, with which the minds of men are want to be agitated.[133]

Part of the power of the Psalter is its raw honesty. It is filled with excruciating pain and confusion, but also with exuberant joy and celebration. Thus, as Calvin asserts, it shows us the validity of every human emotion, and it shows us what to do with those emotions.

HOW TO THINK AND FEEL ABOUT GOD—THE PSALMS OF EXALTATION

The Psalms point us to God, and they tell us how we should think about Him. They are teeming with the names of God (nouns), the attributes of God (adjectives), and the works of God (verbs). They remind us that God is *ours*—our Shepherd, Refuge, and so on. They call us to give Him glorious praise (Psalm 66:2). They call us to awe and wonder (Psalm 8; 139:6).

HOW TO THINK AND FEEL ABOUT SIN—THE PSALMS OF REPENTANCE

Among my favorite psalms are the psalms of confession. They have taught me how to respond to my own sinful failures. 1 John 1:9 invites us to "confess our sins," but Psalms 32 and 51 teach us *how*. Commentators generally list seven "penitential psalms": Psalms 6, 32, 38, 51, 102, 130, and 143. They reveal not only the sorrow of sin unconfessed, but the relief and joy of sin forgiven (32:1). They are invaluable to the church.

---

133. John Calvin, *Calvin's Commentaries*, trans. James Anderson (Grand Rapids: Baker Books, 1999), 4:XXXVII.

HOW TO THINK AND FEEL ABOUT INJUSTICE—THE PSALMS OF IMPRECATION

The Psalms encourage us to be angry in the face of evil. Whereas many Christians feel uncomfortable about the imprecatory psalms, or even ashamed of them as unworthy of God, they are part of the inspired Scriptures. A. C. Gaebelein writes, "The enemies whose destruction is invoked are God's enemies. The measure of their wickedness is full, and a righteous and holy God must deal with them in judgment."[134] Far from relegating them to the Old Testament, Gaebelein suggests that the ultimate fulfillment of the imprecatory psalms is Christ's judgment of the wicked at His second advent.

Frankly, if one is offended by the imprecatory psalms, he will have a hard time with Jesus' actions in Revelation. God teaches us—in songs of praise, no less—that we should long for the judgment of the wicked. If we deem ourselves to be more merciful than God, if we are embarrassed by the Scriptures, the problem is certainly with us. Bernard Anderson advises, "It is hazardous... to edit the psalms theologically by omitting passages that we may find unpalatable.... Seek to understand the Psalms rather than to conform them to our understanding."[135]

HOW TO THINK AND FEEL ABOUT SORROW AND CONFUSION—THE PSALMS OF LAMENT

The modern church doesn't lament well. In fact, we rarely lament at all, despite the fact that *a staggering forty percent of the psalms are expressions of sorrow!* Undeterred by the sheer numbers, we essentially edit lamentations out of the Scriptures. People come to church with excruciating pains, and they sing unrealistically chipper songs. Churches which are theologically

---

134. Arno C. Gaebelein, 12.
135. Bernard W. Anderson, *Out of the Depths: The Psalms Speak for Us Today* (Philadelphia, PA: The Westminster Press, 1974), 165.

opposed to the prosperity gospel in sermonic form portray a Christian life of unrelenting blessings when they sing. We're wrong to omit the psalms of lament—and even unkind. Walter C. Kaiser shows the *mercy* of biblical lamentations, lamenting himself over the church's neglect of them:

> God has placed personal and national laments in Scripture, it would appear, as a corrective against euphoric, celebratory notions of faith, which romantically portray life as consisting only of sweetness and light. Such a one-sided, happiness-only view fails to deal with the realities of life. It drives the hurtful and painful side of life into the corners of faith and practice, leaving few guides or comforts from mortals or the Word of God.[136]

Lament lets people know that Scripture not only acknowledges their pain but offers a salve. We need the psalms of lament to teach us how to hurt, and how to pray when we're hurting. Psalms of lament tell us to "pray angry"—but to *pray*.

The Psalms teach us how to live in a broken world, as Rosaria Butterfield testifies:

> Psalm singing is a daily means of grace that I love, embrace, and practice. When I don't know where to turn, I open up my psalter. You always know where God is in your suffering when you sing the Psalms. In the Psalms, God breaks down the steps of your faith pilgrimage. The Psalms take your brokenheartedness seriously. God gave them to you as a love letter to show that he made you and takes care of you. As you sing the Psalms, you hear your broken vulnerability and God's omnipotent accompaniment."[137]

---

136. Walter C. Kaiser Jr. *Preaching and Teaching from the Old Testament: A Guide for the Church* (Grand Rapids: Baker Academic, 2003), 125.

137. Rosaria Champagne Butterfield, *The Secret Thoughts of an Unlikely Convert: An English Professor's Journey into Christian Faith, Expanded Edition* (Pittsburgh, PA: Crown & Covenant Publications, 2014), 181.

Perhaps one reason why the Western church has forsaken singing psalms—and certainly the psalms of lament—is that we mourn this life so little. Why sing of sorrows and pain—and indeed, why long for the hope of heaven—when we are so very *comfortable*? But as our world becomes more and more secular and more and more antagonistic to our faith, we may find that psalms become more and more precious. Again, Butterfield's words are insightful:

> Singing psalms is real-time intimacy and gives us the gospel grace that we daily need, because singing psalms uses your own body, your voice, the rising and falling of your own breath, to project forward all struggle and pain and loss and gain and profit and joy onto Christ.... When you sing together in worship with your brothers and sisters in Christ, many voices lifting up many words of Christ, you experience a taste of the victory to come, even as you know the intense suffering of today. Psalms are—and have always been—*the hymnbook of the church under persecution.*[138]

THE PSALMS ARE A HYMNBOOK

We should sing songs modeled after biblical psalms, using them as a handbook. But the songs are a *hymnbook* as well. They give us inspired words to sing and to pray. When we sing the Psalms, we're singing songs that God Himself wrote, songs that God Himself commands us to sing:

> "Teaching and admonishing one another in all wisdom, singing psalms and hymns and spiritual songs..." (Colossians 3:16)

---

138.   Rosaria Butterfield, "Why I Sing Psalms," *Challies*, December 21, 2015, https://www.challies.com/sponsored/why-i-sing-psalms. Emphasis added. Chapter 9 will address the importance of *hymns* of lament, modeled after the *psalms* of lament.

"Addressing one another in psalms and hymns and spiritual songs..." (Ephesians 5:19)

"Is any among you afflicted? let him pray. Is any merry? let him sing psalms." (James 5:13 KJV)

The 150 psalms were written to be sung, and they *have been sung* through the ages.

PSALMS WERE SUNG BY ISRAEL IN THE OLD TESTAMENT

The Psalms were sung by Old Testament saints in private and public worship from the time of Moses. (Moses wrote Psalm 90.) Tim Keller writes,

> The Psalms were the divinely inspired hymnbook for the public worship of God in ancient Israel (1 Chronicles 16:8-36). Because psalms were not simply read, but sung, they penetrated the minds and imaginations of the people as only music can do.[139]

PSALMS WERE SUNG BY OUR LORD JESUS

The psalms were sung by our Savior on the night before His crucifixion (Matthew 26:30), quoted by Him from the cross (Matthew 27:46; Psalm 22:1), and cited by Him as having predicted His suffering and eventual glory (Luke 24:44-45). Jesus quoted or alluded to the Psalms more than any other Old Testament book. One way to answer the question "What would Jesus do?" is to sing the Psalms.

139. Tim Keller, *The Songs of Jesus: A Year of Daily Devotions in the Psalms* (New York: Viking, 2015), vii.

PSALMS WERE SUNG BY THE EARLY CHURCH

Charles Foster Kent writes, "These immortal hymns of praise and adoration are… the link that binds the Old to the New Testament."[140] Based on the Savior's example, the disciples took up the Psalms when preaching Christ throughout the book of Acts (2:25-28, 34; 4:11, 24-26; 7:46; 13:22, 33, 35; 14:15). The New Testament letters regularly quote and explain the Psalms.[141] And, as we've noted, they charge the church to sing psalms (Ephesians 5:18; Colossians 3:16; James 5:13). The Psalter "formed the core of the praises of the New Testament church," writes Hughes Oliphant Old.[142]

PSALMS HAVE BEEN SUNG BY THE CHURCH FOR ALMOST TWO MILLENNIA

Matthew Henry writes of the Psalms, "There is no one book of Scripture that is more helpful to the devotions of the saints than this, and it has been so in all ages of the church, ever since it was written."[143] We might well amend Charles Foster Kent's statement, quoted above: "These immortal hymns of praise and adoration are the link *that binds the church to the Old and New Testaments*." Or they should be.

In light of the vital role the Psalms have played in the lives of God's people for the last 3500 years, deeming them obsolete for our modern churches is both audacious and foolish. I can't say it any more clearly: We should sing psalms! Indeed, in order to be obedient to the Scriptures, we

---

140. Charles Foster Kent, *The Songs, Hymns, and Prayers of the Old Testament* (New York: Charles Scribner's Sons, 1914), v.

141. Tremper Longman notes that one-fifth of the apostle Paul's Old Testament citations in his letters come from the Psalms. *How to Read the Psalms* (Downers Grove, IL: IVP Academic, 1988), 65.

142. Hughes Oliphant Old, *Worship That Is Reformed according to Scripture* (Atlanta, GA: John Knox, 1984), 44.

143. Matthew Henry, *Matthew Henry's Commentary on the Whole Bible: Complete and Unabridged in One Volume* (Peabody, MA: Hendrickson Publishers, 1991), 743.

must sing psalms. Yes, we should sing hymns, as well. It need not be either/ or. But as Matt Merker writes, "A Psalm-singing church is a church that is saturated with God's Word."[144]

I've mentioned that my favorite hymn-writers are Watts and Wesley. Who could be better? Well... *God.*

THE PSALMS ARE A SKETCHBOOK

The Psalms are musical prayers. They teach us to pray, and they teach us about the One to Whom we are praying. They demonstrate God's power in creation, in the exodus, in His protection of Israel, and in His care for individuals in times of trouble. Like no other portion of the Scriptures, the Psalms reveal God to us with breathtaking artistry and pathos. The Psalms show us God.

But more than this, the Psalms point us to *Jesus,* as He Himself noted in Luke 24:44-45:

> Then [Jesus] said to them, "These are my words that I spoke to you while I was still with you, that everything written about me in the Law of Moses and the Prophets and the Psalms must be fulfilled." Then he opened their minds to understand the Scriptures.

Some portions of Scripture—including some psalms—point us to Jesus *indirectly.* We don't need to insert Him into every story, artificially, like a sanctified "Where's Waldo?" book. Every tree isn't a prediction of the cross, nor is every sorrow a prediction of Gethsemane. Sound interpretation matters; we mustn't twist or allegorize the Scriptures to get to Christ. Nor should we diminish the value of the Old Testament by making it merely a springboard to devotional thoughts about Jesus. Many psalms

144. Matt Merker, "6 Lessons from Luther on Congregational Singing," *The Gospel Coalition,* October 27, 2017, accessed February 15, 2021, https://www.thegospelcoalition.org/reviews/ the-whole-church-sings.

just contribute to *the overall sweep of the biblical narrative toward Jesus—* our need of a perfect King, a perfect Priest, a perfect Sacrifice, a perfect Prophet, and so on. *Not every Bible passage is immediately Christ-centered, but all of the Bible is ultimately Christ-aiming.*

On the other hand, some psalms point to Christ *very directly.* Scholars cite fifteen psalms which the New Testament identifies as messianic. But there are clearly more allusions to the coming of the Messiah throughout the Psalter. Michael Barrett points out that "sometimes whole Psalms are uniquely messianic and sometimes only part of a Psalm is." He urges the reader to "stay on Christ-Alert as you read the Psalms."[145] Though a full discussion of the messianic Psalms is beyond the scope of this book, Bernard Anderson's words are instructive: "The whole Psalter is to be interpreted and prayed in the light of God's revelation in Christ."[146] Which brings us to our next section...

"CHRISTIANIZING" THE PSALMS

It should be clear that the Psalms point forward to Christ. But should we read Christ *backward* into the Psalms when we sing them?

Isaac Watts thought so. He overtly Christianized the Psalms: "In all places I have kept my grand design in view; and that is to teach my author [the psalmist] to speak like a Christian."[147] Even the (rather verbose) title of Watts' psalter demonstrates his conviction that the Christian church should sing Christian songs, even from the Old Testament: *The Psalms of David Imitated in the Language of the New Testament and Applied to the Christian State and Worship.*

---

145. Michael P. V. Barrett, *Beginning at Moses: A Guide to Finding Christ in the Old Testament* (Grand Rapids, MI: Reformation Heritage Books, 1999), 276.

146. Anderson, 6. Tremper Longman concurs: "The New Testament transforms our understanding of the Psalms as we read it in the light of the coming of Jesus Christ." Longman, 73.

147. Isaac Watts, *The Psalms of David Imitated in the Language of the New Testament and Applied to the Christian State and Worship*, quoted in Horton Davies, *The Worship of the English Puritans* (Morgan, PA: Soli Deo Gloria Publications, 1990), 300. Also see Bond, 102.

I agree with Watts, and this is the approach we take in the metrical psalms published by Church Works Media, essentially due to the influence of my good friend Joe Tyrpak.

The genius of Tyrpak's approach in putting the psalms into a form for modern singing rests on three things: (1) He takes pains to accurately express entire Bible psalms, line upon line, rigorously preserving the psalm's original meaning. Read one of his psalm settings with an open Bible and see if he doesn't faithfully capture the entire psalm. It's difficult work—much harder than writing a hymn—but he does it exceptionally well.[148] (2) He unites his psalm lyrics to familiar hymn tunes, allowing the church to sing the psalms immediately and confidently, without having to learn a new tune. (3) He devotes his final stanza to Christ—not inserting Jesus illegitimately *into* every psalm but showing how Jesus is the ultimate *fulfillment* of the psalm, as Christ Himself expressed in Luke 24:44-45. I believe he strikes exactly the right balance.

I appreciate this word on Christianizing the Psalms from John Frame: "Christian worship demands more than the language of anticipation. It demands the language of fulfillment and completeness, for that is what is distinctive about New Testament faith."[149]

HOW TO SING THE PSALMS

Perhaps one reason why psalm-singing has fallen out of favor in most churches is that many metrical psalms are notoriously *bad*. Edmund S.

---

148. In our efforts to retain a psalm's line-by-line meaning, as with our "Christianizing" of the Psalms, Church Works Media follows the example of Isaac Watts. John R. Tyson writes, "Isaac Watts... was a pioneer in the art of paraphrasing the Psalms and other Bible passages into poetical compositions. Watts's ideal was to follow the biblical text as closely as possible and to restate its message in the best poetical diction he could muster." *Assist Me to Proclaim: The Life and Hymns of Charles Wesley* (Grand Rapids, MI: Wm. B. Eerdmans Publishing Company, 2007), 261.

149. Frame, *Worship*, 126. W. T. Davidson agrees, using almost startling language: "More than any other book of the Old Testament [the Psalter] has been baptized into Christ." Quoted in John Peterson, *The Praises of Israel* (New York, Scribner's, 1950), 7.

Lorenz acknowledges that most metrical psalms are "stiff and mechanical."[150] Donald Hustad remarks that many metrical psalms have been "awkward of construction and unclear in meaning."[151] Joe Tyrpak justifiably jokes that the standard English psalters of ages past sound as though they were written by Yoda: *"Awkward they are. Inverted in ways most unnatural are their words."* There are exceptions, to be sure. But many metrical psalms sacrifice clarity and artistry for forced rhymes. Don't let that discourage you, however. There are better options.

If your church isn't accustomed to singing the Psalms, how can you get started?

SING HYMNS THAT ARE BASED ON THE PSALMS

You may already be singing the Psalms—you just don't know it.

- Luther's "A Mighty Fortress Is Our God" grew out of Psalm 46.
- Watts' "Jesus Shall Reign Where'er the Sun" is a meditation on Psalm 72.
- Watts' "O God, Our Help in Ages Past" unpacks Psalm 90.
- Watts' "Joy to the World" paraphrases ideas from Psalm 98.
- Lyte's "Praise, My Soul, the King of Heaven" is based on Psalm 103.
- Paul Keew's newer gospel song "Shout Out for Joy" is based on Psalm 66.

SING PRAISE CHORUSES AND PERFORMANCE SONGS THAT ARE BASED IN THE PSALMS

I grew up singing praise choruses that quote or paraphrase lines from the Psalms. Not all are of enduring quality, and most use only a few lines from

---

150. Lorenz, 32.
151. Donald P. Hustad, *Jubilate II: Church Music in Worship and Renewal* (Carol Stream, IL: Hope Publishing Company, 1981), 450-51.

a psalm, not the entire psalm. But many are accurate representations of the text that will encourage your soul with simple truth. Some of my favorites include the following:

- "Thy Word" (Psalm 119:105)
- "As the Deer" (Psalm 42:1)
- "He Has Made Me Glad" (Psalm 100:4 and 92:4)
- "The Law of the Lord Is Perfect" (Psalm 19)

Mac Lynch has written lovely performance songs inspired by psalms:

- "This Poor Man Cried" (Psalm 34:6)
- "The Steps of a Good Man" (Psalm 37:23)
- "Create in Me a Clean Heart" (Psalm 51)

USE MODERN PSALTERS—BOTH ONLINE AND BOUND COPIES

Thankfully, there are many exceptional options available today to make psalm-singing easy, understandable, and edifying. The following sources and collections are actually psalms for singing, not simply books about the Psalms:

- Churchworksmedia.com/psalms (various psalms set to known hymn tunes)
- *New Psalter: Psalms for the Church*, edited by Dan Kreider
- *Singing God's Psalms* by Fred Anderson
- *The Psalms* by Martin Leckebusch
- *Psalms for the Common Era* by Adam Carlill
- There is also a new psalter coming from The Master's Seminary as a companion to *Hymns of Grace*.

Pastor and author Terry L. Johnson writes, "Our recommendation is that churches commit to singing at least one psalm in every service of worship."[152] For most churches, that would be an aggressive correction, but we should at least start singing *some* psalms, on purpose. Allen P. Ross concurs: "If the Psalter were restored to a prominent place in worship, it would put more of the Word of God on the lips of worshippers, teach people how to pray and praise, and strengthen and encourage their faith."[153]

Luther agreed, making generous use of both psalms and hymns.

Calvin agreed—allowing nothing but psalms to be sung in his church. We need not adopt his "psalm-only" approach to congregational singing. But shame on us for neglecting the Psalms in our corporate worship and opting instead for what all too often are trite, toothless ditties.

Most importantly, *Scripture* agrees. Scripture commands us to sing the Psalms. So why don't we?

GRACE NOTES FOR WORSHIP LEADERS

- How often does your church sing psalms? Do you see a reason to sing them more often?
- When reading or preaching on the Psalms, do you preach the whole range of genres, including imprecations and lamentations?

---

152. Terry L. Johnson, "Restoring Psalm Singing to Our Worship" in *Give Praise to God: A Vision for Reforming Worship*, ed. Philip Graham Ryken, Derek W. H. Thomas, and J. Ligon Duncan III (Phillipsburg, NJ: P&R Publishing, 2003), 276.

153. Ross, 267.

GRACE NOTES FOR PARENTS AND CHILDREN'S TEACHERS

- Do you have some favorite psalms you can memorize with your children, like Psalm 23 or 100?
- Are you open to reading a psalm a day as a family—and not skipping the difficult ones? Talking through "sad psalms" as a family would demonstrate to your children that God cares about our troubles and sorrows, and He wants us to bring them to Him.

GRACE NOTES FOR EVERYBODY

- Consider starting a "Psalm Journal" in which you record various names of God (nouns), attributes of God (adjectives), and acts of God (verbs).
- Have psalms of lamentation or imprecation made you uncomfortable? If so, why do you think that is?

"And they sing the song of Moses, the servant of God, and the song of the Lamb."
—Revelation 15:3

"We are the stewards of English hymnody. We have been handed an incredible legacy and it's our job to not only preserve it, but to also increase and refine it. We need to do for future generations what past generations did for us. To be faithful stewards we must keep singing the old songs, but also the new songs."
—Tim Challies[154]

"There's an emotional range of praise in the Psalms that involves more than energetic thanksgiving. The Psalms are full of songs that express the pains of living in a fallen world. In fact, many scholars point out that there are more psalms borne out of a desperate cry for help than any other genre.... We and the congregations we serve need to sing songs that remind us, in the dark night of the soul, that God is with us."
—Matt Mason[155]

154. Tim Challies, "Why Your Church Should Sing New Songs (Not Only Old Songs)," *Challies*, October 28, 2019, https://www.challies.com/articles/why-your-church-should-sing-new-songs.

155. Matt Mason, "The Worship Leader and Singing" in *Doxology and Theology: How the Gospel Forms Worship Leaders*, ed. Matt Boswell (Nashville, TN: B&H Publishing Group, 2013), 181.

CHAPTER 9

SING SONGS THAT ARE DIVERSE

My childhood took place during the 1970s and 80s. I remember 8-tracks. I grew up on cassette tapes. I thought I was big-time when I got my first CD player. And I was all about the "mix tape." Rather than listening to one composer or recording artist at a time, I'd record a cassette of my favorites. I did "shuffle" the hard way. But it was worth it, because a recording with back-to-back Bach, or Broadway, or Beetles got old quickly, in my mind. Variety is good.

So it is with hymns. The church needs a "mix tape" of Christian music.

The prime New Testament texts that command us to sing demonstrate a variety of worship music: "psalms, hymns, and spiritual songs" (Ephesians 5:19 and Colossians 3:16). *Psalms* are psalms. (Where else are you going to find exegetical insights like *that*?!) *Hymns* are religious songs—apparently distinct from the 150 God-inspired songs of the Psalter, probably like the hymn samples scattered throughout the New Testament. *Spiritual songs* are yet another genre, and scholarly opinions vary on precisely what they are.[156] (More groundbreaking interpretational

---

156. Robert L. Saucy notes that the obvious distinction is between inspired psalms and the hymns and spiritual songs, which are "products of the church's own spiritual experience." In other words, they are the uninspired but biblical songs of the redeemed. *The Church in God's Program* (Chicago, IL: Moody Press, 1972), 184. John MacArthur notes that the distinctions

genius you'll only get here—they're *not* psalms or hymns.) The diversity of music that Scripture endorses is even broader than these three categories: Consider the varying genres *within* the book of Psalms—from laments to jubilant praise, from imprecations to royal songs. The point is, Scripture commends a menagerie of melodies.

Now, since we have a collection of inspired songs in the Psalms, it makes sense to use them as *templates* for our hymns and spiritual songs. Our songs, if modeled after the Psalter, should be as diverse as the Psalms, as varied as the Christian experience, and as broad as our Christian heritage.

Truly biblical worship, modeled after the Psalms, will cover a vast array of *eras*, *genres*, and *themes*.

SING SONGS FROM DISTINCT ERAS

We usually associate the book of Psalms with David. But the earliest psalm was written nearly half a millennium before David lived, in 1500-1400 BC by a man named Moses. You've heard of him? He wrote Psalm 90, which contrasts man's few years with God's eternality. God has been doing what He does forever—and His people have been writing about it for millennia. When we read or sing Psalm 90, we're making use of a song that is 3500 years old! That's significant.

One of the most important hymnals of the nineteenth and twentieth centuries was titled *Hymns Ancient and Modern*. It was an attempt by the Anglican church to unite the hymnody of the church's two factions: the formalists and the evangelicals. The hymnal was groundbreaking in its combination of both old and new texts with fresh, stately tunes, and many of its songs are still sung today. Beyond its importance in hymn history, I love the name, and I appreciate the tip-of-the-hat given to it by those who recently published *Hymns Modern and Ancient*. Both titles highlight

between the three terms aren't precise, nor are they essential, "or Scripture would have recorded those distinctions for us." *Worship: The Ultimate Priority* (Chicago: Moody Press, 2012), 203. The point of "psalms and hymns and spiritual songs" is diversity of expression in worship.

a distinctive of biblical worship: True worship isn't the monopoly of a particular time, place, or culture. And our selection of songs should evidence that.

To put a sharp point on it, it leaves me uneasy when I'm in a worship service and every song we sing has been written during my lifetime, or even during the last decade or two. Ignoring the great hymns (and books! and creeds!) of the past communicates to the church that newer is better.[157] That may be the case with cars and cell phones, but it's not necessarily the case with music. C. S. Lewis aptly charged the church with "chronological snobbery" because we are so negligent of the contributions made by saints of the past.[158] Gerald Hiestand and Todd Wilson agree: "It is either ignorance or hubris (or some combination of the two) that causes us to neglect the theological scholarship of the past."[159] They're not wrong. A philosopher from my childhood by the name of Bob Seger made essentially the same point: "Today's music ain't got the same soul."

Actually, with respect to Dr. Seger, some of "today's music" is exceptional. And some of it is awful. Similarly, some "old-time" music is exceptional, and some of it is awful. So, pick the best songs of many eras. On purpose. Still, my initial point stands: *If you're never singing songs written by dead people, something's wrong.* Listen to Robert Morgan:

> As we sing a new song to the Lord, let's not forget the old ones. It's the sturdy old hymns of the faith that strengthen and steady me when I'm weary and worn.... Hymns, especially those chock full of theology, such as Watts' and Wesley's, permeate our souls with the timeless

---

157. Even retaining some of the archaic language of old hymns—"Thee" and "Thou" and "Thy"—can be good for the church. On occasion I have written with archaic pronouns on purpose, like a photographer printing pictures in black-and-white for artistic effect. As John Frame comments, "Ancient language can also convey to worshipers a sense of unity with the church of past centuries, and that is a good thing." *Contemporary*, 19.

158. C. S. Lewis, *Surprised by Joy: The Shape of My Early Life* (Orlando, FL: Harcourt, Brace, Jovanovich, 1966), 207-08.

159. Gerald Hiestand and Todd Wilson, *The Pastor Theologian* (Grand Rapids, MI: Zondervan, 2015), 95.

veracities of Scripture.... And hymns connect us with generations now gone. Each week millions of Christians in local settings around the world, using hymns composed by believers from every era and branch of Christendom, join voices in united bursts of praise.[160]

My goal for the churches I have pastored has been to expose them to *great* songs—both ancient and modern. So we would sing "Is He Worthy?" (written by Andrew Peterson in 2018), then "Arise, My Soul, Arise" (written by Charles Wesley in 1742), then "O Sacred Head, Now Wounded" (written by Saint Bernard around 1100), then "All I Have Is Christ" (written by Jordan Kauflin in 2008). And we would do it consecutively, spanning nearly 1,000 years of church history and noticing that each of the songs exalts the same eternal Savior.

While I'm on the topic of diverse selections of hymns, the four songs in my illustration above represent not only different eras, but different *traditions*: The lyrics were written by an Anglican (Peterson), a Methodist (Wesley), a pre-Reformation Catholic (Bernard), and a Bible-toting reformed Charismatic (Kauflin). How cool is that!

If you just raised your eyebrows, Charles Spurgeon (a Baptist, for those keeping score) defended the idea of singing the best songs available to us, regardless of their origin. In his introduction to the hymnal his church published (creatively titled *Our Own Hymn-Book*), he wrote the following:

> The area of our researches has been as wide as the bounds of existing religious literature—American and British, Protestant and Romish, ancient and modern. Whatever may be thought of our taste, we have exercised it without prejudice; and a good hymn has not been rejected because of the character of its author, or the heresies of the church in whose hymnal it first appeared; so long as the language and the

---

160. Robert J. Morgan, *Then Sings My Soul: 150 of the World's Greatest Hymn Stories* (Nashville, TN: Thomas Nelson, 2003), xi.

spirit of it commended the hymn to our heart, we included it and we believe that we have thereby enriched our collection.[161]

There is great value in teaching our congregations, our children, and ourselves that the gospel wasn't copyrighted in the twentieth or twenty-first centuries. The church is 2000 years old, not 200 or 20. The Dean of American hymnologists, Donald Hustad, made this point eloquently even as he mourned the modern church's willingness to abandon that heritage:

> Until recently, evangelicals acknowledged in their music their identity with the same family tree, and we added the hymns of Luther, Gerhardt, Calvin, Wesley, Newton, Bonar, and many others. When we stood to sing their songs, we were joining our own spirits and voices with theirs and the thousands of believers who followed in their train, exulting in the glory and redeeming love of God. And our faith was strengthened. Today, some of our family of faith seem to be willing, even eager, to discard this heritage for a simpler fare that may disappear as suddenly as it has flowered.[162]

On the other hand, singing *only* ancient songs leads to the opposite error: It communicates to the church that God has worked through His people in the past but is not continuing to do so in our day. God is still at work, and we're living during a time when many wonderful "new songs" are being written, as the Psalms themselves command (33:3; 40:3; 96:1; 98:1; 144:9; 149:1). Matt Boswell is exactly right: "The hymnal of the church has no back cover."[163] We should feed our souls on songs that span the history of the church, including our own time.

161. Charles Spurgeon, *The Autobiography of Charles H. Spurgeon, Compiled from His Letters, Diaries, and Records by His Wife and Private Secretary* (Cincinnati, OH: Curtis & Jennings, 1900), 320.

162. Donald P. Hustad, "Let's Not Just Praise the Lord," *Christianity Today*, November 6, 1987, https://www.christianitytoday.com/ct/1987/november-6/lets-not-just-praise-lord.html.

163. Boswell, "Reforming," 12. What a creative way to describe the need for new songs!

As I was researching for this book, I flipped through a number of hymnals I have acquired during my time in the ministry. One is a Lutheran hymnal published in 1899. It's old, but not ancient. Still, it moved me. I turned its brittle pages in the midnight quiet of my study, and I was overwhelmed at the treasure I held in my hands. Godly believers, now dead and forgotten, had labored to provide for their denomination a book of psalms and hymns. Without modern conveniences, they had reviewed, compiled, and printed what they esteemed to be the songs best suited to nourish the people under their care. It was a labor of love. And while they are long gone, the fruit of their work remains. I thanked God for them that evening, and for others like them who have served the Lord and the church so well. The treasury of Christian hymns is a legacy entrusted to us by God's people in the past. May it not be lost on our watch.

Sing great songs from distinct eras.

SING SONGS FROM DISTINCT GENRES

I mentioned in the introduction to this book that my musical tastes are eclectic. The church's should be, too. We should sing a wide variety of songs—not just praise choruses and not just triumphant anthems, but a healthy mix. The goal is stylistic and thematic breadth as wide as the Scriptures. Allen P. Ross explains:

> Church music should have a balance of hymns, praise songs, doxologies, choruses, and litanies. A steady run of subjective, experiential songs without the doctrinal hymns will not be as edifying as the music should be; and an absence of the songs will not help the congregation express their spiritual experiences in harmony with the historic faith.[164]

---

164. Ross, 442.

I love that balance. Yes, we should sing doctrinal hymns. And yes, we should sing experiential testimonies of our walk with the Lord. Speaking as a father, I want my daughters (and in time, my grandkids) to know a wide swath of Christian music, including oratorios by Handel, anthems by John Rutter, hymns by Charles Wesley, gospel songs by Fanny Crosby, and reflective songs of testimony by Laura Story. After all, the New Testament calls us to sing "psalms and hymns and spiritual songs"—not just one type.

Donald Hustad regrets the tendency of the church to be iconoclastic, demolishing what is old and replacing it with what is new and shiny:

- The church once sang only psalms.
- When the church began singing hymns, it stopped singing psalms.
- When the church began singing gospel songs, it stopped singing hymns.
- Whenever we begin singing new songs, we stop singing old songs.[165]

Terry L. Johnson sees the same trend, and he notes that with each step we have jettisoned more and more doctrine:

> The transitions in the church from the metrical psalms of the six-teenth–eighteenth centuries to the classic hymns of the eighteenth century (e.g. Watts, Newton, Cowper, Wesley) to the gospel songs of the late nineteenth to mid-twentieth centuries to the Scripture songs of today demonstrate a dramatic reduction of the theological and biblical content of the church's songs.... a spiritually disastrous development that begs to be reversed.[166]

165. Donald Hustad, "Don Hustad, Musician, Composer, and Teacher: On Hymnology," posted August 11, 2015, https://youtu.be/2viinJrB6Ko. The language which historian Sydney E. Ahlstrom uses to describe the move from hymns to gospel songs is more jarring. He says that the gospel songs embraced by American Protestants between 1860 and 1920 "swept much of Isaac Watts, the older Reformed 'psalms,' and even much of British Methodism's fine treasury into *disuse and oblivion*." *A Religious History of the American People* (New Haven, CT: Yale University Press, 1972), 846. Emphasis added.

166. Johnson, 275.

Beyond singing a blend of psalms and hymns, old songs and new songs, we should be singing songs with a variety of moods. Once again the Psalms are a reliable guide. As I discussed in chapter 8, we tend to "cherry-pick" the Psalms. We sing happy songs about God's goodness and care. And we should! But we've already noted that 40% of the Psalms are songs of lament, dealing with hardship, confusion, and sorrow. Do the songs you sing in church reflect that?

Do 40% of the songs you sing in church or listen to in your car deal candidly with the reality of pain and depression? If not, why not? The most obvious answer, I think, is that we assume that people need to feel happy. Happiness is an addiction for evangelical Christians—and a delusion, many times. The stark reality is that we live in a broken world. It has its joys and beauties, as Louie Armstrong's "What a Wonderful World" reminds us. But we're not in Eden anymore, Toto. Creation is "groaning" (Romans 8:22). The wonderful world we inhabit is violent—"red in tooth and claw" in the words of Alfred Lord Tennyson.[167]

"True," says the typical worship leader. "So we need *happy* songs to make people feel better."

Actually, we don't. Not exclusively, anyway. As the late David Powlison put it in his moving book *God's Grace in Your Suffering*, what you need in life's most excruciating times are hymns that "speak to your suffering."[168]

By neglecting songs of lament, we give the impression that the Christian experience is always "happy all the day."[169] That's not true. People need

---

167. Alfred Lord Tennyson, *In Memoriam A. H. H.*, 1850, Canto 56.
168. David Powlison, *God's Grace in Your Suffering* (Wheaton, IL: Crossway, 2018), 25. This profound little book meditates on the hymn "How Firm a Foundation" and finds in it light to help in life's dark seasons.
169. Adding a happy tune and a happier refrain to Isaac Watts' somber text "Alas! and Did My Savior Bleed?" is one example of our efforts to be relentlessly upbeat. The song "At the Cross" weds a brooding, solemn text by Watts to a tune and refrain by Ralph E. Hudson, and the two are entirely at odds with each other. The tune is too chipper. Worse, singing of being a "worm" and of griefs that "melt mine eyes to tears" moments before singing of being "happy all the day" feels like either whiplash or schizophrenia. Christians need not be morose all the day, but we're not always happy either. Try singing "Alas! and Did My Savior Bleed?" to the tune MARTYRDOM by Hugh Wilson instead.

to learn biblical ways to respond to disappointment and grief. Songs of lament do that. As Dale Ralph Davis teaches, sorrowful songs (especially in the Psalter) "let people know that *they're not crazy*"—that they're not the only people who feel this way.[170] They legitimize the deep and confusing emotions we experience and teach us how to deal with them. They show us how real people respond to real life.

Carl Trueman agrees:

> A diet of unremittingly jolly choruses and hymns inevitably creates an unrealistic horizon of expectation which sees the normative Christian life as one long triumphalist street party—a theologically incorrect and pastorally disastrous scenario in a world of broken individuals.[171]

God's people suffer. *Godly* people suffer. If someone doesn't know this, it's because he or she isn't reading the Bible—or even the newspaper. Our worship—including both our singing and preaching—must neither deny the reality of pain nor quickly rush to simplistic solutions. An approach to religion that tries to distract people from their problems instead of sensitively addressing those challenges is useless. We must not give the impression that Scripture teaches an "escapist" approach to life's problems. Warren Wiersbe explains:

---

170. Dale Ralph Davis in a lecture to Doctor of Ministry students at The Master's Seminary in July 2019.

171. Carl Trueman, *The Wages of Spin: Critical Writings on Historical and Contemporary Evangelicalism* (Tain, Scotland: Mentor, 2004), 159. Contrast Trueman's call for lament with Homer Rodeheaver's instructions to music students to keep the song service intentionally chipper: "In the musical part of our service it is our aim always to make it as cheery and bright and sunshiny as we can, at the same time not losing sight of the reverential, devotional power of gospel song. If we can show the sunshine in our own faces it will recommend our religion to other folks more than anything else we do." Mungons and Yeo, 72. The result of this approach is songs like "Brighten the Corner Where You Are," or salt-in-the-wound lyrics like "Every cloud will wear a rainbow if your heart keeps right." Ibid., 101.

When our people assemble to worship, they move out of the confusion, ugliness, and disarray of everyday life into the order and beauty of liturgy.... But for too many people, the experience of worship is an *escape* from reality instead of an *encounter* with reality, an encounter that might give them a deeper understanding of God and His will for their lives.[172]

But won't singing songs about suffering be depressing? Hardly. It's uplifting. Well-written songs of lament are a balm to hurting people. Let me give an example. Perhaps no song written in the last several years has caught on with God's people as readily as Andrew Peterson's "Is He Worthy?" I could cite it as an example of almost every chapter in this book. It's biblical, doctrinal, Christ-centered, Trinitarian, and even congregational due to its ingenious antiphonal question-and-answer format. But here I'm using it as an example of biblical lament. Consider the lyrics of the first stanza:

> *Do you feel the world is broken? (We do.)*
> *Do you feel the shadows deepen? (We do.)*
> *But do you know that all the dark won't*
> *Stop the light from getting through? (We do.)*
> *Do you wish that you could see it all made new? (We do.)*[173]

From the very first phrase, Peterson's text acknowledges that we live in a broken world. He later uses biblical allusions, like "Is all creation groaning?" (Romans 8:22). But he doesn't just leave us to ponder our misery. Rather, He points us to Jesus Christ as our Help in hard times and our Hope for the future: "Is a new creation coming?" (Revelation 21-22). It is!

---

172. Warren Wiersbe, *Preaching & Teaching with Imagination: The Quest for Biblical Ministry* (Wheaton, IL: Victor Book, 1994), 225.

173. Lyrics from "Is He Worthy?" by Andrew Peterson and Ben Shive. © 2018 Junkbox Music (ASCAP) / Vamos Publishing (ASCAP) / Capitol CMG Genesis (ASCAP) / Jakedog Music (ASCAP) (adm. at CapitolCMGPublishing.com). All rights reserved. Used by permission.

This song is a favorite of churches around the world, and with good reason. It's real. It deals with our pain. And it points us to the Solution. That's much, much more encouraging than clapping our way through "This Is the Day" during hard times.

SING OTHER SONGS OF LAMENT

- "It Is Well with My Soul" (Spafford and Bliss)
- "Jesus, Lover of My Soul" (Wesley and Parry)
- "We Rest on Thee" (Cherry and Sibelius)
- "Be Still, My Soul" (von Schlegel and Sibelius)
- "Still, My Soul, Be Still" (Townend, Getty, and Getty)
- "Come, My Soul, with Every Care" (Newton and Coleman)
- "How Firm a Foundation" (traditional)
- "Come, Ye Disconsolate" (Moore, Hastings, and Webbe)
- "Turn Your Eyes Upon Jesus" (Lemmel)
- "Jesus, Draw Me Ever Nearer" (Becker and Getty)
- "He Will Hold Me Fast" (Habershon and Merker)
- "Yet Not I But through Christ in Me" (Farren, Robinson, and Thompson)
- "O Lord, My Rock and My Redeemer" (Stiff)
- "My Soul Finds Rest" (Keyes and Townend)
- "All Your Anxiety" (Joy)
- "Lord, I Need You" (Nockels, Carson, Reeves, Stanfill, and Maher)
- "Rejoice in the Lord" (Hamilton)
- "How Can I Fear?" (Hamilton)
- "You Are Always Good" (Anderson and Hamilton)
- "I Run to Christ" (Anderson and Habegger)

I included more songs here than in other lists in order to show how many songs of lament you already know and sing. I don't have space to give similar lists for every genre of Christian music, but it's important to sing anthems of praise, songs of confession, and so on. And again, it doesn't hurt to mix in a gospel song or praise chorus alongside a deep, doctrinal hymn. The point is to make an intentional effort to sing a wide variety of songs from a wide variety of genres—without settling for dumb stuff, of course.

SING SONGS FROM DISTINCT THEMES

Daniel Block notes that "truly worshipful music is rich in variety and comprehensive in scope."[174] The Gettys similarly challenge church leaders: "Ensure that your church's song list includes hymns and songs that touch on all the major doctrines and seasons of life, just as the Psalms and historical hymnals do."[175]

In order to serve the church a "well-balanced diet" of hymns—indeed, in order to teach "the whole counsel of God" (Acts 20:27)—we need to be intentional about addressing the many themes we find in the Scriptures.

This isn't essential, but I think it's useful for church leaders to prepare a Sunday "menu"—call it a *liturgy* or an *order of service*—that considers a single biblical theme, incorporating the Scripture reading, the songs, and even the pastoral prayer. Don't sing about heaven, then the Bible, then the resurrection, then God's love. There are rare talents like John Daker who can transition seamlessly from "Christ the Lord Is Risen Today" into "That's Amore." (Google it.) But most of us are better served by singing songs that focus on one key idea. Don't choose songs just because they move from "upbeat" to "slow" or because they're all in the key of G. Pursue a single biblical theme.

Why does this matter? Well, it's how we think. It's how we process information. You've probably been in a conversation with someone who said apparently random, disjointed things, and it made you scratch your head. "It's a nice day. I like potato salad. Brian Regan is funny. Someone should mow that lawn." You probably think to yourself, "Someone should

---

174. Block, 233.
175. Getty and Getty, 108.

get back on his meds." We expect communication to be orderly, not to lurch from one idea to the next. So why not choose hymns that build on a theme rather than wandering aimlessly through a service?

QUICK THOUGHTS ON SERVICE PLANNING

The church I most recently pastored had a weekly worship theme that connected the Scripture reading, the congregational songs, the choral song, the solo or ensemble (when we had one), and the pastoral prayer of adoration. We didn't try to connect the theme to the sermon, in part because doing so would be redundant during long expositional series through a single book, and in part (frankly) because my sermons were almost always completed after the songs had been selected.[176] We did end the service with a song that responded to the sermon's theme, however.

Let me recommend two other ways we highlighted our weekly worship theme: (1) We would send out a weekly "Preparing for Sunday" email on Friday that informed the congregation of the theme, Scripture reading, and songs we would be singing Sunday. It's easy to do, and it allows church members to prepare their hearts ahead of time. (2) We would introduce the theme toward the beginning of our service, usually before the reading of Scripture, with a brief, devotional introduction. This time provided a great opportunity to pastor our flock by showing them how the Scriptures related to our hymns—and to their everyday lives.

EXAMPLES OF COMPELLING THEMES

- Redemption
- The New Birth
- The Blood of Christ

---

176. R. Kent Hughes provides an alternative opinion. When he pastored College Church in Wheaton, Illinois, he *did* try to connect the songs to the text he was preaching. Hughes, 167, 169.

- God's Fatherly Care
- God's Wisdom
- The Five *Solas*
- The Ministry of the Spirit
- Christ's Intercession for Us
- Jesus' Current Reign and Jesus' Coming Reign
- Comfort for the Weary

I've included in Appendix F a few sample orders of service prepared by Greg Habegger, who collaborates with me on new hymns and who pastored with me at Killian Hill Baptist Church. This book already lists many hymns by doctrinal themes, experiential themes, and so on. Go ahead and borrow brains, networking with friends who plan services for their churches. It's not that difficult to plan a unified service, and it will be *great* for your church.

For what it's worth, Spurgeon urged his students toward this kind on intentional service planning:

> There is a way of taking a line of prayer, if the Holy Spirit shall guide you therein, which will make the service all of a piece, and harmonize with the hymns and discourse. It is very useful to maintain unity in the service where you can; not slavishly, but wisely, so that the effect is one.... [E]xhibit a degree of unity in the service, being careful in both the hymn, and the prayer, and the chapter, to keep the same subject prominent.[177]

To Spurgeon, such planning was ideal, though not mandatory. His goal wasn't just to have a well-crafted service, but to serve the people well:

> I trust, my brethren, that we all feel very deeply the importance of conducting every part of divine worship with the utmost possible

---

177. Charles H. Spurgeon, *Lectures*, 1:77.

efficiency. When we remember that the salvation of a soul may hang, instrumentally, upon the choice of a hymn, we should not consider so small a matter as the selection of the psalms and hymns to be a trifle.[178]

I can't improve on Spurgeon. Don't make the selection of songs and the planning of the service "to be a trifle." Choose wisely and broadly.

GRACE NOTES FOR WORSHIP LEADERS

- Do you take care to cover a variety of eras, genres, and themes in your orders of service? How can you do better?
- Do you organize your services around a particular theme? If so, are you avoiding redundancy? If not, are you ready to try?
- Do you notify the congregation of the theme, Scripture reading, and song selections ahead of time, allowing them to arrive with prepared hearts?

GRACE NOTES FOR PARENTS AND CHILDREN'S TEACHERS

- C. S. Lewis' charge of "chronological snobbery" is a challenge to parents. How can you better teach your children about the faithful people, books, and hymns of previous generations?
- Perhaps you could play a game with your children, challenging each other to think of Christian songs on the theme of God's power, or God's love, or Jesus' blood. Go back and forth until someone is stumped. Find creative ways to get them thinking of and singing Christian songs.

178. Ibid., 1:92.

GRACE NOTES FOR EVERYBODY

- Are you conversant with the great Christians, great books, and great hymns of the past? Most of us aren't. How can you become more informed about church history and the legacy we share and advance as Christians?
- Have you considered the various themes of our songs and how they address the various needs of our lives? How can you take notice of this more intentionally, both during worship services and the rest of the week?

"Sing aloud to God our strength; shout for joy to the God of Jacob!"
—Psalm 81:1

"Praise the Lord! I will give thanks to the Lord with my whole heart, in the company of the upright, in the congregation."
—Psalm 111:1

"Let us not present old worn-out praise, but put life, and soul, and heart, into every song, since we have new mercies every day, and see new beauties in the work and word of our Lord."
—Charles Spurgeon[179]

"Sing lustily and with good courage. Beware of singing as if you were half dead, or half asleep; but lift up your voice with strength."
—John Wesley[180]

179. Charles Spurgeon, *The Treasury of David* (Peabody, MA: Hendrickson Publishers, 1988), 1:105.
180. Wesley, *"Directions."*

CHAPTER 10

SING SONGS THAT ARE EMOTIVE

We were a church plant: Tri-County Bible Church in Madison, Ohio. I was only 26 at the time—"too young to be a pastor" as the church plant's matriarch "Granny" said the first time she met me. She was probably right. But I learned to be a pastor as that small group of Christians learned to be a church. Our first service took place on October 4, 1998, in the auditorium of Madison High School.

We would meet in the high school for the next twelve years. Every Sunday morning we put out a temporary sign and carried in hymnals, nursery supplies, and a second-hand, second-rate sound system. It was exhausting. But watching the Lord build His church was *exhilarating*. We had no building—but we had a vibrant, growing church.

The room we met in was made to kill sound. It did. Singing didn't resonate at all. And the piano we used made the clunky old sound system seem posh by comparison. It was out of tune. It had broken and sticking keys. It was just bad.

But we sang nonetheless. My parents donated a Kurzweil keyboard, which at least stayed in tune. Eventually we became a church that delighted to sing together, and over time we had a great infusion of musical talent. Tri-County Bible Church can *sing*! But early on, our singing was cringey.

And yet, one Sunday morning during our first year, as we prepared for the Lord's Table, a young man quietly wept. We were singing "O Sacred Head, Now Wounded," with our dying piano and dead acoustics. As we sang "Mine, mine was the transgression, but Thine the deadly pain," David melted into tears, overwhelmed by the words of the song. He was a new believer—the first convert in the church's history. He was an All-American kid; he played football, was an honor student, and was popular. But he had been lost. When God finally opened David's eyes to the gospel, He opened them *wide*.

David had an insatiable appetite for the Word. He was a bold evangelist, leading his Italian Catholic grandmother and his Uncle Joe to Christ. Baptizing the three of them was a highlight of my ministry. David is a trophy of God's grace, and he's a joyful Christian. But that day, moved by the hymn's depiction of Jesus' suffering in his place, David wept.

Singing summons our emotions in a unique way. I've been choked up by books. I've cried while watching plays, movies, and musical performances. But all of those activities are passive—I'm taking images and sounds in, not actively participating. Singing is different. You don't just think or feel your joy, your burden, your grief when you sing. You *express* it. Rosaria Butterfield explains, "Singing intertwines text with tune: It makes you dwell a little longer in the hard and vulnerable places as you hear your very own voice settle your wandering heart."[181]

When is the last time a hymn made you weep—either for joy or for sorrow? When is the last time you wanted to stretch out your hands or pump your fists in response to truth set to music? If it's been a while, or if music has never summoned a deep emotional response, why is that?

Music is inherently emotive. And Christian music is irresistibly, irreducibly emotive. Harry Eskew and Hugh McElrath write, "A hymn by its very nature as poetry is *passionate*. It appeals to the heart as well as to the mind. A hymn stirs the emotions and lifts the soul, comforting,

---

181. Butterfield, "Why I Sing Psalms."

challenging, making joyful or sorrowful, exalting sentiment, and quickening genuine feeling."[182]

Perhaps that sounds Charismatic to you. Maybe it sounds put on—an unhealthy, contrived emotionalism. If so, John Calvin has something to say to you: "Singing has great power and vigor to move and inflame men's hearts to call upon and praise God with a more vehement and burning zeal."[183] I'm slightly worried that Calvin's sentence might set this book on fire with its intensity: "power... vigor... move... inflame... vehement and burning zeal." Mercy. Calvin certainly didn't call for stoic detachment when we sing.

Hymnologists and historical figures tell us that worship music is— and must be—emotive. Good. But what does Scripture say? I'm glad you asked.

THE PSALMS CALL FOR EMOTIVE WORSHIP

The Psalms—the songbook of the redeemed for three millennia—invite and exemplify passionate, expressive worship. Look at some expressions of worship in the Psalms:

- *Bowing* or *kneeling* as an indication of reverence, submission, and even fear before the Lord. *"Oh come, let us worship and bow down; let us kneel before the Lord, our Maker!" (Psalm 95:6).*
- *Mourning*, as evidenced by torn garments, sackcloth, ashes, weeping, and fasting. *"I am weary with my moaning; every night I flood my bed with tears; I drench my couch with my weeping" (Psalm 6:6).*
- *Shouting* in joyful, exuberant, celebratory praise to God. Worship need not be docile, and enthusiasm need not be carnal. *"Shout for joy in the Lord, O you righteous!... Sing to him a new song; play skillfully on the strings, with loud shouts" (Psalm 33:1, 3).*

182. Eskew and McElrath, 17-18.
183. John Calvin, preface to *The Genevan Psalter*, 1542.

- *Clapping*, another expression of joy, participation, and agreement—a universal response to mirth and music. *"Clap your hands, all peoples! Shout to God with loud songs of joy!" (Psalm 47:1).*[184]

- *Raising hands*, a common biblical expression of petition, dependence, yearning, or joy. *"Hear the voice of my pleas for mercy, when I cry to you for help, when I lift up my hands toward your most holy sanctuary" (Psalm 28:2).*

- *Dancing*, an expression of praise so glad and so intense that it can neither be contained nor adequately expressed by mere words. Dancing before the Lord showed delight and gratitude, especially in times of victory. It certainly wasn't sensual; but it *was* joyful. *"Let them praise his name with dancing, making melody to him with tambourine and lyre!" (Psalm 149:3).*[185]

I'm not necessarily arguing that our Sunday services need to include all of these elements. Some may indeed be cultural expressions. Fine. But I'd challenge those who approach congregational singing with staid stoicism to tell me this: *Just what are our cultural expressions of exuberant, celebratory joy or deep, heartbreaking sorrow?* Whatever our answer, there can be

---

184. I will note here that although I spent much of my life in circles that considered music with a "backbeat" or contemporary sound to be carnal, the arguments I and others made were noticeably extrabiblical. Scripture explicitly endorses songs—with percussion—that are emotive, energetic, and celebratory. It will not do to dismiss all contemporary music as carnal and all celebratory music as sensual. Discernment, charity, and a commitment to the sufficiency of Scripture are essential as we address this issue. Adding to Scripture is as sinful as subtracting from it.

185. Because this is the most controversial of the worship expressions in the Scriptures, this definition from Allen P. Ross may be helpful: "The dancing... was the natural joy of the human spirit in response to God. The words used indicate that it consisted of whirling and turning, probably a round dance in which the dancers danced in circles." Ross, 260. J. Barton Payne explains that, following the examples of Miriam after the Red Sea deliverance (Exodus 15:20) and David's exultant dance at the ark's entry into Jerusalem (2 Samuel 6:14), "such group activity became a natural expression of Israel's faith in God." *The Theology of the Older Testament* (Grand Rapids, MI: Zondervan Publishing House, 1962), 427.

no mistake that the Psalms call the church to wholehearted and expressive praise in celebration of our great God.

I smile when I remember a conversation I had with Brenda, a delightfully spry older lady I was privileged to pastor in our noticeably conservative church. She shared with me how moved she was when we closed a service by singing "Before the Throne of God Above." She teased, "Pastor, I *tried* to raise my hands, but they just wouldn't go up!" I laughed and urged her not to pull a muscle. But I sincerely rejoiced that her *heart* was moved even if her *hands* stayed put. It is a spiritual victory when Christians are moved by the truths they sing!

THE SCRIPTURES MODEL EMOTIVE WORSHIP

Some might argue that the Psalms, as poetry, are hyperbolic in their calls for exuberant praise. I'd disagree, but let's go ahead and go down that path. Does the rest of Scripture also describe worship in such celebratory and emotive terms? Let's look at a few examples.

- Moses led the nation of Israel, and Miriam led the women of Israel in praise to Jehovah for His deliverance from their bondage in Egypt—praise that included singing, tambourines, and dancing (Exodus 15:1-21).
- David danced with all his might when the ark of the covenant was brought to Jerusalem (2 Samuel 6:14).
- The worship and thankfulness for the completion of the wall in Nehemiah's day was loud and proud: "And they offered great sacrifices that day and rejoiced, for God had made them rejoice with great joy; the women and children also rejoiced. *And the joy of Jerusalem was heard far away*" (Nehemiah 12:43, emphasis added).
- Of course, we also have examples of reverent quiet, of mourning, and of bowing down before the Lord. These examples include private worship (Nehemiah 1:4; Matthew 2:11; Luke 5:8), but also corporate worship (1 Kings 8:54; Nehemiah 8:9; Acts 20:36).

- The book of Revelation pictures worship in heaven as uber-expressive: falling down (1:17; 4:10; 5:8, 14; 19:4), casting crowns (4:10), shouting praise to God (6:10; 7:10)—shouts so loud that they sound "like the roar of many waters and like the sound of mighty peals of thunder" (19:1, 3, 4, 6).

Some argue that the New Testament is relatively silent on emotive worship. To the degree that that's true, I believe it's because proper worship was assumed based on the foundation set in the Old Testament. We don't really know how expressive worship was in the New Testament church. But we do know it was based on the Psalms. We know that tears regularly accompanied preaching and praying (Acts 20:19, 31; 2 Corinthians 2:4). We know that an erstwhile lame man responded to his healing with unbridled joy that would have made King David proud: "And leaping up, he stood and began to walk, and entered the temple with them, walking and leaping and praising God" (Acts 3:8). And we know that the worship in Revelation is undeniably expressive.

So I ask a question: Why would the church today worship with measured restraint when the worship of God's people in the past and in the future is so effusive?

WHY ARE EVANGELICALS AFRAID OF EMOTIVE WORSHIP?

Many evangelicals today affirm at least some approximation of the Regulative Principle of worship. This essentially means that only elements of worship commended by the Scriptures are valid for use in public worship. The *Second London Baptist Confession* describes it this way:

The acceptable way of worshiping the true God is instituted by himself, and so limited by his own revealed will, that he may not be worshiped according to the imagination and devices of men, nor the suggestions of Satan, under any visible representations, or any other way not prescribed in the Holy Scriptures.[186]

Very good. But if we genuinely intend to align our worship with Scripture, why is much of our singing so dispassionate and stoic? I'd argue that our emotional passivity is *learned*, primarily by years of watching fellow church members sing with folded arms, pocketed hands, or rigid spines. Some of this, to be sure, is a corrective to some fanatical abuses. That's understandable. But that doesn't mean it's good.

I've spent my entire Christian life in conservative churches. Most people didn't raise their hands in worship. They didn't sway, nod in agreement, or shout "Yes! Amen!" during a song. They didn't clap. They certainly didn't dance in church. I was taught to sing with complete restraint—hands at my sides, one foot slightly in front of the other for good breath support, and "dignity, always dignity" (to quote Don Lockwood).

Ironically, I was taught to *preach* with vim and vigor, raising my voice, gesturing with my hands, and unleashing my passion. In my college homiletics classes you would receive poor grades if you didn't show legitimate, demonstrable emotion as you preached. We expect preachers to preach their hearts out—to speak like they *mean* it. Conservative pulpits have been home to acrobatic preachers like Billy Sunday, to brooding preachers like Paul Washer, David Platt, and John Piper, and even to theatrical preachers like George Whitefield, whose eloquence and earnestness moved throngs of his hearers to tears.

And yet *singing by its very nature is more emotive than speech*. With its poetic language, its imagery, its music, its communal and participatory nature, music was designed by God to summon and set sail our affections. Allen P. Ross writes, "When the people come together to sing praises to God, they come out of themselves and elevate their voices above normal speech in celebration."[187] Yes! Singing lifts our communication "above

186. The Second London Baptist Confession of 1689, 22.1.
187. Ross, 438.

normal speech." Our emotionally disengaged singing is contrary to Scripture and to the very nature of both communication and music. Edmund Clowney writes, "Song is not only memorable but moving, expressing emotional depth as well as reflective breadth."[188] I would venture to say that song is memorable in part *because* it is moving. Biblical worship was wholehearted, passionate, and expressive. Is ours?

JONATHAN EDWARDS ON EMOTIONAL WORSHIP

I've heard Mark Dever share the farcical definition of a Puritan as "one who has a phobia that someone, somewhere, is happy." We picture the Puritans as dour and depressed. The word *puritanical* certainly has a negative connotation. But that's fake news. The Puritans found deep joy in God, His creation, and life in general. They were students of the Word and surgeons of the soul; their insight into the needs of sinful hearts is astounding. The Puritans were heroes, and they were anything but staid and stoic.

Chief among the Puritan theologians was Jonathan Edwards. I'll be honest: the very mention of his name is intimidating. But Edwards was a champion of the human affections.[189] Edwards valued the emotions, especially when stirred by Christian music:

---

188. Edmund P. Clowney, *The Church: Contours of Christian Theology*, ed. Gerald Bray (Downers Grove, IL: InterVarsity Press, 1995), 134.

189. Edwards commonly wrote about human *affections*—a word with more depth, value, and stability than our concept of *emotions*. His goal was to defend the Great Awakening against those who wrote it off as mere emotionalism. Not so, said Edwards. Heightened affections are essential when God is at work. W. Robert Godfrey defines the affections as "the will at work in a vigorous manner." "Worship and the Emotions" in *Give Praise to God: A Vision for Reforming Worship*, ed. Philip Graham Ryken, Derek W. H. Thomas, and J. Ligon Duncan III (Phillipsburg, NJ: P&R Publishing, 2003), 363. Affections are, then, a matter of *volition* even more than an issue of *feelings*. Still, for simplicity, I will use *affections* and *emotions* as approximate synonyms. I call for expressive (or emotive) worship that involves the entirety of the inner person—mind, will, and emotions.

The duty of singing praises to God seems to be wholly to excite and express religious affections. There is no other reason why we should express ourselves to God in verse rather than in prose and with music, except that these things have a tendency to move our affections.[190]

Exciting and expressing genuine religious emotion was a good thing to Edwards—indeed, a "duty." And poetry (*verse* in Edwards' statement) and music are used to intentionally "move our affections." Let's consider what this looks like.

EDWARDS SAYS YOU SHOULD BE MOVED BY THE WORDS OF SACRED MUSIC

The beautiful juxtaposition in a phrase like "Mine, mine was the transgression, but Thine the deadly pain" should affect you. Climaxing the crucifixion story by switching from "Took the blame, bore the wrath" to "What a love! What a cost!" in the final stanza of "The Power of the Cross" should summon tears of gratitude. Surveying the wondrous cross should move my will to conclude that "Love so amazing, so divine, demands my soul, my life, my all."

EDWARDS SAYS YOU SHOULD BE MOVED BY THE MELODIES OF SACRED MUSIC

Poetry moves us, he says. But so does music. Being moved by music doesn't mean you're being manipulated. It means you're being human and that the music which God created to affect you is doing its job. This is true of great melodies of the past, like ST. COLUMBA and O WALY WALY. And this is true of great melodies of the present. The best modern hymn tunes—like Getty's "In Christ Alone," Kauflin's "All I Have Is Christ," Habegger's "His

---

190. Quoted in John Piper, *A God-Entranced Vision of All Things: The Legacy of Jonathan Edwards* (Wheaton, IL: Crossway Books, 2004), 242.

Robes for Mine," and Cook's "Before the Throne of God Above"—all climax musically just as they climax lyrically, allowing the congregation to almost *shout* the truth. This is good!

We should be moved by music. More importantly, we should be moved by *the gospel*. I completely agree with this assessment from Jonathan Edwards:

> If we are going to be emotional about anything, shouldn't it be our spiritual lives? Is anything more inspiring, more exciting, more loveable and desirable in heaven or earth than the gospel of Jesus Christ?... The gospel story is designed to affect us emotionally—and our emotions are designed to be affected by its beauty and glory. It touches our hearts at their tenderest parts, shaking us deeply to the core. *We should be utterly humbled that we are not more emotionally affected than we are.*[191]

Calvin agreed: "How then is it possible for thee to know God, and to be moved by no feeling?"[192]

How indeed?

HOW HYMNS HELP

Hymns should be sung with emotion. Most of this chapter has focused on us as singers, not on the songs themselves. But if what we've studied about the importance of emotional engagement is true, we should select *songs* that effectively and appropriately move us—and we should avoid songs which either bore or manipulate us. What we sing must be biblically accurate; that's a given. But lyrics are poetry, not just cold, hard facts. What hymns say and how they say it should *move* us.

191.   Jonathan Edwards, *Religious Affections*, abridged and updated by Ellyn Sanna (Uhrichsville, OH: Barbour Publishing, 1999), 46-48. Emphasis added.
192.   John Calvin, *Calvin's Commentaries*, trans. John Owen (Grand Rapids: Baker Books, 1999), 22:174.

I've mentioned that my hymn-writing heroes are Watts and Wesley. The two are recognized by most as the preeminent lyricists in the history of English hymnody. But while they both wrote exquisite texts to point people to Christ, the two men couldn't have been more different.

Watts was reserved, unattractive, and incessantly sick. As for his preaching, he was commended by a contemporary for "the gravity and propriety of his utterance."[193] His hymn texts reveal a brilliant mind and a warm heart. They are elegant and precise, like a gazelle that glides and leaps with astounding ease. He marveled that, despite his sin, he was welcomed by the Savior: "Lord, why was I a guest?" Watts was at his best when he soberly contemplated the cross work of Christ, as in "When I Survey the Wondrous Cross" and "Alas! and Did My Savior Bleed?"

Wesley was different. He was intense and prone to passionate displays. Biographer John R. Tyson describes him as "impetuous, short-tempered, and given to outbursts of feeling."[194] His brother's biographer, Stephen Tomkins, writes of Charles' "volatility" and relational scrapes, making me think that it's just as well that God didn't grant him the "thousand tongues" he coveted. A witness of Charles' preaching described it as "all thunder and lightning."[195] And so are his hymns! Wesley was no gazelle; he was a grizzly, and it came out in his hymn texts. They are exceptional poetry, and they are worshipful, but they are anything but subdued: *"Hark!" "Hallelujah!" "Arise!" "Amazing!" "Rejoice!"* His texts are an absolute force—"the most exuberant and emotional hymns that had been written in English" in Tomkins' estimation.[196]

Watts crawls to Christ's throne as an unworthy "worm"; Wesley approaches Christ's throne "boldly" to claim his blood-bought crown. Watts calls us to humility; Wesley calls us to courage. Watts makes us ponder; Wesley helps us revel. And both of them are right! Both are essential!

193. Bond, 42.
194. Tyson, 6.
195. Tomkins, 95.
196. Ibid.

What we gain from exceptional hymns is the help to say what we want to, but sometimes can't. Hymns give words to our otherwise imprecise thoughts. We sing them and say, "Yes, that's true; that's exactly what I wanted to say." The goal of the lyricist is to supply true expressions of what the people of God believe and feel but struggle to adequately express in their own words. Robert Guy McCutchan explains:

> The religious poet, the hymn writer, comes to our aid and says for us those things which are in our thinking but which we lack the capacity to express. He couches in appropriate language many of the finer religious thoughts which many of us would never be able to utter except through him. We feel a responsibility for expressing our devotion but lack words to do so. The fact is, hymns aid us in making articulate our convictions; they draw out what is already there.[197]

Great hymns stir and shape and express our emotions.

EMOTIONS MUST FOLLOW THOUGHT, NOT DISPLACE OR DRIVE IT

Bob Kauflin leads singing with emotion, sometimes for thousands of people at a time. But he does so carefully, incessantly quoting Scripture and highlighting the meaning of the song's lyrics, never just pulling the audience's heartstrings through music. There's a reason for this, he writes: "Vibrant singing enables us to combine truth *about* God seamlessly with passion *for* God. Doctrine and devotion. Mind and heart."[198] Yes!—and the

197. McCutchan, 28. I think this statement is helpful. However, I find it inadequate in this sense: Great hymns don't merely draw out of us "what is already there"—what we believe—but actually pour into us what we *ought to* believe. And it might be a bit optimistic to believe that even Christians' hearts are just brimming with good thoughts awaiting good words to release them. Still, I do believe that hymn-writers have a role in helping the church say what we mean and need to say but otherwise couldn't.

198. Kauflin, *Worship Matters*, 99.

order of those things matters, as we'll see. David Doran teaches the same thing: "Right affection for God flows from right thinking about God."[199]

We are not after emotion for emotion's sake. It's not hard to manipulate people into feeling something. But mere emotion isn't worship. Emotion unhinged from thought is dangerous. Notice the subtle error in this statement about music by Rick Warren in his best-selling book *The Purpose-Driven Church*: "A song can often touch people in a way that a sermon can't. Music can bypass intellectual barriers and take the message straight to the heart."[200]

I called Warren's statement an error. That's probably a bit hasty. For one thing, I spent the first couple chapters of this book arguing that music *sticks* in a way that sermons don't. And he's probably right that "music can bypass intellectual barriers." That's probably true. But it's *not good*, and it's not something the church should *try* to do. God wants us to feel deeply about what we believe, but He commands us to love Him with our *mind* as well as with our heart, soul, and strength (Matthew 22:37). Paul expressed his intent to "sing with his mind" (1 Corinthians 14:15). So, the last thing we want religious music to do is to bypass the mind. We want to *think* while we sing!

Godly emotion must grow out of our understanding of biblical truth. That sequence is important. First, we understand; then we emote *in response to the truth*. Emotions must be the caboose of the soul train, not the engine. MacArthur explains: "When the words [of worship music] are teeming with rich theological life and biblical accuracy, they inform the mind and that launches a legitimate experience of glorifying God."[201]

Kauflin agrees, and he urges Christian musicians to be serious students of biblical theology: "Mind and heart belong together. Strong, passionate desires for God flow from and encourage the faithful, thoughtful

---

199. Doran, "Three Qualities."
200. Rick Warren, *The Purpose-Driven Church: Growing Without Compromising Your Message & Mission* (Grand Rapids, MI: Zondervan, 1995), 279.
201. John MacArthur, *The Master's Plan for the Church* (Chicago: Moody Press, 2008), 314.

study of God—his nature, character, and works."[202] Excellent. But it gets even better. Kauflin later clarifies that the truth that ultimately moves us and makes our worship fervent is the very heart of the Christian faith:

> No facet of God's truth should move our affections more than the gospel.... Calvary is always in our view. One of the aspects of biblical worship we desperately need to recover today is *a passionate, scripturally informed exaltation of Jesus Christ and his redemptive work.*[203]

Christians have every reason to respond to God's saving work with deep, thoughtful emotion. John Piper captures this beautifully: "Strong affections for God rooted in truth are the bone and marrow of biblical worship."[204]

Exceptional hymns don't just help us sing. They make us *think* and *feel* for God's glory.

GRACE NOTES FOR WORSHIP LEADERS

- What's the difference between legitimately moving the church toward deeper affections for Christ and illegitimately manipulating the church's emotions?
- How have you seen the emotive power of music used for good? How about for evil?

---

202. Kauflin, *Worship Matters,* 32.
203. Ibid., 78.
204. John Piper, *Desiring God: Meditations of a Christian Hedonist* (Colorado Springs: Multnomah, 2001), 81.

GRACE NOTES FOR PARENTS AND CHILDREN'S TEACHERS

- How do you shepherd the emotions of your children—showing them that there is a time for exuberant joy and a time for sorrow and mourning?
- Do you think children's emotional reactions to Bible stories and songs are innate or learned?

GRACE NOTES FOR EVERYBODY

- How does the expressiveness of your worship compare to that of Scripture?
- Are you moved by truth that you sing? Why? How do you express it?
- Explain in your own words what the relationship should be between biblical truth and human emotion.

"I will sing to the Lord, because he has dealt bountifully with me."
—PSALM 13:6

"Singing is the expression of a heart affected by truth."
—MICHAEL BARRETT[205]

"If our hymnal does not look at least something like the Hebrew psalter, we probably should tinker with it a bit."
—MARK SNOEBERGER[206]

---

205. Barrett, *Beauty*, 98.
206. Mark Snoeberger, "Singing the Christian Experience," *Detroit Baptist Theological Seminary*, February 18, 2020, https://dbts.edu/2020/02/18/singing-the-christian-experience.

CHAPTER 11

SING SONGS THAT ARE EXPERIENTIAL

"Today's songs are all about the singer. They talk about the worshiper more than about God. Just look at all the first-person personal pronouns: 'I... me... my...' They're positively narcissistic."

Ever heard that critique of contemporary worship songs? I have—often![207] Christopher Wordsworth would certainly agree. He complained that whereas ancient songs were self-forgetful, newer songs were self-focused.

The kicker? Wordsworth lived in the nineteenth century, and the songs he critiqued as self-absorbed included Watts' "When I Survey the Wondrous Cross" and Wesley's "Jesus, Lover of My Soul." Oops.[208]

---

207. Examples: Mark Dever and Paul Alexander, *The Deliberate Church*, 120. Douglas Sean O'Donnell, *God's Lyrics*, 128. Frank Garlock and Kurt Woetzel, *Music in the Balance* (Greenville, SC: Majesty Music, 1992), 120. Philip Graham Ryken, *City on a Hill: Reclaiming the Biblical Pattern for the Church in the 21ˢᵗ Century* (Chicago, IL: Moody Publishers, 2003), 57. In fairness, I've made that argument myself, as well. Bob Kauflin offers a good counterargument: *Worship Matters*, 101.

208. Lorenz, 38.

OBJECTIVE TRUTH AND SUBJECTIVE EXPERIENCE

In English, we highlight the contrast between the objective and the subjective. Things that are *objective* are settled and certain—matters of truth and fact. Things that are *subjective* are open to opinion—matters of experience and feeling.

Hymnologists use those terms to describe songs.

There are sacred songs that highlight *objective truth*—they tell us facts about what God is like or what God has done. Think of Sergeant Joe Friday: "Just the facts, ma'am." On the other hand, there are sacred songs that emphasize *subjective experience*—they tell us how we respond to what God has done. Joe Friday is replaced by Andy Williams: "Feelings, nothing more than feelings." It's common to think of traditional hymns as objective songs and to think of gospel songs as subjective songs. Let's consider an example of each.

Think of the hymn "Immortal, Invisible, God Only Wise"—an astoundingly good lyric by Walter C. Smith. It rehearses attributes of God, emphasizing through beautiful poetry God's transcendence. It makes God big—or rather, it reveals the bigness of God. The church needs songs like this.

Now consider "I'd Rather Have Jesus," a gospel song written by Rhea F. Miller in 1922. It's a testimonial, sharing the singer's desire for Jesus above all that the world offers. It's aspirational, singing about what *should* be true, although sometimes it's not. The song's theology is fairly light, but it provides a moving exhortation. The church needs songs like this as well.

Now, much of the contemporary church has turned its attention to experience *over* theology—focusing on God's immanence (nearness) to the neglect of His transcendence (loftiness). Modern songs are often focused on God's healing our wounds, accepting us despite our flaws, comforting us in our sorrows, and so on. And God does those things! But we can't turn the Most High God into an Omnipotent Therapist or Omnipresent Concierge. That's why many conservative pastors and scholars are understandably concerned about too much "*I, me,* and *my*" in worship songs, as I mentioned at the beginning of the chapter. Their warnings are justified, if a bit too simplistic. But *hear them*. Here's Donald Hustad's summary of what was lost when churches stopped singing hymns with laser-like focus on our great God:

> Many American evangelicals continued to exhibit a considerable gap between the materials they sang and the theology they preached. They confessed to believe in a transcendent God who is above all creation, yet they sang few hymns which properly revealed God's excellences. Some congregations expected "strong meat" in biblical preaching, but seemed to be satisfied with "milk" or even lollipops in song.[209]

That's not good.

But here's the thing: The best hymns and gospel songs *combine the two*; they are *both* objective and subjective. Is "Before the Throne of God Above" about Christ or me? Both! Is "Jesus Paid It All" about Jesus' sacrifice or my forgiveness and devotion? Both! Is "And Can It Be" about the Savior or the saved? Both! In fact, think through the very songs I cited earlier as examples of objective and subjective hymns:

- "Immortal, Invisible, God Only Wise" focuses on our awesome God. But it also unpacks our interaction with God. He is "hid from our eyes." He has made us: "To all life Thou givest, to both great and small." He is eternal, whereas we are timebound: "We blossom and flourish as leaves on the tree, / And whither and perish, but nought changeth Thee." As a result of God's greatness, we worship Him: "All praise we would render...." The depiction of the worshiper is humbling, to be sure—and accurate—but the worshiper is there.
- "I'd Rather Have Jesus" testifies of the believer's devotion to Jesus. But in doing so, it inherently proclaims *the immeasurable worthiness of God*. Why would I "rather have Jesus than anything"? Because He

---

209. Hustad, *Jubilate II*, 461.

is so good, so gracious, and so much better than anything the world offers. And while the first two stanzas and the refrain imply Jesus' worth, the final stanza actively proclaims it, pivoting to objective praise: "He's fairer than lilies.... He's sweeter than honey...."

It's a false dichotomy to say that we must sing about God and not about ourselves. Timothy Dudley-Smith rightly suggests that hymns should be "a marriage of truth and experience."[210]

SING SONGS ABOUT GOD... AND YOURSELF

Of course, there are songs that focus on the singer to the exclusion of the Savior, and those songs should be rejected. But merely counting first-person personal pronouns is an inadequate measure of a song's message. Such a standard would have us rejecting many of the Psalms. Here's a good rule of thumb: If a criticism of music could be leveled against the Psalms—too much repetition, too much emotion, too many personal references, and so on—it's not a sound argument. Worship is deeply, inescapably personal. And worship songs need to focus on the Christian *experience*.

One of the great values of the Psalms is that they personalize our worship and our relationship with God. Their focus on the believer's experience is one of the things that makes them so powerful. God isn't just *a* Shepherd, Rock, or Redeemer—He is *mine*!

- God is my king. (Psalm 2:6; 5:2)
- God is my strength. (Psalm 18:1)
- God is my rock, my fortress, my deliverer, my God, my rock, my shield, the horn of my salvation, my stronghold. (Psalm 18:2)
- God is my support. (Psalm 18:18)
- God is my redeemer. (Psalm 19:14)
- God is my shepherd. (Psalm 23:1)

210. Dudley-Smith, 147.

- God is my light and my salvation. (Psalm 27:1)
- God is my refuge, my strength, my help, my fortress. (Psalm 46:1, 7, 11)
- God is my God and my Lord. (over 60 times)

That's only the start of what would be a very long list. What's more, the psalmist speaks constantly of "my heart," "my enemies," "my troubles," "my prayer," "my words," and so on. And these inspired prayers and songs are intended to be a model for our own! Don't tell me that our songs should take on some disinterested air that ignores the worshiper! We need songs that are intensely personal, including great hymns, gospel songs, praise choruses, and testimonials.

Charles Wesley's hymns are remarkably personal. During the year after his conversion, he wrote the following lyrics, from multiple hymns:

- *"Still the small inward voice I hear, / That whispers all my sins forgiven; / Still the atoning blood is near, / That quench'd the wrath of hostile Heaven: / I feel the life His wounds impart; / I feel my Savior in my heart."* (This is a little-known stanza from the remarkably personal hymn "And Can It Be.")
- *"Come, Divine, and peaceful Guest, / Enter our devoted breast; / Holy Ghost, our hearts inspire, / Kindle there the Gospel-fire."*
- *"I felt my Lord's atoning blood / Close to my soul applied; / Me, me He loved—the Son of God / For me, for me, He died!"*

Note how often Wesley repeats his wonder that Jesus' death was "for *me*, for *me*!" Biographer John R. Tyson explains why:

His hymns were born in his own spiritual pilgrimage, life experiences, and personal study of the Bible. They were loaded with biblical phrases and doctrines, as well as vibrant emotion. Set in first-person form, they placed biblical words and experiences upon the singer's lips. In this way, Wesley's hymns, like his sermons, were intended not simply to narrate evangelical doctrines and experience, but to induce them. By taking up the first-person language he had learned from the Moravians and Martin Luther, Wesley was able to make the singers of his hymns participants in the experiences they sang about. This was a relatively new development in hymnody, one that broke pattern with Wesley's evangelical precursors like Isaac Watts and added a new vitality to singing in church. It brought his hymns their hallmark sense of immediacy that has helped them endure through the ages.[211]

SING ABOUT SALVATION... AND ABOUT LIFE

The Christian's justification is often highlighted in modern hymns. It's what I write about in "His Robes for Mine." It's what I love to preach about. But we—myself included—might be neglecting our ongoing, sometimes mundane *Christian walk*. That's concerning to Dr. Mark Snoeberger, a systematic theologian *par excellence*. You would think he'd be all about objective hymns. Yet, he writes passionately and convincingly about the need to sing of the entire Christian life, not just conversion:

> Most newer hymnody, where it exists, tends to be dominated by songs about the Gospel, and more specifically, the Gospel as justification. There is nothing wrong, of course, with singing about justification. The New Testament itself seems to commend this practice in its occasional hymnic outbursts. I wonder, though, whether we moderns may be neglecting something that the majority church (historically speaking) rightly emphasized....
>
> The Apostle Paul tells us in his epistles both to the Ephesians and to the Colossians that we ought to sing "psalms, hymns, and spiritual songs".... There are psalms about the human condition, sin, repentance, forgiveness, sickness, persecution, discouragement, want, grief, frustration, trials, loss, death, the afterlife, children, grandchildren,

211. Tyson, 57-58.

industry, learning, nature, providence, contentment, gratitude, redemption, the law, grace, hope, joy, peace, triumph, and on and on and on. The psalms address, more comprehensively and incisively than any human hymnal ever has, the full range of human sentiments experienced in the life of faith. Israel sang about these things, and according to Paul, so should we. And if our hymnal does not look at least something like the Hebrew psalter, we probably should tinker with it a bit.[212]

Part of the solution is to sing psalms, as I argue in chapter 8. But again, the Psalter should be *the pattern for our non-inspired songs*—our handbook for worship in addition to our hymnbook. We have biblical precedence for singing about going to work, cleaning the house, and other ho-hum adventures. We should write and sing songs like this—like the Gettys' "Before You I Kneel (A Worker's Prayer)." "Great Is Thy Faithfulness" certainly focuses on God. But it also rejoices in His blessings—not only pardon for sin (which is primary), but also ongoing peace, God's presence, daily strength, and future hope—"blessings all mine, with ten thousand beside."

Another example: We all thrill to sing the third stanza of "How Great Thou Art," about salvation through Christ. But I've endured the comparatively shallow second stanza for most of my life. Yet, as I age—and possibly, mature—I find it beautiful to sing about taking time to rejoice in the greatness and goodness of God we experience during a walk through the forest or a hike in the mountains. The stanza doesn't seem so shallow now. We *should* praise God for gifts like this, not only for (ahem) "soteriology." It's a good thing to sing, "For the joy of human love: brother, sister, parent, child." Do it. Don't belittle it. Don't feel guilty about it. It's the stuff of *life*—the stuff sung through the ages via the Psalter.

For what it's worth, my devotional song "I Run to Christ" aims to address the normalcies of life. I wrote it with an eye on my own fatigue but also with empathy for the burned-out accountant, the diaper-changing

212. Snoeberger, "Singing."

mother, and the stressed-out student. It finishes with God's provision of forgiveness through Christ. But much of the song deals with the mundane stuff of life: fear, grief, temptation, strife, and discouragement. We all face these things. Why not sing about them?

> *I run to Christ when chased by fear / And find a refuge sure.*
> *"Believe in me," His voice I hear; / His words and wounds secure.*
> *I run to Christ when torn by grief / And find abundant peace.*
> *"I too had tears," He gently speaks; / Thus joy and sorrow meet.*
>
> *I run to Christ when worn by life / And find my soul refreshed.*
> *"Come unto Me," He calls through strife; / Fatigue gives way to rest.*
> *I run to Christ when vexed by hell / And find a mighty arm.*
> *"The Devil flees," the Scriptures tell; / He roars, but cannot harm.*
>
> *I run to Christ when stalked by sin / And find a sure escape.*
> *"Deliver me," I cry to Him; / Temptation yields to grace.*
> *I run to Christ when plagued by shame / And find my one defense.*
> *"I bore God's wrath," He pleads my case— / My Advocate and Friend.*

Let me cite a few more examples. "O Great God"—my favorite Bob Kauflin hymn—pictures my struggle with sin as divine warfare, and it pleads with God to conquer me. (Note how it addresses sanctification, not just justification.) "All I Have Is Christ"—my favorite Jordan Kauflin hymn—gives the testimony of every true believer, from the hopelessness of sin to the wonder of salvation to the ongoing desire to be used by God. Edward Joy's gospel song "All Your Anxiety" is a salve to weary and worrying Christians, as are Civilia Martin's "His Eye Is on the Sparrow" and William Cushing's "Under His Wings." These songs are all about God. But they're also about *us*—about our real-life Christian experience.

SING WELL-CHOSEN GOSPEL SONGS

We've noted that one genre which regularly addresses the Christian experience is the gospel song—the red-headed stepchild of many hymnologists. Again, there was a time when I would roll my eyes at the gospel songs written in the nineteenth and twentieth centuries. I was so sophisticated. So smart. So... well, *arrogant*, to be honest. There's a reason why people so enjoy the songs of Fanny Crosby, Frances Ridley Havergal, John W. Peterson, the Gaithers, and others. I'm not endorsing all of them, of course, any more than I endorse all hymns. But many gospel songs are deeply meaningful. Please listen to this counsel: *As you strive to choose exceptional hymns, beware of an elitism that disdains the worthy songs of God's people.*

I've heard people blame the popularity of gospel songs on mental laziness in the church. But Donald Hustad insightfully suggests that gospel songs filled the void of personal-experience songs that the church lost when it stopped singing the Psalms.[213] It's not lazy or shallow to sing songs of testimony—whether psalms, hymns, gospel songs, or songs intended for performance rather than the entire congregation.

Let me give a personal example from that last category—performance songs. Not long ago I came to church with a shattered heart. A friend of my daughter's had died, unexpectedly and tragically. We were devastated. My daughter, still a college student at the time, ended up being the primary comforter for the grieving family through the first indescribably awful night after the tragedy. I grieved for the young lady. I grieved for her family. And I grieved for my daughter to be in such a high-pressured situation with no warning and little preparation apart from her own walk with the Lord. Still, it was Saturday, so in the middle of all that grief, I prepared to preach. I went to church the next day absolutely numb.

The service started. I tried to sing the hymns, but my voice refused, and tears streamed down my face. Just before I was to get up and preach, a soloist sang a beautiful song by Laura Story: "He Will Not Let Go."

213. Donald Hustad, recorded lecture on hymns: https://youtu.be/2viinJrB6Ko.

It described perfectly the suffocating sorrow that I was feeling. It was a lament. But it also reminded me of God's unfailing love and unslipping grip: "I am not alone, / For He will not let go."

It wasn't a congregational song. It didn't fit all of the categories we've covered over the first ten chapters of this book. But it was true; it was *personal*; and it was a balm.

Yes, Christianity is rooted in the objective truths of what God has accomplished in the past. But it is also a personal and ongoing relationship with our God and Savior, every day. There are subjective elements to our faith, as well. The Christian walk isn't "Just the facts, ma'am." It's facts and faith. Facts and frustrations. Facts and failures. And yes, facts and feelings.

SING FOR GOD'S PLEASURE... AND YOUR OWN

We rightly emphasize the importance of directing our worship to God. The primary goal of worship music is not "to get a blessing." It's not about us. It's been said that we sing for "an Audience of One." That sounds spiritual, for sure. But we might be overstating the case to say that our pleasure is inconsequential. Our enjoyment of worship isn't primary, but it isn't irrelevant either. God gave us music for our enjoyment as surely as for His. In my experience, worship music is one of earth's greatest pleasures, and it will be one of heaven's as well!

John Frame is helpful here. He acknowledges that our singing is done for the pleasure of God, but he also notes the flipside: "If our congregation does not *enjoy* hearing and singing of God's incomparable love to us in Jesus, surely something important is missing."[214]

Right. We don't merely praise as a duty; worship must be our delight. God is not honored when we sing great music from a cold heart—even when our theology is icily correct. In fact, repeating words of adoration that we don't mean is a breach of the Fourth Commandment—it's taking God's name in vain. Worship is—worship *must be*—experiential.

214. Frame, *Contemporary*, 61.

Otherwise, no matter how carefully we choose our songs, our worship is dead.

Scripture could not be clearer about this point: God detests it when we honor Him with our lips but our hearts are far from Him (Matthew 15:8; Isaiah 29:13). God is "wearied" by our letter-of-the-law offerings when they come from legalistic, idolatrous, or bored hearts (Isaiah 1:10-15). As Bob Kauflin astutely observes, "Worship isn't primarily about music, techniques, songs or methodologies. It's about our hearts. It's about what and who we love more than anything."[215]

The Shop Around the Corner's Kathleen Kelly tells us, "Whatever else anything is, it ought to *begin* by being personal." Just so. Whatever else worship is, it ought to begin by being personal.

SING SONGS THAT TELL YOUR SPIRITUAL BIOGRAPHY

It's important to sing songs about your walk with God. We've established that. But what does that look like? What songs should we sing? Well, I'm going to give a partial list to prime the pump. You'll notice that I include more gospel songs and praise choruses here than in other sections. That's okay. This is where those genres shine.

SING ABOUT YOUR CONVERSION

- "And Can It Be" (Wesley and Campbell)
- "Blessed Assurance" (Crosby and Knapp)
- "Satisfied" (Williams and Hudson)
- "Just As I Am [I Come Broken]" (Elliott, Williams, Bradbury, and Holland)
- "Complete in Thee" (Wolfe, Gray, and Nyce)
- "All I Have Is Christ" (Kauflin)
- "Now I Belong to Jesus" (Clayton)

215. Kauflin, *Worship Matters*, 25.

SING ABOUT YOUR DEVOTIONAL LIFE AND WORSHIP OF CHRIST

- "Be Thou My Vision" (traditional Irish hymn and melody / Byre and Hull)
- "I Need Thee Every Hour" (Hawks and Lowry)
- "Jesus, I Am Resting, Resting" (Pigott and Mountain)
- "My Jesus, I Love Thee" (Featherston and Gordon)
- "I'd Rather Have Jesus" (Miller and Shea)
- "I Will Follow" (Lynch)
- "All the Way" (Crosby and Lynch)
- "We Are Heirs of God Almighty" (Townend)
- "Bow the Knee" (Hamilton and Reid)
- "O How He Loves You and Me" (Kaiser)
- "I Love You, Lord" (Klein and Thomas)
- "As the Deer" (Nystrom)

SING ABOUT GOD'S HELPING YOU THROUGH TRIALS

- "Like a River Glorious" (Havergal and Mountain)
- "It Is Well with My Soul" (Spafford and Bliss)
- "His Eye Is on the Sparrow" (Martin and Gabriel)
- "Under His Wings" (Cushing and Sankey)
- "Be Strong in the Lord" (Johnson and Fettke)
- "O Lord, My Rock and My Redeemer" (Stiff)
- "He Will Hold Me Fast" (Habershon and Merker)
- "Yet Not I But through Christ in Me" (Farren, Robinson, and Thompson)
- "Ancient of Days" (Robinson, Thompson, Farren, and Reeves)
- "He Hideth My Soul" (Crosby and Kirkpatrick)
- "Turn Your Eyes Upon Jesus" (Lemmel)
- "He Is Able, More than Able" (Ferguson and Noland)

- "I Run to Christ" (Anderson and Habegger)
(See chapter 9 for a fuller list of hymns of lament.)

SING ABOUT YOUR SIN, REPENTANCE, AND GROWTH
TOWARD CHRISTLIKENESS

- "Come, Ye Sinners, Poor and Needy" (Hart / Walker's *Southern Melody*)
- "The Blood of Jesus Speaks for Me" (Moffitt and Cottrell)
- "Nothing Between" (Tindley)
- "Have Thine Own Way, Lord" (Pollard and Stebbins)
- "O God, My Joy" (Keew and Pinner)
- "Take My Life, and Let It Be Consecrated" (Havergal and Malan)
- "A Tender Heart" (Hamilton)

SING ABOUT YOUR LONGING FOR HEAVEN

- "Hark, I Hear the Harps Eternal" (Warren / traditional melody)[216]
- "My Faith Looks Up to Thee" (Palmer and Mason)
- "I Shall Know Him" (Crosby and Sweney)
- "The Sands of Time Are Sinking" (Cousin and Urhan)
- "It Is Not Death to Die" (Malan and Kauflin)
- "Christ Our Hope in Life and Death" (Getty, Boswell, J. Kauflin, Merker, and Papa)
- "One Day [When We All Get to Heaven]" (Hewitt, Redman, Redman, and Jarman)
- "Abide with Me" (Lyte and Monk)
- "To Live or Die" (Anderson and Habegger)

216. This beautiful song sings better congregationally than you'd expect. Try it!

SING ON YOUR DARKEST DAYS

Christian music is a lifeboat for the soul. In our darkest, hardest, saddest moments, the songs we've learned in better times support us.

So, Paul and Silas, beaten and imprisoned, sang.

So, John Hus, tied to a pyre and engulfed in flames, sang "Jesus, Thou Son of David, have mercy on me."

So, the five missionaries to Ecuador, risking their lives to take the gospel to the unreached, encouraged each other and their wives by singing "We Rest on Thee."

So, dying saints ask to hear hymns in their last moments. And bereaved saints find solace in songs at their loved ones' memorials.

And even when every other memory fades, hymns are there. The "theology that sticks" is resilient. You've probably seen this. An elderly Christian walks through the thick fog of Alzheimer's disease or dementia. She can't remember conversations, faces, or even children. Then, reminded of a beloved hymn, without straining or even realizing it, she bursts into song. The fog lifts, at least momentarily. Confusion may reign everywhere else, but the words and tunes that have sustained her faith for a lifetime are still there.

This is explained beautifully by the Evangelical Lutheran Church in America:

> Through the songs sung in worship, God's people, including children and those new to the faith, learn their language about God and the story of salvation. These songs remain with people through life, persist when memory fades, give meaning in later life, and are a comfort in death.[217]

---

217. Evangelical Lutheran Church in America, *Principles for Worship* (Minneapolis, MN: Augsburg Fortress Press, 2001), 30. While the statement is true and inspiring, the ELCA, sadly, does not stand on orthodox doctrine.

Hymns help you every day. They give vent to your joys on your best days. They give words to your groanings on your worst days. And they will help you on your last day.

GRACE NOTES FOR WORSHIP LEADERS

- How do you balance objective (factual) songs and subjective (experiential) songs in your church? Can you give several examples of each? Do you intentionally include songs that are both objective and subjective?
- Can you think of a time when a song met an urgent need for you or for a church member?

GRACE NOTES FOR PARENTS AND CHILDREN'S TEACHERS

- How can you teach your children to deal with the gaps between what they believe and what they feel?
- What songs are you teaching your children now that will help them on their darkest days throughout the rest of their lives, even decades from now?

GRACE NOTES FOR EVERYBODY

- Can you think of songs you sing or listen to that exalt human experience and feelings above Bible doctrine in an unhelpful way?
- Can you recall a time when hymns have kept you or loved ones afloat during floods of trouble or grief?

"Sing to him a new song; play skillfully on the strings, with loud shouts."
—PSALM 33:3

"Shout for joy to God, all the earth; sing the glory of his name; give to him glorious praise!"
—PSALM 66:1-2

"Hymns should be beautiful; mere expressions of piety are not enough."
—ROBERT GUY McCUTCHAN[218]

"Christ is the Lord of our whole life and the Christian life should produce not only truth—flaming truth—but also beauty."
—FRANCIS SCHAEFFER[219]

218. McCutchan, 26.
219. Francis A. Schaeffer, *Art and the Bible: Two Essays* (Downers Grove, IL: IVP Books, 1973), 48.

CHAPTER 12

SING SONGS THAT ARE BEAUTIFUL

"A good hymn is the most difficult thing in the world to write."

I didn't say that. The renowned poet Alfred, Lord Tennyson did.[220]

But I agree. Writing a hymn isn't hard. But writing a *good* hymn is hard. And writing a *great* hymn is catching lightning in a bottle. Charles Wesley, for example, wrote well over six thousand hymns, and most of us sing maybe six of them.

But let's be clear: There are good hymns, great hymns, and bad hymns—and God deserves to be praised with hymns that are great.

Our hymns should never be less than true. But I believe they should be *more*. Our hymns should be beautiful. Sacred songs must demonstrate artistry and excellence consistent with the nobility of worship and the grandeur of God.

Unconvinced? Okay. I actually expect this chapter to be the most controversial for many readers. Let's lean into it a bit.

In the Old Testament, God's people were forbidden to bring their disabled animals as a sacrifice. They were to bring animals "without blemish" as an acceptable offering to God (Exodus 12:5; 29:1; and nearly 40 times

---

220. Hallam Tennyson, *Alfred Lord Tennyson: A Memoir* (New York: The MacMillan Company, 1897), 2:401.

in Leviticus and Numbers). Why this stipulation? Because the sacrifices prefigured our unblemished Savior (Hebrews 9:14; 1 Peter 1:19). Because God is supremely worthy of the best we have—not offerings which cost us nothing (2 Samuel 24:24). And, perhaps most pointedly, because people are incurably selfish and conniving. The temptation for Israelites was to sacrifice to God an animal that was either useless or going to die anyway (Malachi 1:8; Leviticus 22:22). That's shrewd—and blasphemous. God deserves our best, not our leftovers, and not things we deem "good enough."

I believe this principle applies to our music as well. British Poet Laureate Robert Bridges longed for the church to have better music—"a music worthy of the fair temples in which we meet."[221] That idea moves me. I love to visit the stunning cathedrals of Europe, and I can see how it would be motivating to write something "worthy of Westminster Abbey." But our goal is actually much, much higher. Our music should be worthy of *God*. Our God deserves what is best and beautiful.

Of course, the challenge is defining what "best" and "beautiful" even mean. But the basic principle certainly stands, and it's heralded by the Psalms: God deserves music that is "skillful" (Psalm 33:3) and praise that is "glorious" (Psalm 66:2).

BEAUTY, ARTISTRY, AND WORSHIP

Allen P. Ross says, simply, "Praise should be well prepared because it is an offering to God."[222] Our worship is to be consistent with the One we're worshiping. How we worship is actually a reflection on *Him*. That's the point of Psalm 145:3: "*Great* is the LORD, and *greatly to be praised*, and his greatness is unsearchable." Because God is great, his praise should be great. Because God is holy, His praise (and those who offer it) should be holy. Because God is beautiful, His praise should be beautiful. Donald

---

221.   Robert Bridges, *A Practical Discourse on some Principles of Hymn Singing* (Oxford, England: B. H. Blackwell, 1901), 43. The context of this quotation is included in Appendix A.

222.   Ross, 441.

Whitney writes, "We worship God as He is revealed in the Bible, not as we might want Him to be."[223]

Now, what about the notion of art in worship? Doesn't art belong in museums rather than in the adoration of God?

- Ask Moses, who was given explicit instructions for the building of the dazzlingly beautiful tabernacle (Exodus 25-31). God prescribed ornate carvings, detailed embroidery, and gold-plated beams and furniture. Even the high priest's clothes were exquisite: "And you shall make holy garments for Aaron your brother, *for glory and for beauty*" (Exodus 28:2, emphasis added).
- Ask Bezalel and Oholiab, who were uniquely enabled by God to craft the beautiful objects God designed for the tabernacle and to teach others to work under their artistic supervision (Exodus 35:30-35).
- Ask Solomon, who hired a humongous staff and invested incredible wealth to build a temple as a fitting display of Jehovah's grandeur (2 Chronicles 2-4).
- Ask the psalmists, who were inspired by the Spirit to write gorgeous, imaginative poetry—literary art that speaks of a God Who wears light as a garment (Psalm 104:2), pitches the heavens as His tent (104:2), rides the clouds as a chariot (104:3), and performs innumerable exploits. This audacious imagery still stirs the imagination three thousand years after its composition.
- Ask Jesus, Who spoke with remarkable vividness and creativity, captivating His hearers with "language arts"—proverbs, parables, and paradoxes.
- Ask every reader of Psalm 33:3 (cf. 1 Chronicles 15:22 and 2 Chronicles 34:12) who is commanded to make music "skillfully."

---

223. Donald S. Whitney, *Spiritual Disciplines for the Christian Life* (Colorado Springs, CO: Nav-Press, 1991), 89.

James S. Spiegel writes,

> Both implicitly and explicitly, the Bible sanctions the arts. And these matters are important not merely for their utility but for the immediate glory of God.... We must strive not only for true worship, but for true worship done *well*.[224]

Are we meeting that goal? Don't answer quickly.

Too often, I believe, we settle for that which is merely adequate—if that. Harold M. Best, the long-time director of the Wheaton College Conservatory of Music, laments our unwillingness to strive for what is truly excellent:

> Contentment with mediocrity as a would-be carrier of truth looms as a major hindrance to true creative vision among evangelicals.... We have reduced Christianity and what we mistakenly call Christian music to the level of market research and audience response.[225]

That's not flattering. But is it false? Clyde S. Kilby doesn't think so. He contrasts God's creativity with our boring predictability in a rather stinging challenge:

> How can it be that with a God who created birds and the blue of the sky, and who before the foundation of the world wrought out a salvation more romantic than Cinderella, with a Christ who encompasses the highest heaven and deepest hell, with the very hairs of our

224. James S. Spiegel, "Aesthetics and Worship" in *The Southern Baptist Journal of Theology* 2, no. 4 (1998), 50. See also a compelling blog article by renowned choral composer Dan Forrest, "The Art of Worship," *Desiring God*, August 16, 2015. https://www.desiringgod.org/articles/the-art-of-worship.

225. Harold M. Best, "Christian Responsibility in Music" in *The Christian Imagination: Essays on Literature and the Arts*, ed. Leland Ryken (Grand Rapids, MI: Baker Book House, 1981), 402.

heads numbered, with God closer than hands and feet, Christians often turn out to have an unenviable corner on the unimaginative and the commonplace?[226]

The importance of pursuing true beauty for God's glory is such a crucial issue, and it's been addressed capably by writers like Abraham Kuyper, C. S. Lewis, Francis Schaeffer, Calvin M. Johansson, Leland Ryken, his son Philip Graham Ryken, Jeremy Begbie, and many others. God willing, I hope to return to the topic and write on it more extensively in time.

For now, let us give full attention to a wonderful truth—that God is the Creator of beauty. He made us in His image, and thus we are capable of creating beauty as well. Indeed, we are *responsible* to create beauty, especially as it relates to worship. Ecclesiastes 9:10 is as germane to our singing as to the rest of life: "Whatever your hand finds to do, *do it with your might.*"

SO... WHAT DOES BEAUTIFUL WORSHIP LOOK LIKE?

It is good to aspire for beautiful worship music. But there is often a great disparity between ideals and reality. Let me anticipate some questions and objections:

- "Should we be performing Bach cantatas or Handel oratorios each Sunday? I want good congregational singing, not a reenactment of the Renaissance. Give me a break."
- "You sound like a cultural elitist... and maybe even an idolater. What next—vestments, incense, and icons?"

226. Clyde S. Kilby, "Christian Imagination" in *The Christian Imagination: Essays on Literature and the Arts*, ed. Leland Ryken (Grand Rapids, MI: Baker Book House, 1981), 41. Kilby is quite severe regarding evangelical attempts at the arts, dismissing our efforts as "cliché... reactionary, static, and hackneyed... trite and... static... functional and prosaic," 41-42. It's a dour analysis, to be sure. But much of it is true. We can and should do better.

- "Frankly, this is discouraging. Our musicians can barely make it through praise choruses that have three chords. Our singing is already rough. Now you're telling me that God deserves *excellence*? Go ahead and kick me while I'm down."

First, I admit that I've experienced those same feelings. No, I'm not calling for a renewed Renaissance. But yes, I am calling for excellence. I believe that God deserves *the best we're capable of*—and that's relative. Not every church or individual is capable of the same "best." I've lived on both ends of the spectrum, and I believe God was as pleased with both our musically challenged church plant as He was with our musically gifted choir and orchestra.

But more importantly, I'm encouraging excellent *hymns*. Excellent *gospel songs*. Excellent *choruses*. Excellent Christian *children's music*. That makes all the difference. An excellent hymn is very different from an excellent aria. It's simpler. It's more accessible. It's easy to learn, even for non-musicians. I'm saying that when it comes to congregational singing, God is deserving of great *hymns*—not Puccini; and great *singing*—not Pavarotti.

Let me give an example that I think will help. My friend Dan Forrest has once-in-a-generation talent as a composer. His music is performed by the best choirs in the world. His pieces appear regularly in Carnegie Hall, European cathedrals, and so on. He has to steward the gifts and the platform God has given him. He'd be sinning to be a computer programmer, as important and noble as that vocation is. Dan was made to compose beautiful and complex music.

But when Dan goes to church on a typical Lord's Day, his congregation doesn't usually sing his *Requiem for the Living* or *Jubilate Deo*. They sing great *hymns*—simple, true, artistically composed hymns. Now, the church *choir* might labor over a beautiful piece like Dan's arrangement of "And Can It Be" or even his *Requiem* on occasion. But the entire congregation strives to sing great "psalms and hymns and spiritual songs"—not songs that are merely adequate.

"A FUNCTIONAL ART"

Apple has mastered the concept of *functional art*. Their products are sleek and beautiful. But they're meant for constant use, not display in museums. Functional art describes objects which are well-designed and aesthetically pleasing, but which also serve a utilitarian purpose. Sculpture is art, intended only to be gazed upon. Architecture is *functional* art, intended to be visually pleasing, but also to provide shelter for the people inside, preferably without falling down.

Hymns are a functional art. C. S. Lewis called them "an extreme case of literature as an applied art."[227] As art, hymns must adhere to established musical and literary principles. But they are also intended for a very narrow and important function: *Hymns are designed to be sung (unrehearsed) and comprehended (unexplained) by a diverse assembly of Christian singers (untrained).* Erik Routley describes hymns as "songs for unmusical people to sing together."[228] Oh, and a hymn has literally *three minutes* to accomplish its desired goals.

Sure, people may consider the subtle beauties and deeper meanings at their leisure outside of the worship service—as we're doing with several hymns in this book. But if a hymn's text cannot be understood and its tune retained—basically upon a first reading—the art isn't functioning. It's like a beautiful building that falls down. So how do we pursue beauty and still maintain the accessibility that corporate singing requires? *Very carefully.*

GOD IS WORTHY OF BEAUTIFUL TEXTS

I've argued that hymn lyrics should be overtly biblical, doctrinal, Christian, and so on. Now I'm arguing that they should be well written. Not pretentious. Not Pulitzer-Prize winners. But also not shoddy. May the

---

227. C. S. Lewis, *English Literature in the Sixteenth Century excluding Drama* (Oxford, England: Oxford University Press, 1954), 112.
228. Erik Routley, *Christian Hymns Observed: When in Our Music God Is Glorified* (Princeton, NJ: Prestige Publications, 1982), 1.

Lord deliver us from the unimaginative, the clichéd, the trite, the banal, and the grammatically skewed.

We're almost finished with a book on hymns, so this seems like a good place to finally *define* them. I'll lean on the experts, The Hymn Society of the United States and Canada, who offered this definition of a hymn nearly a century ago:

> A Christian hymn is a lyric poem, reverently conceived, designed to be sung, which expresses the worshiper's attitude to God or God's purposes in human life. It should be simple and metrical in form, genuinely emotional, poetic and literary in style, and its idea so direct and so immediately apparent as to unify a congregation while singing it.[229]

That's pretty good. Notice that hymns are to be "poetic and literary in style." Timothy Dudley-Smith calls them "a marriage of poetry and piety."[230] You might not think of a hymn as *literature*, but it is. That's important, and it's not a secular or academic concept. It's biblical. God enjoys literature. Indeed, He inspired it. He gave us the Bible not as an encyclopedia, but as poems, proverbs, narratives, and prophecies. If worship is a human response to divine, biblical revelation—and it is—our hymns should be as imaginative as God's Word. When He has spoken to us in high-def color, why would we respond in blurry black-and-white?

The lyrics of Christian songs should be so painstakingly imaginative that we see ancient truths in new ways. They should be so stirring that our hearts are stirred by them to love God even more. They should illumine our understanding, deepen our devotion, and elevate our worship.

Go back with me to the year 1923. Imagine a fifty-year-old man, pen in hand, laboring to find *just the right words* to express what's in his heart. The man is Frederick Martin Lehman, an immigrant to the United States. He's been a Christian for many years, and, in fact, is a pastor. But today,

---

229. Carl F. Price, "What Is a Hymn?" *Hymn Society Paper* VI, 1937.
230. Dudley-Smith, 146.

more than any time in his life, he's impressed anew with the immensity of God's love. He wants to write a hymn about it.

Now, Lehman could have written that God's love is big. *Yawn.* He could have said that God's love is vast. *That's better.* He could have just riffed on synonyms for big: God's love is humongous. Whopping. Gargantuan.

That would all have been true. And we wouldn't be talking about it a century later.

But instead of merely telling us of God's love, Lehman *showed* us. He turned our ears into eyes. He sparked our imagination without sacrificing our orthodoxy:

> *Could we with ink the ocean fill,*
> *And were the skies of parchment made;*
> *Were every stalk on earth a quill,*
> *And every man a scribe by trade—*
> *To write the love of God above*
> *Would drain the ocean dry;*
> *Nor could the scroll contain the whole*
> *Though spread from sky to sky.*[231]

That's not a good hymn lyric. That's a *great* hymn lyric. In my mind, it's one of the most vivid and memorable ever written. And *that's* the kind of song we should be singing. Compare it to many contemporary ditties and you'll be embarrassed for them. Of course, not all the songs we sing will be *that* picturesque, but many will be if you search and don't settle.

See, great hymn-writing is an art. In fact, it's almost an obsession. Douglas Bond writes of Isaac Watts' genius:

231. This is masterful poetry. In addition to the unsurpassed imagery, there are beautiful internal rhymes in lines 5 and 7, so that the rhyme scheme is unexpected: abab, ccd, eed. Magnificent, and he does it in every verse!

There is a childlike enchantment to Watts' poetry, as if it were penned by a man who is discovering the glories of the gospel for the very first time, almost as if he is beside himself with excitement at divine truth, a man intoxicated with the free mercy of God in Christ.[232]

Childlike enchantment. Beside himself with excitement. A man intoxicated by God. Those effusive descriptions tell not only of immense skill, but of passion so deep that it's almost painful.

Doctrinal accuracy and depth are essential. But our singing shouldn't sound like we're merely reading a theology book. Scott Aniol writes, "We must be careful not to concern ourselves with clarity to the neglect of poetic beauty that touches the affections."[233]

Writing orthodox and artistic lyrics is harder than it may sound. The church needs *theologian-poets*, not one or the other. Literary elements like alliteration, consonance, irony, parallelism, syntax, and punctuation are essential to beautiful lyric writing. Listed like this, those things may bore you—but put into skillful practice by a gifted hymn-writer, they can *captivate* and *thrill* you. And so the Gettys charge hymn-writers, "It is your responsibility to make sure the lyrics are as excellent and true and life-giving as you can possibly make them."[234]

GOD IS WORTHY OF BEAUTIFUL TUNES

"The style of music we use in directing our songs to God has everything to do with how we conceive of God," says William S. Smith.[235] What a sobering sentence. I've focused primarily on beautiful lyrics. But even the music—the notes, chords, and tunes—carry meaning.

---

232. Bond, 82.
233. Scott Aniol, *Worship in Song: A Biblical Approach to Music and Worship* (Winona Lake, IN: BMH Books, 2009), 217.
234. Getty and Getty, 137.
235. William S. Smith, 28.

The music that carries our words of worship should strain for beauty and artistry just as the lyrics do. But another essential factor in creating beautiful music is *consistency*. The music must, at the very least, *match the text*—and hopefully even elevate it. It certainly shouldn't contradict it. The tune needs to fit the pathos of the lyrics or the song won't make any sense. Michael Barrett is correct: "There must be such a wedding of words and tune that the message is conveyed without distraction."[236]

Let me give a couple negative examples. I've already noted how Ralph E. Hudson's gospel song "At the Cross" does a disservice to Isaac Watts' mournful text "Alas! and Did My Savior Bleed?" The two just don't fit. I think the same is true of the gospel song "Love Lifted Me." I grew up singing and enjoying it. But the tune doesn't fit the text.

James Rowe's lyric says serious things about the plight of the sinner: "I was sinking deep in sin, / Far from the peaceful shore, / Very deeply stained within, / Sinking to rise no more." That's an accurate and moving depiction—like David stuck in a miry pit (Psalm 40:2). The problem is that the tune by Howard E. Smith is toe-tappingly upbeat, almost like a carnival. And that's *fine*—except that it doesn't fit the very serious lyric. Hymnologist and hymn-writer Margaret Clarkston writes, "The best hymn tunes are those that best illuminate their text."[237] This one doesn't.

Now let me give a positive example. One of my favorite hymn lyrics languished for over a century for want of a good tune. Charitie Lees Bancroft's brilliant text "Before the Throne of God Above" was written in the nineteenth century. Yet, it was relatively unknown until Vikki Cook wrote a practically perfect tune for it in 1997. Other tunes had been tried, but none stuck until Cook's tune breathed new life into a profound but obscure text. Music matters! (Gifted composers should look for a similarly neglected text to set to a new, noble, and emotive tune. Godspeed!)

236. Barrett, *Beauty*, 99.

237. E. Margaret Clarkston, "Christian Hymnody" in *The Christian Imagination: Essays on Literature and the Arts*, ed. Leland Ryken (Grand Rapids, MI: Baker Book House, 1981), 419.

Much more could be said about music styles. This is where the "worship wars" have raged. Personally, I'm not primarily concerned about whether the sound is traditional or contemporary. I've already said that many arguments in opposition to contemporary music are extrabiblical and flawed. But I do think the words of Calvin deserve to be heeded:

> Care must always be taken that the song be neither light nor frivolous, but that it have weight and majesty (as St. Augustine says), and also, there is a great difference between music which one makes to entertain men at table and in their houses, and the Psalms which are sung in the Church in the presence of God and his angels.[238]

Give it some thought. The music we use should be (a) consistent with the text, (b) appropriate for the worship of a holy God, (c) of excellent musical quality, and (d) designed to enable great congregational singing. And I believe that those conditions can be met by a praise band, a pipe organ, or—if necessary—a rickety old piano in a dirty high school auditorium.

BEAUTIFUL MUSIC IS PART OF OUR
CHRISTIAN WITNESS

The way we worship reflects on God. And the way we worship reflects on *Christianity*. That's the point of the hypothetical situation Paul describes in 1 Corinthians 14:23-25. An unbeliever who attends a Christian worship service may feel like an outsider—and *should* in some ways—but our worship should have an intelligible, convicting, and winsome influence on her, drawing her to Christ. I use those words on purpose: *Intelligible. Convicting. Winsome.* Our worship should make an impression on the lost among us, and it should be an attraction to our faith, not a deterrent.

How could our music be a deterrent to an unbeliever? C. S. Lewis provides a compelling example. In his search for truth, he was initially

---

238. John Calvin, preface to *The Genevan Psalter*, 1565.

turned off to Christianity *by Christian music*. Odd? He explains: "The 'sentimentality and cheapness' of much Christian hymnody had been a strong point in my own resistance to conversion."[239] You can call Lewis a snob. But his point stands: Silly or shmaltzy music communicates that the Christian God and the Christian faith are similarly silly and schmaltzy. As Erik Routley notes, "There is... an uncomfortably close connection between cheap music and cheap faith."[240]

Thankfully, the opposite is true as well. Dane Ortlund writes, "Human beings are created with a built-in pull toward beauty. We are arrested by it."[241] That gives us an opportunity. Worship music is a means by which we may simultaneously *exalt the Lord, edify the church*, and *evangelize the lost*. It's a way to display God's beauty in a bland world. The Gettys argue that it's worth months and years of work to compose a song that's *just right*. Why? Because "singing together organizes notes and words in beautiful ways to shine God's dazzling truths into the relativistic gray of our culture."[242] Yes! Our beautiful, colorful songs should stand out in this ugly, gray world.

Even the lost should notice a distinct excellence in our songs and a distinct earnestness in our singing—and it should make them want what we have, by God's grace. That's the meaning of Psalm 40:3, after all: "He put a new song in my mouth, a song of praise to our God. *Many will see and fear, and put their trust in the* Lord."

SING BEAUTIFUL MUSIC BEAUTIFULLY

Professor T. David Gordon is unabashed in proclaiming the superiority of traditional hymns over modern songs. He loves the organ and loathes the

239. C. S. Lewis, "Christianity and Culture" in *The Christian Imagination: Essays on Literature and the Arts*, ed. Leland Ryken (Grand Rapids, MI: Baker Book House, 1981), 24.

240. Erik Routley, *Music, Sacred and Profane* (London: Independent Press, 1960), 22.

241. Dane Ortlund, *Gentle and Lowly: The Heart of Christ for Sinners and Sufferers* (Wheaton, IL: Crossway, 2020), 96.

242. Getty and Getty, 6-8.

guitar, from what I can tell. I don't share his perspective. But I find this insight of his particularly compelling: *Most who reject traditional hymns do so because they've seen them sung badly.*[243] (And I would counter that the same could be said of those who reject contemporary songs.)

This is important. Arguing for great old hymns isn't the same as arguing for the *status quo*—for dead, uninspired singing of great old hymns. The sad reality is that congregational singing is lacking in most churches; but *changing from old songs sung badly to new songs sung badly isn't the solution.* We need to sing better songs... *better.* We need to sing beautiful music... *beautifully.*

"THINK, MEN. THINK."

A big part of beautiful congregational singing boils down to *interest* and *effort.* Thoughtful selection and intentional engagement would improve our singing immediately. But part of what's needed is gifted and trained musicians. R. Kent Hughes offers this modern beatitude: "Happy is the congregation led by godly, competent musicians."[244] Musicians make a difference. If you have such musicians in your church, thank God for them. And thank *them*!

But what if you're *not* a "happy congregation led by competent musicians"? What if you're in a musical wilderness? That's tough. I've been there.

One of my favorite scenes from one of my favorite musicals is when Professor Harold Hill's charade is up at the end of *The Music Man.* He's been outed as a huckster, and he's about to feel the wrath of the angry River City mob he's been fleecing. But he's given a final chance—he can rescue himself by conducting the "brass band" of boys he's neglected to

---

243. T. David Gordon, *Why Johnny Can't Sing Hymns: How Pop Culture Rewrote the Hymnal* (Phillipsburg, NJ: P&R Publishing, 2010), 162-164. Paul S. Jones says much the same: "Musicians must also share the blame for the decline of hymnody. Musicians have failed when they have chosen poor hymns or played good ones like dirges." *Singing*, 193.

244. Hughes, 171.

teach all summer. As the director's baton is offered to him, he shrinks from it like it's a miniature guillotine. He knows that the band is hopeless, and he fears that their awful performance will seal his fate. Just before waving the baton, he looks pleadingly at the untrained boys and begs them: "Think, men. *Think.*"

Perhaps you can relate. It's good to desire beautiful music. "Play skillfully," Psalm 33:3 says. But for many churches, skillfully played music would take a Pentecost-like miracle. "Lord, teach them to play notes they never learned." Music ministry can try one's courage, especially in a small church. So what do you do in the absence of capable musicians?

You do the best you can. You persevere. You pray for help. You love and value people for their inherent worth, regardless of their abilities. You keep at it, week after week and year after year. And you enjoy singing God's praises wholeheartedly with God's people.

There are practical ways to improve, however. Sing fewer hymns, and sing them well. Get music to your novice musicians *weeks in advance*, and encourage them to practice. Don't surprise them with an unnecessary change. Ever. If instrumental accompaniment is still too cringe-inducing to be helpful, sing *a cappella* or with a recorded accompaniment. Keep things as simple as necessary.

Perhaps you can borrow a pianist or guitarist from a like-minded church. As far as a song leader goes, most churches really don't need an arm-waving song leader to conduct them, so just keep your hands at your side and lead the congregation in song with your face and voice.

It will get better. In the meantime, guard your own heart. Pray for contentment. *Use the church to build people, not vice versa.* And be easily blessed.

Finally, rest in Psalm 149:4. In the middle of a psalm about glorious praise, the psalmist encourages us with this motivation to sing: "For the LORD takes pleasure in his people." The ESV *Study Bible* comments, "This idea would be unbearably arrogant had not the Lord himself declared it."[245] And yet, I can't tell you what a relief that is to me. God *delights* in us and our praise even when it's out of tune. The wise counsel of Paul S. Jones is to give to God "the best the congregation can offer."[246] If that's what you're doing—*the best your congregation can do*—God is delighted. Just like the proud parents of River City who absolutely reveled to hear their sons play (poorly) in Harold Hill's ragtag marching band.

REMEMBER GRACE

Parents, do you (or did you) adorn your refrigerator with the crayon-colored "artwork" of your toddlers and elementary students? Kids aren't usually skillful; a stranger would toss those pictures. But those scribbles display the hard work and creativity of *your little girl*, so you love them. *That's* how God delights in our praise.

We do our best because God deserves no less. We plan and practice. But let's be real: God is serenaded night and day by angels whose full-time job is to sing (Revelation 4:8). Our songs are unlikely to impress Him. Our best is still embarrassingly poor. But just like parents treasure the outside-the-lines coloring of their doing-their-best children, God delights in our songs... in spite of us. "As a father shows compassion to his children, so the LORD shows compassion to those who fear him" (Psalm 103:13). He applauds our sincere singing. He appreciates our best artistic efforts, flawed as they are.

This is essential to remember, friends. None of us will *ever* be worthy of God's approval. Not on our best day. We are in constant need of grace every moment of our lives. Worship, like the rest of life, is all of grace. God deserves our best. But our best will always be unworthy of Him. Our worship is accepted because of *Christ*, not because of how we sound.

---

245. C. John Collins, Psalms notes in the *ESV Study Bible*, ed. Lane T. Davis and Wayne Grudem (Wheaton, IL: Crossway, 2008), 1127.

246. Jones, *Singing*, 282.

"Through him then let us continually offer up a sacrifice of praise to God, that is, the fruit of lips that acknowledge his name." (Hebrews 13:15)

Through whom? Through Christ. So pursue excellence. Strive after beauty. But do so in humble dependence, offering to God the "fruit of your lips"—your psalms and hymns and spiritual songs—in the name of our true Worship Leader, the Lord Jesus.

GRACE NOTES FOR WORSHIP LEADERS

- Are the songs you choose for worship excellent, both lyrically and musically? Is your preparation? How could you do better, whether in selection, rehearsal, or execution?
- How can you practice contentment with your church's music capabilities even as you reach for improvement?

GRACE NOTES FOR PARENTS AND CHILDREN'S TEACHERS

- How do you teach unconditional love to your children even as you encourage them to improve through diligent effort? What insight does that give into God's estimation of our worship?
- Are you willing to invest the time, money, and patience required to give your children access to the music lessons that will open for them a lifetime of opportunities? Have you considered this as a serious matter of stewardship?

GRACE NOTES FOR EVERYBODY

- If God accepts our worship because of Christ (Hebrews 13:15), why should we labor to give Him our best?
- Is it possible that you've settled into some music that's "good enough" rather than stretching for that which is "skillful" (Psalm 33:3) and "glorious" (Psalm 66:2)?

"Great is the Lord, and greatly to be praised, and his greatness is unsearchable."
—PSALM 145:3

"We want to sing songs that raise our view of God, that present Him in all His glory and grace."
—MARK DEVER AND PAUL ALEXANDER[247]

"In a day when there is such shallowness in corporate worship, the church must recapture a high view of God that leads to transcendent worship. In the final analysis, it is theology that inevitably produces doxology."
—STEVEN J. LAWSON[248]

247. Dever and Alexander, 118.
248. Steven J. Lawson, preface to Douglas Bond's book, *The Poetic Wonder of Isaac Watts* (Orlando, FL: Reformation Trust, 2013), xiii.

CHAPTER 13

SING SONGS THAT ARE DOXOLOGICAL[249]

Wonder.

That's one of the essential elements of biblical worship. I've said that we need to cultivate *thought* in modern worship. We also need to cultivate *wonder*. We're unamazed. We're too busy to marvel. We're too stimulated to be astounded. God's grace no longer amazes us.[250]

And yet, our God is awesome. I'm using the word in its pre-1980s sense: God inspires *awe*. He is magnificent. Breathtaking. Captivating. Exhilarating. Overwhelming. Mind-blowing.

My flimsy adjectives can't begin to do God justice, so listen to His self-revelation:

• "The LORD is slow to anger and abounding in steadfast love, forgiving iniquity and transgression, but he will by no means clear

---

249. I use this relatively unfamiliar word because it's exactly right. The word "doxology" comes from the Greek word for *glory*. Any song we sing in praise to God—including "The Doxology" ("Praise God from Whom all blessings flow...") is doxological. We sing for God's glory. That's the reason we were made, the reason we were saved, and the unimprovable purpose of the church: "that we should be to the praise of His glory" (Ephesians 1:6, 12, 14; see also 3:20-21).

250. William Plumer writes, "A religion without wonders is false. A theology without wonders is heretical." Plumer, 880.

the guilty, visiting the iniquity of the fathers on the children, to the third and the fourth generation." (Numbers 14:18)

- "O LORD, the God of Israel, enthroned above the cherubim, you are the God, you alone, of all the kingdoms of the earth; you have made heaven and earth." (2 Kings 19:15)
- "For you, O Lord, are good and forgiving, abounding in steadfast love to all who call upon you.... For you are great and do wondrous things; you alone are God.... But you, O Lord, are a God merciful and gracious, slow to anger and abounding in steadfast love and faithfulness." (Psalm 86:5, 10, 15)
- "Oh, the depth of the riches and wisdom and knowledge of God! How unsearchable are his judgments and how inscrutable his ways! 'For who has known the mind of the Lord, or who has been his counselor?' 'Or who has given a gift to him that he might be repaid?' For from him and through him and to him are all things. To him be glory forever. Amen." (Romans 11:33-36)
- "Now to him who is able to do far more abundantly than all that we ask or think, according to the power at work within us, to him be glory in the church and in Christ Jesus throughout all generations, forever and ever. Amen." (Ephesians 3:20-21)
- "Now to him who is able to keep you from stumbling and to present you blameless before the presence of his glory with great joy, to the only God, our Savior, through Jesus Christ our Lord, be glory, majesty, dominion, and authority, before all time and now and forever. Amen." (Jude 24-25)
- "Worthy are you, our Lord and God, to receive glory and honor and power, for you created all things, and by your will they existed and were created." (Revelation 4:11)
- "Worthy is the Lamb who was slain, to receive power and wealth and wisdom and might and honor and glory and blessing!" (Revelation 5:12)
- "Hallelujah! For the Lord our God the Almighty reigns." (Revelation 19:6)

Is that your view of God? Does pondering Him ever leave you speechless, just shaking your head in astonishment? Does God amaze you? If not, you're not thinking of Him correctly. Listen to A. W. Tozer:

> When we come into this sweet relationship, we are beginning to learn astonished reverence, breathless adoration, awesome fascination, lofty admiration of the attributes of God and something of the breathless silence that we know when God is near.[251]

SINGING, WORSHIP, AND IDOLATRY

Tozer, the Bible-quoting mystic of the first half of the twentieth century, wrote often of reverent worship. He begins his book on the attributes of God with this sobering statement: "What comes into our minds when we think about God is the most important thing about us."[252] That's true. And yet, it's so easy to think wrongly about God.

We're prone to create a god of our own design, a god we make in our own image, as we'd prefer him to be. Kind, perhaps, but not holy. Generous, but not severe. Merciful, but not just. Attentive when we need His help, but willing to look the other way when we want a little privacy. Or—conversely—we can invent a God who endorses our extrabiblical preferences and is as conservative as we want Him to be. As Calvin astutely observed, "Man's nature… is a perpetual factory of idols."[253]

The only way to avoid idolatry—even unintentional idolatry—is to draw our understanding of God from the Scriptures. The Second Commandment (Exodus 20:4-6) doesn't only forbid idol craft. It tells us that our view of God must come from the Scriptures not the culture around

---

251. A. W. Tozer, *Whatever Happened to Worship*, ed. Gerald B. Smith (Camp Hill, PA: Christian Publications, 1985), 30.
252. A. W. Tozer, *The Knowledge of the Holy* (New York, HarperCollins, 1961), i. I'd add "awestruck singing" to Tozer's "breathless silence" as an appropriate response to God's majesty.
253. John Calvin, *Institutes of the Christian Religion*, ed. John T. McNeill, trans. Ford Lewis Battles (Philadelphia: The Westminster Press, 1960), 1:108.

us or our own imaginations. It informs us that we can't just worship God willy-nilly, however we choose. Worshipping our own "customized" Jesus is as idolatrous as worshipping Baal or Molech or Dagon.

Jim Berg, one of my college professors, used to say, "If you're not thinking in King-James English, you're leaning on your own understanding." I now try to think in English-Standard English, but his point stands: If we deviate from the Scriptures, our thinking about God will be wrong. And to the point of this book, if the Word of Christ doesn't dwell deeply, lavishly, pervasively in our hearts, our songs will be wrong.

Great songs, born and bred in the Scriptures, set before us the greatness of God. Trite songs, in contrast, set before us a puny god. What we sing *shows* our thinking about God, but it also *shapes* our thinking about God. We need to sing songs which "make God big"—that is, which remind us of God's inherent greatness.

Margaret Clarkston writes, "A hymn is a persuasive thing; it makes us feel that this is what *we* think, not just what the writer thinks."[254] This can be a boon to sound teaching. But it can go the other way, too, as Erik Routley urgently warns:

> A congregation's... disposition toward right belief or away from it, is subtly influenced by the habitual use of hymns. Therefore it is right to call for caution in their use and choice, because there is no single influence in public worship that can so surely condition a congregation to self-deception, to fugitive follies, to religious perversities, as thoughtlessly chosen hymns.[255]

254. Clarkston, 420.
255. Erik Routley, *Hymns Today and Tomorrow* (Nashville, TN: Abingdon, 1964), 22. This is such a powerful statement. Sadly, Routley himself falls short of "right belief," arguing in favor of "demythologizing" Scripture and in opposition to hymns that speak of Christ's atonement as a vicarious substitution for sinners. *Hymns*, 60-70.

Hymns must place before believers the unrivaled majesty of our Creator, Redeemer, and King. Great songs lead us to worship. Poor songs lead us to idolatry. Not just inferior worship—*idolatry*. It's that important.

GOD-DRIVEN OR PURPOSE-DRIVEN SONGS?

Perhaps no book has influenced the strategies of evangelical churches in the last twenty-five years more than Rick Warren's blockbuster, *The Purpose-Driven Church*. The book teaches some good things. But it teaches a consumerism approach to ministry that shapes every part of church life, including worship music. Here are a couple samples of Warren's take on church music:

> "You must decide who you're trying to reach, identify their preferred style of music, and then stick with it."

> "The style of music you choose to use in your services will be one of the most critical (and controversial) decisions you make in the life of your church. It may also be *the* most influential factor in determining who your church reaches for Christ and whether or not your church grows. You must match your music to the kind of people God wants your church to reach."

> "If you were to tell me the kind of music you are currently using in your services I could describe the kind of people you are reaching without even visiting your church. I could also tell you the kind of people your church will never be able to reach."[256]

My point isn't to critique Warren's music. I'm not going to argue with Warren's research. He's certainly correct that musical style is a huge factor

---

256. Rick Warren, *The Purpose-Driven Church: Growing Without Compromising Your Message and Mission* (Grand Rapids, MI: Zondervan, 1995), 280-85.

in church growth. My main hesitation—in addition to the poor theology of sinners and salvation behind the overall ministry approach—is that he is telling churches to choose their music *based on the tastes of the unsaved.* Where is God in the whole market-research strategy? Are the church's songs we sing really supposed to be determined by polling lost people?

The Bible describes a better way. Here's my attempt at a summary of a Scriptural approach to music selection for corporate worship: *Our music must aim at God's glory, in the name of God's Son, by the enablement of God's Spirit, through the singing of God's Word, for the good of God's church.*

John MacArthur, commenting on Colossians 3:16, writes, "Singing is to be directed to God as praise and worship offered to Him for His pleasure and glory. That it is edifying to believers is a byproduct of its main purpose."[257] Pastor and hymn-writer Matt Boswell concurs:

> When the church is gathered together in the name of God, only singing which glorifies Him is appropriate. We don't sing corporately because it was our idea. We sing because it was God's idea for His people. Since it is God who has commanded us to sing, it is God who will also determine what kind of songs we will sing. We are to sing to Him and for Him. Our songs are not meant to be entertainment, or a distraction from God.[258]

ISAAC WATTS' "BIG GOD"

Let's contrast Warren's view of worship music with Watts', though it's hardly a fair fight.

Isaac Watts was a diminutive man, standing only five feet in height. Movie-makers would probably typecast him as a milquetoast prig. So what allows his hymns to tower over the best efforts of any songwriter not

257. John MacArthur, *The MacArthur New Testament Commentary: Colossians and Philemon* (Chicago: Moody Publishers, 1992), 160.
258. Matt Boswell, "5 Marks of the Worship of the Church," *Crossway*, July 1, 2013, https://www. lifeway.com/en/articles/music-marks-worship-church-theology-doxology.

named Wesley even centuries after his death? It's more than his creative genius. *Watts had a high view of God*, and he shares that view with all who sing his hymns.

We sing of Watts' "big God" in the joyful triumph of "I Sing the Mighty Power of God" and "Joy to the World." We sing of his "big God" in the solemn wonder of "Alas! and Did My Savior Bleed?" and "When I Survey the Wondrous Cross." Watts' God is *massive*, and his hymns endure for that very reason. Steven J. Lawson captures the secret of Watts' genius:

> By his extraordinary literary skill, he made hymn-singing a devotional force in the Protestant church. Captured by a towering vision of God, this gifted composer revitalized congregational singing by restating rich theology in lyrics that matched the musical style with the weightiness of the biblical message. All this—the rise and fall of a phrase, striking metaphors, the cadence of the line—conveyed the majesty and transcendence of God in unforgettable words.[259]

I hope those words leapt off the page: "A towering vision of God." "Rich theology." "The weightiness of the biblical message." "The majesty and transcendence of God."

Sadly, the opposite is also true. You can sing songs that make God small. ("Make" here means, of course, that these songs *portray* Him as small—which in no way threatens or erodes His unchanging greatness.) If you feed your soul on clever or clichéd songs that describe God as merely personal, friendly, accepting, and permissive, you're singing a caricature of God. Heed this warning from Calvin M. Johansson:

> A steady diet of music that is only intellectualized, clever, astute, brilliant, and ingenious, or only escapist, amusing, cloying, entertaining,

---

259. Lawson, XII-XIII.

standardized, uncreative, sensational, and trite, will gradually lead
believers to believe that the Christian faith is the same.[260]

Ouch. We should avoid stupid songs. So, what do songs that accurately depict God's grandeur look like? We've already highlighted many
throughout this book, but let's finish well.

SING "THE MIGHTY POWER OF GOD"

One of my favorite motifs of worship music is the theme of God's perfec-
tions. How many songs can you list which focus on the attributes of the
Most High God? Here are a few of my favorites.

- "Holy, Holy, Holy" (Heber and Dykes)
- "Immortal, Invisible, God Only Wise" (Smith / traditional
  Welsh melody)
- "I Sing the Mighty Power of God" (Watts / ELLACOMBE)
- "How Great Thou Art" (Hine / Swedish folk melody)
- "O Great God" (Kauflin)
- "O Worship the King" (Grant and Haydn)
- "How Deep the Father's Love for Us" (Townend)
- "Grace Greater than Our Sin" (Johnston and Towner)
- "Wonderful, Merciful Savior" (Rodgers and Wyse)
- "Mercies Anew" (Kauflin and Altrogge)
- "Only a Holy God" (Farren, Robinson, Smith, and Thompson)
- "Holy, Mighty, Worthy" (Anderson and Habegger)

Sing songs *about* God, *to* God, and *for* God.

David Breed makes this Godward focus an essential measure of a
hymn. It must be biblical, first and foremost. But it must also be *devotional*
in the sense that it points us to God:

260. Johansson, 99.

True devotion contemplates God in the various relations which he sustains towards his earthly creatures. The true hymn must therefore have a motion Godward.... The true hymn must tend towards God; bring him to mind; exalt his name and seek his glory. Those which are simply introspective, didactic, dogmatic, sentimental, egotistical, and the like, are not hymns.[261]

That's precisely what the 150 inspired hymns in the Psalter do. With relentless repetition and irresistible imagery, they show us God in all of His magnificence. Our songs should do no less.

SING, "LOST IN WONDER"

As I said when this chapter began, I love that word: *wonder*. I love to think of the worshiper being so thrilled by God that he is "*lost* in wonder, love, and praise," as Charles Wesley wrote in his hymn "Love Divine, All Loves Excelling." But I didn't always think this way.

I used to roll my eyes at John Jacob Niles' Christmas hymn "I Wonder As I Wander." *Why didn't he just say, "I think as I walk"?* Ah, but there's a difference. First, the wordplay between *wonder* and *wander* is lovely. But at what does the hymn-writer call us to marvel? "How Jesus the Savior did come for to die, / For poor, orn'ry people like you and like I." That *does* cause you to wonder. The death of Christ for sinners is indeed a mystery of grace. It is—quite literally—*wonder*-ful.

261. Breed, 91.

The amazement of the redeemed is often expressed more subtly in our hymns through the use of rhetorical questions. It's an effective, artful technique.[262]

- "Was it for crimes that I have done / He groaned upon the tree?" (Watts, "Alas! and Did My Savior Bleed?")
- "O, can it be, upon a tree, / The Savior died for me?" (Newton, "I Saw One Hanging on a Tree")
- "Who has held the oceans in His hands? / Who has numbered every grain of sand?... / Who has given counsel to the Lord? / Who can question any of his words?... / Who has felt the nails upon his hands / Bearing all the guilt of sinful man?" (Baird, Baird, Baird, and Altrogge, "Behold Our God")[263]
- "Does the Father truly love us?... Does the Spirit move among us?... And does Jesus, our Messiah, hold forever those He loves?...Does our God intend to dwell again with us?" (Peterson and Shive, "Is He Worthy?")[264]
- "The peace of Christ makes fresh my heart, / A fountain ever springing! / All things are mine since I am his! / How can I keep from singing?" (Lowry, "How Can I Keep from Singing?")

I love that rhetorical question: "How can I keep from singing?" It reminds me of Watts' lyric: "Let those refuse to sing / Who never knew our God; / But children of the heav'nly King / May speak their joys abroad." Yes. It is *Christian* to sing. Calvin Johansson writes, "The regenerate sing and

262. Acknowledging that posing rhetorical questions is a legitimate poetic technique means, among other things, that we should stop piling on Mark Lowry for asking, "Mary, did you know?" An exasperated "Of course she did!" misses the point. It's a poetical device which is put to good use in this moving, thought-provoking song.

263. Lyrics from "Behold Our God" by Jonathan Baird, Meghan Baird, Ryan Baird, and Stephen Altrogge. © 2011 Sovereign Grace Praise (BMI), Sovereign Grace Worship (ASCAP) (adm at IntegratedRights.com). All rights reserved. Used by permission.

264. Used by permission. See p. 146.

sing well because they of all people have something to sing about."[265] We do! If you know God the Father through the saving work of Jesus and the indwelling of the Holy Spirit, you can't *help* but sing His praises!

SING FOR GOD'S PLEASURE

We began this book by studying Colossians 3:16. We will end there as well. This musical mandate calls us to sing biblical, doctrinal, Christ-centered songs. It tells us to sing to one another, teaching and admonishing each other with our songs. It shows how hymn-singing is a congregational and unifying activity. There's a lot packed into this little verse.

But it concludes by telling us that our songs are ultimately directed "to God." Music must be tethered to God—*His* attributes, *His* names, *His* works, *His* purposes, and *His* glory. This is vital, perhaps more important than anything else I've said.

Throughout this book I've emphasized the importance of music as a teaching tool. And so it is. The danger, however, is that we can come to see singing as merely utilitarian. We should choose great hymns because they teach people about God. True. But that's not the main motivation.

We should choose great hymns first and foremost because God is great!

Biblical worship fixates on God. We sing not only to teach, to find comfort, or to get a blessing, but to *praise*. Timothy Dudley-Smith calls the benefits we receive from singing together "side-effects." They're a blessing, to be sure, but "they can never be the main purpose of the hymn, which remains 'the praise of God.'"[266] We're not in love with hymns— we're in love with *God*. We don't gather to worship—we gather to worship *God*. There's a difference. It's possible to be so enamored by "praise and worship" that inviting God to the gathering slips our minds.

The key to worship isn't great songs—and I say that at the end of a book on the importance of exceptional hymns! Neither does worship rise

---

265. Johansson, 145.
266. Dudley-Smith, 5.

and fall with well-rehearsed musicians or an enthusiastic congregation—
as desirable as those things are. No, *the key to worship is deep wonder and
adoration of God as we see Him in Scripture and as we meet Him in Christ.*
To worship, Tozer tells us, is "to be astonished at the inconceivable eleva-
tion and magnitude and splendor of Almighty God!"[267] It is, Piper writes,
"being satisfied with Christ, prizing Christ, cherishing Christ, treasuring
Christ.... 'going hard after God.'"[268] Songs can help. But they can only help.

CONCLUSION: SOLI DEO GLORIA!

I've offered my thoughts on worship songs, and I've done so as a lover of
hymns, a lover of the church, and especially a lover of our Triune God. I'm
not naïve enough to assume that such a study will lead us all to the same
conclusions. I'm fine with that. It's my sincere hope that what I've shared
will be a help, not only to inform you, but to inspire you—to encourage
you to "go hard after God" with the help of sacred songs.

I've tried to make this book a positive look at what is best in worship music. It's easy to critique; it's hard to contribute. Discussions about
church music most certainly need more light and less heat. I want to celebrate what's great.

That said, I do believe that many of the songs Christians are singing
pale in comparison to the best songs of the past. Douglas Bond laments our
dismissal of rich hymnody: "I pity a world without Watts. I pity a church
without him. Why would Christians want to cut themselves off from rich
theological passion skillfully adorned, as in Watts' finest hymns?"[269]

Why indeed? Why, when such grand expressions of God's greatness
are available, do we cast them aside in favor of obviously inferior songs?

There is a problem with the contemporary church and its music.
There are encouraging exceptions, like the Gettys, Sovereign Grace, City

---

267. Tozer, *Whatever Happened*, 26.
268. John Piper, *Brothers, We Are Not Professionals: A Plea to Pastors for Radical Ministry* (Nash-
     ville: Broadman & Holman, 2002), 26.
269. Bond, xxiv.

Alight, the "Three Matts" (Boswell, Papa, and Merker), Travis Cottrell, and others. It's a great time for sound, fresh hymns! But the momentum of music in the evangelical church at large is still moving away from serious doctrinal content.

James Montgomery Boice calls us back with this sober assessment:

> One of the saddest features of contemporary worship is that the great hymns of the church are on the way out. They are not gone entirely, but they are going. And in their place have come trite jingles that have more in common with contemporary advertising ditties than with the psalms. The problem here is not so much the style of the music, though trite words fit best with trite tunes and harmonies. Rather the problem is with the content of the songs. The old hymns expressed the theology of the church in profound and perceptive ways and with winsome, memorable language. They lifted the worshiper's thoughts to God and gave him striking words by which to remember God's attributes. Today's songs reflect our shallow or nonexistent theology and do almost nothing to elevate one's thoughts about God.[270]

Keith and Kristyn Getty see the same crisis, and they too call the church to attention: "May it not be on our watch that good congregational singing is taken from or given away by the congregation, or that we do not carefully watch over what we sing."[271]

Not on our watch. Not without our best efforts to stem the tide. Not without our ensuring that the songs we choose to sing are *the most beautiful, the most biblical, the most edifying, the most Christ-saturated, and the most God-exalting songs we can find.*

---

270. James Montgomery Boice, *Whatever Happened to the Gospel of Grace? Recovering the Doctrines That Shook the World* (Wheaton, IL: Crossway, 2001), 178-80.
271. Getty and Getty, 80.

May the Lord increase our love, our devotion, and our discernment as we seek to honor Him through exceptional sacred music—*theology that sticks.*

Soli Deo gloria.

GRACE NOTES FOR WORSHIP LEADERS

- Hopefully this book has been encouraging, not overwhelming. What are the main takeaways you can apply to improve corporate worship in the church you lead?
- This book has presented twelve criteria for choosing exceptional songs for worship. Sometimes there is tension between these criteria—as with the need for songs that are "experiential" and for others that are "doxological." How can you balance those tensions?

GRACE NOTES FOR PARENTS AND CHILDREN'S TEACHERS

- Your young children aren't yet ready to wade through a book like this. What main lessons can you pass on to them from what you've learned?
- Pray now that the Lord will help you give your children a legacy of music that will be fuel for a lifetime of joyful, hope-building worship.

GRACE NOTES FOR EVERYBODY

- What are your favorite songs that tether your attention to God?
- How can you use the principles in this book to improve your corporate worship experience when you sing in church?

- How can you use the principles in this book to improve your private worship experience when you sing in your home or car?

PART 4

ADDITIONAL RESOURCES

"BONUS TRACKS": WISE WORDS ON THE THEME OF EACH CHAPTER

CHAPTER 1: THE STICKING POWER OF CHRISTIAN MUSIC

"The fundamental difficulty is that we do not realize how much sacred song is to us—what it means, what it expresses, and what it is capable of accomplishing. And therefore it is pitiably neglected."

David R. Breed, *The History and Use of Hymns and Hymn-Tunes* (New York: Fleming H. Revell Company, 1903), 347.

"Nowhere is God's gift of music more appropriate than in the church at worship."

Robert L. Saucy, *The Church in God's Program* (Chicago, IL: Moody Press, 1972), 187.

"When truth gets in a hymnbook, it becomes the confident possession of the whole church."

J. Alec Motyer, *Look to the Rock: An Old Testament Background to Our Understanding of Christ* (Grand Rapids, MI: Kregel, 2004), 222.

"What a church sings has often more impact upon the theology, devotion, and behavior of its members than the church's doctrinal confession or even what a pastor preaches."

Scott Aniol and Ryan J. Martin, preface to *Hymns of the Living God*, ed. Scott Aniol and Ryan J. Martin (Fort Worth, TX: Religious Affections Ministries, 2017), ii.

"People tend to believe what they sing which makes singing in the church of utmost importance. The message of a song becomes internalized by those who sing it thoughtfully and wholeheartedly."

Tom Ascol, "Singing in the Church," *The Founders Journal* 90 (Fall 2012), 1.

"Those who know God must sing. This attitude and spirit has resonated wherever the church of Jesus Christ has been found walking in spiritual health and vitality. People who are happy in God sing praises to God and for God."

Tom Ascol, "Songs of Salvation," *The Founders Journal* 90 (Fall 2012), 4.

"I strongly hold that holy thoughts often abide for ever in men's memories under the form of poetry, which pass away and are forgotten under the form of prose."

J. C. Ryle. Quoted in Eric Russell, *J. C. Ryle: That Man of Granite with the Heart of a Child* (Fearn, Scotland: Christian Focus, 2001), 89-90.

"Nothing, in fact, nothing so uplifts the soul, gives it wings, liberates it from the earth, looses the shackles of the body, promotes its values and its scorn for everything in this world as harmonious music and a divine song rhythmically composed."

John Chrysostom, *Old Testament Homilies*, trans. Robert Charles Hill (Brookline, MA: Holy Cross Orthodox Press, 2003), 3:69.

"When Charles Simeon of Cambridge used to hold sermon classes for young clergy on the art of preaching he would borrow a phrase from Richard Baxter a century before, and talk of 'screwing the word of God into the hearers', adding that 'the very hymn... is a turn of the screw.'"

Timothy Dudley-Smith, *A Functional Art: Reflections of a Hymn Writer* (Oxford, UK: Oxford University Press, 2017), 5.

"Worship leaders are singing theologians. We communicate truth with poetry and verse; we organize doctrine with rhythm and rhyme; we proclaim the good news through melody and harmony. With every stanza of every hymn, we are articulating and teaching what we believe, intentional or not."

Matt Boswell, "Reforming the Role of the Worship Leader" in *Doxology and Theology: How the Gospel Forms Worship Leaders*, ed. Matt Boswell (Nashville, TN: B&H Publishing Group, 2013), 9.

"Don't base your [song] choices on popularity or the latest hits, but choose songs based on what will feed people's souls."

Ken Boer, "The Worship Leader and the Gospel" in *Doxology and Theology: How the Gospel Forms Worship Leaders*, ed. Matt Boswell (Nashville, TN: B&H Publishing Group, 2013), 195.

"Every song is a teaching tool. Our songs either anchor us in truth, or they lead us astray."

Matt Merker, "Help! I Don't Like the Music at My Church," *Crossway*, February 27, 2001, accessed March 1, 2021, https://www.crossway.org/articles/help-i-dont-like-the-music-at-my-church.

"One of the major contributing factors of the superficiality of the lives of evangelical Christians in our country today is the failure of the churches to teach and use the great hymns of the church universal in their services of worship."

Robert G. Rayburn, *O Come, Let Us Worship: Corporate Worship for the Evangelical Church* (Grand Rapids, MI: Baker, 1980), 223.

"I love the grand old hymns. Throughout my Christian life I have treasured their historic statement of the church's faith, having committed many of them to memory. They have been my dearest companions in dark hours of loneliness and discouragement and my greatest encouragers in times of celebration and adoration.... The theology of hymns is far too rich and beneficial to lose."

Charles R. Swindoll, *The Church Awakening: An Urgent Call for Renewal* (New York: Faith Words, 2010), 122-23.

"A good hymnal contains many paraphrases of Scripture and is a compact handbook of Christian theology in poetic form. It also includes noble examples of all the forms of prayer with which we respond to God's self-revealing—adoration, confession, thanksgiving, petition, supplication, surrender, and dedication. It can supply thoughts and words to express our devotion when we have difficulty finding our own. Used regularly, it enlarges and enriches our personal vocabulary of worship, and—when we meet in church on Sunday—helps us sing the hymns with joy and understanding."

> Donald P. Hustad, "Let's Not Just Praise the Lord," *Christianity Today*. November 6, 1987, accessed February 9, 2021, https://www.christianitytoday.com/ct/1987/november-6/lets-not-just-praise-lord.html.

"Church music is not merely the preliminary for the serious part of the service. It does not merely set the mood for the preaching. It is not an appendage or an option. Music is a key element [in the worship service] that is capable of expressing worship and instructing the saints. It must be taken as seriously in its own right as praying or preaching."

> Kevin Bauder, "Why Pastors Should Be Learned in Worship and Music," *The Artistic Theologian* 1 (2012), 12.

"It is a well-worn saying that people tend to leave church humming the songs and not the sermon."

> Philip Pervical, *Then Sings My Soul: Rediscovering God's Purposes for Singing in Church* (Sydney, Australia: Matthias Media, 2015), 58.

CHAPTER 2: SING SONGS THAT ARE BIBLICAL

"Biblical worship inherently entails a response to revelation."

> J. Ligon Duncan III, "Foundations for Biblically Directed Worship" in *Give Praise to God: A Vision for Reforming Worship*, ed. Philip Graham Ryken, Derek W. H. Thomas, and J. Ligon Duncan III (Phillipsburg, NJ: P&R Publishing, 2003), 54.

"Our services should not separate singing from the Word, but the church should hear the Word through singing."

> Matt Boswell, "Reforming the Role of the Worship Leader" in *Doxology and Theology: How the Gospel Forms Worship Leaders*, ed. Matt Boswell (Nashville, TN: B&H Publishing Group, 2013), 11.

"Music should be seen as an element of the ministry of the Word, just like preaching. Therefore, the songwriter ought to be as skilled in Scripture and as concerned for theological precision as the preacher. Even more so, because the songs he writes are likely to be sung again and again (unlike a sermon that is preached only once)."

> John MacArthur, *Worship: The Ultimate Priority* (Chicago: Moody Press, 2012), 206.

"If it is the Word of God that brings the church about, that builds it up, and that adds to its numbers, then it must be our task to be as faithful and as accurate as we can in communicating that Word, even when we sing."

> Mark Ashton with C. J. Davis, "Following in Cranmer's Footsteps" in *Worship by the Book*, ed. D. A. Carson (Grand Rapids, MI: Zondervan, 2002), 90.

"Hymns should never be sung because they are customary. They should only be sung because they express Christian teaching, and promote Christian teaching, in a manner which will communicate itself to the congregation for whom they are chosen. To this rule there are no exceptions."

Erik Routley, *Hymns Today and Tomorrow* (Nashville, TN: Abingdon, 1964), 127-28.

"Next to the Word of God, music deserves the highest praise. She is a mistress and governess of those human emotions... which govern men as masters or more often overwhelm them. No greater commendation than this can be found—at least, not by us. For whether you wish to comfort the sad, to terrify the happy, encourage the despairing, to humble the proud, to calm the passionate, or to appease those full of hate—and who could number all these masters of the human heart, namely, the emotions, inclinations, and affections that impel me to evil or good?—what more effective means than music could you find?... Thus *it was not without reason that the fathers and prophets wanted nothing else to be associated as closely with the Word of God as music. Therefore, we have so many hymns and Psalms where message and music join to move the listener's soul....* After all, the gift of language combined with the gift of song was only given to man to let him know that he should praise God with both word and music, namely, *by proclaiming [the Word of God] through music* and by providing sweet melodies with words."

Martin Luther, *Luther's Works*, ed. Ulrich S. Leupold, trans. Paul Zeller Strodach (Philadelphia, PA: Fortress Press, 1965), 53:323-24. Emphasis added.

"Luther did not so much paraphrase Scripture in his hymns, as he did sermonize. In other words, what you find in the hymns, such as in 'A Mighty

Fortress,' is not just the interpretation of the Psalm; it is instead more a homiletical exercise that has been expanded into a hymn."

> R. Albert Mohler Jr., "Satan Cannot Sing: Martin Luther's Celebration of the Gospel in Christian Hymn," Sermon Audio, October 30, 2011, https://www.sermonaudio.com/sermoninfo.asp?SID= 10301122443110.

"A skillful man, if the Bible were lost, might extract it from Wesley's hymns. They contain it in solution."

> John Rattenbury, cited by John R. Tyson, *Assist Me to Proclaim: The Life and Hymns of Charles Wesley* (Grand Rapids, MI: William B. Eerdmans Publishing Company, 2007), 258. The statement is whimsical hyperbole, but it highlights the overt biblical content of Wesley's hymns.

CHAPTER 3: SING SONGS THAT ARE DOCTRINAL

"Congregational song is part of the teaching ministry of the church. Church musicians and pastors should ask themselves: if our people learned their theology from our songs what would they know in twenty years about God, the cross, the resurrection, the offices of Christ, the Holy Spirit, the Trinity, creation, justification, election, regeneration, the church, the sacraments, and all the other fundamental doctrines of the faith?"

> Kevin DeYoung, "Ten Principles for Church Song," *The Founders Journal* 90 (Fall 2012), 16.

"The songs we sing not only reflect our theology; they also shape it. That is, congregational singing is both a cause and effect."

> Dan Kreider, preface to *Sing the Wonders: Hymns and Psalms for the Church*, ed. Dan Kreider (Jupiter, FL: Grace Immanuel Bible Church, 2016).

"It is well known that the character of its song, almost equal with the character of its preaching, controls the theology of a church."

> *Trinity Hymnal* (Philadelphia, PA: Great Commission Publications, 1961), vi.

"Show me a church's songs and I'll show you their theology."

> Gordon Fee, quoted in Douglas Sean O'Donnell, *God's Lyrics: Rediscovering Worship through Old Testament Songs* (Phillipsburg, NJ: P&R Publishing, 2010), xii.

"The hymnody of the church reveals much of what is dear to a congregation and a church's tradition."

> Bryan Chapell, *Christ-Centered Preaching: Redeeming the Expository Sermon* (Grand Rapids, MI: Baker Academic, 2005), 61.

"Hymns are a theological repository of the church. Through hymns we make a catechism for the generations. As time goes on, hymns come to contain the doctrines most well known and most closely cherished by the people of God. By setting the truth of God to music, the church of God is united not only in orthodoxy of belief, but in worship."

> Daniel Stevens, "Hymns as Pillars for the Church," *The Master's Seminary Blog*, May 18, 2016, accessed December 12, 2021, https://blog.tms.edu/pillars-for-the-church.

"The foundation of doxology is theology, and the goal of theology is doxology."

> Matt Boswell, "Reforming the Role of the Worship Leader" in *Doxology and Theology: How the Gospel Forms Worship Leaders*, ed. Matt Boswell (Nashville, TN: B&H Publishing Group, 2013), 9.

"Generation upon generation of Christ-followers have stood to their feet and turned to a particular selection in a hymnal to direct their adoration toward God. They've been guided to the throne of our God Most High singing or speaking words written by gifted poets with a theologian's heart and a musician's ear."

> Thom S. Rainer, Preface to *Baptist Hymnal*, ed. Mike Harland (Nashville, TN: LifeWay Worship, 2008).

"Classic hymns were written to teach and reinforce biblical and doctrinal concepts in the context of worship directed to God. The kind of worship they embodied made demands on the human intellect. Those hymns aimed to praise God by extolling and proclaiming His truth in a way that enhanced the worshiper's comprehension of the truth. They set a standard of worship that was as cerebral as it was emotional. And that was perfectly biblical. After all, the first and great commandment teaches us to love God with all our heart, soul, *and mind* (Matthew 22:37).... It may be the case that modern church music has done more than anything else to pave the way for the sort of superficial, flippant, content-starved preaching that is rife today."

John MacArthur, *Worship: The Ultimate Priority* (Chicago: Moody Press, 2012), 201-02.

CHAPTER 4: SING SONGS THAT ARE CHRISTIAN

"God has made our hearts and spirits happy through His... Son, whom He has delivered up that we might be redeemed from sin, death, and the devil. He who believes this sincerely and earnestly cannot help but be happy; he must cheerfully sing and talk about this, that others might hear it and come to Christ. If any would not sing and talk of what Christ has wrought for us, he shows thereby that he does not really believe and that he belongs not [to the realm of] New Testament [religion]."

Martin Luther, introduction to the *Baptsche Gesangbuch*, WA 35:476f. Textual clarifications made by Tom Ascol, "Songs of Salvation," *The Founders Journal* 90 (Fall 2012), 3.

"The great services of the Catholic Church in which Luther had been reared came likewise over into the German under his direction. The service of the Mass, the central point in Lutheran worship, was set in the familiar tongue under Luther's own editorship, and for the use of public worship he produced a series of noble hymns.... Luther adds hymn after hymn to his Church's worship. They are bold, militant, confident, triumphant expressions; *covering chiefly the doctrine of redemption, they swing freely around the blood and sacrifice of Jesus.*

Edwin P. Booth, *Martin Luther: Oak of Saxony* (Westwood, NJ: Barbour and Company, Inc., 1988), 231-32. Emphasis added.

"Hear our loss of focus on the gospel in our songs. This is no comment on musical styles and tastes, but simply an observation about the lyrical content of much that is being sung in churches today. In many cases, congregations have unwittingly begun to sing about themselves and how they are feeling rather than about God and His glory."

> Alistair Begg, foreword to Sinclair Ferguson, *In Christ Alone: Living the Gospel-Centered Life* (Lake Mary, FL: Reformation Trust, 2007), 3.

"In all our worship, the good news that Jesus has died for our sins and risen gloriously from the dead should be central."

> John M. Frame, *Worship in Spirit and Truth: A Refreshing Study of the Principles and Practice of Biblical Worship* (Phillipsburg, PA: P&R Publishing, 1996), 6.

"Lyrics set to music have formative power because they are memorable. Use songs that fill our minds with God's character, that form our worldview by God's truth, and that teach us about the biblical meaning and personal implications of His Gospel.... As the main teaching pastor, it is therefore your responsibility to shepherd the congregation into the green pastures of God-centered, Gospel-centered songs, and away from the arid plains of theological vacuity, meditations on human experience, and emotional frenzy. The best of the hymns and the best of the more modern worship choruses are those that direct our focus away from ourselves and onto the character and Gospel of God. Practice discerning the difference, and be careful about what you're teaching through the music you encourage people to sing."

> Mark Dever and Paul Alexander, *The Deliberate Church: Building Your Ministry on the Gospel* (Wheaton, IL: Crossway Books, 2005), 85.

CHAPTER 5: SING SONGS THAT ARE TRINITARIAN

"Some recent scholarship, evaluating the most popular songs in the CCLI database, has revealed that American evangelicals aren't as Trinitarian in song as we are in our confessions. This is a travesty! Our creeds and our songs shouldn't be at theological odds with one another. We need to view a richer picture of God the Father, Jesus the Son, and God the Holy Spirit illustrated in our hymnology and in our people's mouths, brains, and hearts!"

> Bruce Benedict, "The Worship Leader and Liturgy" in *Doxology and Theology: How the Gospel Forms Worship Leaders*, ed. Matt Boswell (Nashville, TN: B&H Publishing Group, 2013), 115-16.

"The Christian God, to be savior, must then be Father, Son, and Holy Spirit.... Disregard the Trinity and you necessarily undermine salvation.... Christian worship is inherently trinitarian."

> Bruce A. Ware, *Father, Son, & Holy Spirit: Relationship, Roles, & Relevance* (Wheaton, IL: Crossway Books, 2005), 17-18.

"The voice must express the praise of the heart if the singing is to be really addressed to God."

> F. F. Bruce, *The Epistles to the Colossians, to Philemon, and to the Ephesians* (Grand Rapids, MI: William B. Eerdmans Publishing Company, 1984), 159.

CHAPTER 6: SING SONGS THAT ARE CONGREGATIONAL

"At every opportunity Luther and his colleagues were concerned to get the whole congregation—not just part of it—involved in the singing, teaching them of the need to sing the scriptural Word, giving them the texts and melodies to sing, and supplying the musical means by which an antiphony of unison and harmony graced their services of worship."

> Robin A. Leaver, *The Whole Church Sings: Congregational Singing in Luther's Wittenberg* (Grand Rapids, MI: William B. Eerdmans Publishing Co., 2017), 162.

"The congregation of a church is the ultimate choir."

> Keith Getty and Kristyn Getty, *Sing!: How Worship Transforms Your Life, Family, and Church* (Nashville, TN: B&H Publishing Group, 2017), 3.

"Congregational singing is the most important, the only indispensable, church music."

> Donald P. Hustad, *Jubilate II: Church Music in Worship and Renewal* (Carol Stream, IL: Hope Publishing Company, 1981), 476.

"The congregation itself needs to be unified.... It needs more than this—it needs to be stirred, uplifted, moved toward God. It is not a mere aggregation of individuals, each of whom imparts nothing to the others and receives nothing from them. It constitutes, or should constitute, a vitalized whole."

> David R. Breed, *The History and Use of Hymns and Hymn-Tunes* (New York: Fleming H. Revell Company, 1903), 347-48.

"It seems to us totally inconsistent to be a joyful believer and a non-singer! When a non-singer becomes a Christian, he or she becomes a singer."

Ronald Allen and Gordon Borror, *Worship: Rediscovering the Missing Jewel* (Portland, OR: Multnomah Press, 1982), 157.

Congregational worship is "a unified chorus of spiritual response toward God expressed publicly to God, as a result of understanding biblical truth about God."

Scott Aniol, *Worship in Song: A Biblical Approach to Music and Worship* (Winona Lake, IN: BMH Books, 2009), 155.

"Like the compilers of *Hymns Ancient and Modern* and generations of Christians before them, I affirm congregational singing as both prayer and creed. I am convinced that congregational singing is the best musical venue for accomplishing the purposes of gathered Christian worship."

Fred R. Coleman, preface to *Hymns Modern and Ancient*, ed. Fred R. Coleman (Milwaukee, WI: Heart Publications, 2011).

"[A hymn] must be of such character as regards both text and tune as to make it suitable for congregational singing. This requirement requires that it must not only read well but sing well."

Robert Guy McCutchan, *Hymns in the Lives of Men* (New York: Abingdon-Cokesbury Press, 1945), 26.

"The musical expression of the church involves 'speaking to one another.' In contrast to some contemporary teaching that says that our worship is to be directed entirely to God, Paul presumes [in Ephesians 5:19] that there is a horizontal dimension to our worship. In praising God we consciously should be directing our worship to the edification of others."

> Bryan Chapell, *Ephesians* (Phillipsburg, NJ: P&R Publishing, 2009), 263.

"If our one God truly is a Community of Persons, then true Christian worship is, at its core, inherently communal and corporate. The Trinitarian essence is multi-personal, and worship shaped like the Trinity should be multi-personal. This doesn't minimize the need for our individual communion with Father, Son, and Holy Spirit.... Nevertheless, if God exists as a community, then the core of our faith, too, is expressed not as individuals, but as a church body. And if this is true, then corporate worship is one of the most fundamental elements of our faith.... When we sing *together* we reflect the Trinity—many disparate voices join together in harmonic oneness."

> Zac Hicks, "The Worship Leader and the Trinity" in *Doxology and Theology: How the Gospel Forms Worship Leaders*, ed. Matt Boswell (Nashville, TN: B&H Publishing Group, 2013), 46, 51. This explanation bridges the gap between Chapter 5 of this book (on Trinitarian songs) and Chapter 6 of this book (on congregational songs). Fellowship in the church is an echo of fellowship in the Trinity. I've not heard it described this way before, but it's accurate and profound.

CHAPTER 7: SING SONGS THAT ARE UNIFYING

"It is by the grace of God that a congregation is permitted to gather visibly in this world to share God's word and sacrament. Not all Christians receive this blessing. The imprisoned, the sick, the scattered lonely, the proclaimers of the Gospel in heathen lands stand alone. They know that visible fellowship is a blessing... The physical presence of other Christians is a source of incomparable joy and strength to the believer."

Dietrich Bonhoeffer, *Life Together: The Classic Exploration of Christian Community* (New York: HarperOne, 1954), 18-19.

"Music furnishes one of the most exquisite, elevating, unwearying pleasures of which our nature is capable. But it does much more. Song and music are a *language* distinct from speech—the language of *feeling.* This language supplies the means by which multitudes may express their thoughts as well as their feelings as with one voice. Let a thousand people speak at once; all thought and feeling are drowned in hubbub. But let them sing together in perfect time and tune; both thought and feeling are raised to a pitch of energy else inconceivable."

E. R. Conder and W. Clarkson, *The Pulpit Commentary*, ed. H. D. M. Spence and Joseph S. Exell (Peabody, MA: Hendrickson Publishers), VIII:366.

"Learn... the real unity of believers. Whatever differences there may be amongst them as regards lesser things, when they utter their hearts in prayer and praise, we find that they are one. The hymns of the Church for ever witness to the unity of the Church."

W. Forsyth, *The Pulpit Commentary*, ed. H. D. M. Spence and Joseph S. Exell (Peabody, MA: Hendrickson Publishers), VIII:370.

"One of the church's greatest treasures is congregational singing. When you join your voice to those of your brothers and sisters in praise of King

Jesus, you are looking up to God as Redeemer and around to the people who have been redeemed."

Trevin Wax, endorsement for Keith and Kristyn Getty, *Sing!: How Worship Transforms Your Life, Family, and Church* (Nashville, TN: B&H Publishing Group, 2017).

"When God's people gather in worship, their music expresses a common faith and helps them to vocalize their collective praise, thanksgiving, sorrow, and trust."

Jonathan Blackmon, "Scripture, Shekinah, and Sacred Song: How God's Word and God's Presence Should Shape the Song of God's People" in *The Artistic Theologian* 1 (2012), 33.

"Many Christians approach the topic of music from a very individualistic perspective. 'What kind of music will help me worship God the best?' But, of course, the diversity of our backgrounds—and especially our cultural backgrounds—mean that we'll have many different answers to that common question."

Mark Dever and Jamie Dunlop, *The Compelling Community: Where God's Power Makes a Church Attractive* (Wheaton, IL: Crossway, 2015), 80.

"The specific contribution of music to the building up of community in worship includes its encouragement of alertness to others, immediate responsiveness to changes in tone, tune and rhythm, and sharing in the confidence that can come from joint singing. Singing together embodies joint responsibility in which each singer waits on the others, is attentive with the intention of serving the common harmony."

David F. Ford, *Self and Salvation: Being Transformed* (Cambridge, UK: Cambridge University Press, 1999), 122.

"It's the gospel that blends us together, not music."

Bob Kauflin, *Worship Matters: Leading Others to Encounter the Greatness of God* (Wheaton, IL: Crossway, 2008), 105.

"Every person—young and old, homemaker, business executive, teacher, storekeeper—all—are included in the work of singing praise."

Harry Eskew and Hugh T. McElrath, *Sing with Understanding: An Introduction to Christian Hymnody* (Nashville, TN: Broadman Press, 1980), 224.

"The true beauty of such a congregational choir is that our voices and our hearts are knit *together* in praise. It is exhilarating to be part of a body of believers singing truth *together*."

Keith Getty and Kristyn Getty, *Sing!: How Worship Transforms Your Life, Family, and Church* (Nashville, TN: B&H Publishing Group, 2017), 4.

"Christians should show crosscultural *grace* toward those whose tastes and practices are different from their own."

Donald P. Hustad, *Jubilate II: Church Music in Worship and Renewal* (Carol Stream, IL: Hope Publishing Company, 1981), 64.

"Unless it can be shown to be inappropriate for worship, everyone's music should be heard: old people's and young people's music; European, African American, and other ethnic people's music; complex music and simple music. This is how we defer to one another—serve one another—in the body of Jesus Christ."

John M. Frame, *Contemporary Worship Music: A Biblical Defense* (Phillipsburg, PA: P&R Publishing, 1997), 25.

CHAPTER 8: SING SONGS THAT ARE INSPIRED

Luther, in a letter recruiting help to turn Bible psalms into metrical psalms for congregational singing, provides a fascinating look into his approach to the psalter: "Everywhere we are looking for poets. Now since you are so skillful and eloquent in German, I would like to ask you to work with us in this and to turn a Psalm into a hymn as in the enclosed sample of my own work. But I would like you to avoid new-fangled, fancied words and to use expressions simple and common enough for the people to understand, yet pure and fitting. The meaning should also be clear and as close as possible to the Psalm. Irrespective of the exact wording, one must freely render the sense by suitable words. I myself am not sufficiently gifted to do these things as I would. But you may be a Heman, Asaph, or Jeduthun."

Martin Luther, *Luther's Works*, ed. Ulrich S. Leupold (Philadelphia, PA: Fortress, 1965), 53:221.

"From ancient times in the Church a special significance has been attached to the common use of psalms. In many churches to this day the Psalter constitutes the beginning of every service of common worship. The custom has been largely lost and we must find our way back to its prayers."

Dietrich Bonhoeffer, *Life Together: The Classic Exploration of Christian Community* (New York: HarperOne, 1954), 44.

"Part of the Psalms' power to move people comes from their simplicity. They use short, concrete words, familiar, everyday images—sheep and shepherds, the beasts of the field, the fowls of the air, night and day, mountains, valleys, thunder and rain, the proud and haughty and the put-upon. When the Psalm-singer says he thirsts for God as parched earth thirsts for rain, his meaning is clear to everyone. When he says he feels as alone as a solitary sparrow on a housetop, who does not think of a tiny bird he has seen sitting forlornly by itself?"

> Daniel James, "The Psalter: Hymnbook of Humanity," *Christianity Today*, April 15, 1966, accessed February 3, 2021, https://www.christianitytoday.com/ct/1966/april-15/psalter-hymnbook-of-humanity.html.

"In the divinely-inspired hymn book, the Psalms, we not only have songs of praise, but we also have examples of songs on many other aspects of the Christian life. There are prayers for forgiveness, mercy, deliverance, and strength; there are testimonies of God's grace and provision; there are words of exhortation and instruction. Modern congregations certainly have need of all these kinds of songs."

> Preface to *Hymns of Grace and Glory*, ed. Joan J. Pinkston and Sharalynn E. Hicks (Greenville, SC: Ambassador Emerald International, 2002).

"The Bible has a built-in hymnal, the book of Psalms, comprised of 150 songs, written over a period of about fifteen hundred years. These songs communicate truth about the character and the mighty deeds of the God of Israel. And these songs are responsive expressions of dependence on, reverence before, and delight in God."

> Matt Mason, "The Worship Leader and Singing" in *Doxology and Theology: How the Gospel Forms Worship Leaders*, ed. Matt Boswell (Nashville, TN: B&H Publishing Group, 2013), 176.

"Because they are Holy Spirit-inspired biblical songs, we would be well advised to sing them."

> Paul S. Jones, "Hymnody in a Post-Hymnody World" in *Give Praise to God: A Vision for Reforming Worship*, ed. Philip Graham Ryken, Derek W. H. Thomas, and J. Ligon Duncan III (Phillipsburg, NJ: P&R Publishing, 2003), 227.

"We must deliberately include more Scripture in our singing, or we are disobeying the model (if not the clear commands) of Scripture."

> Tim Fisher, *The Battle for Christian Music* (Greenville, SC: Sacred Music Services, 1992), 46.

"The Psalter contains a vast collection of liturgies, meditations, prayers, and hymns, not only to be used in corporate worship but also to inspire and guide believers in every circumstance: when in need of rescue from enemies, healing from illness, vindication in the face of false accusations, and forgiveness for sin; when celebrating personal or communal experiences of divine grace; when bringing sacrifices to the temple; and when the nation was gathered in Jerusalem for the annual pilgrim festivals" (Passover, Weeks, Booths).

> Daniel I. Block, *For the Glory of God: Recovering a Biblical Theology of Worship* (Grand Rapids, MI: Baker Academic, 2014), 230.

"It has been said that next to Scripture itself a good Psalter-Hymnal is the richest fountain of edification. Not only are its songs a source of daily nourishment for the church, but they also serve as a very effective vehicle for the outpouring of confession of sin, gratitude, spiritual joy, rapture. Whether sung in the regular worship-service on the Lord's Day, at a midweek meeting, in social gatherings, in connection with family-worship, at a festive occasion, or privately, they are a tonic for the soul and promote the glory of God."

William Hendriksen, *New Testament Commentary: Exposition of Colossians and Philemon* (Grand Rapids, MI: Baker Academic, 1964), 163.

"It is reported that Athanasius, an outstanding Christian leader of the fourth century, declared that the Psalms have a unique place in the Bible because most of Scripture speaks *to* us, while the Psalms speak *for* us."

Bernard W. Anderson, *Out of the Depths: The Psalms Speak for Us Today* (Philadelphia, PA: The Westminster Press, 1974), x.

CHAPTER 9: SING SONGS THAT ARE DIVERSE

"It is an expression of extreme hubris and folly to think we have nothing to gain from older songs and nothing to lose when we throw out the songs Christians have been singing for hundreds of years."

Kevin DeYoung, "Ten Principles for Church Song," *The Founders Journal* 90 (Fall 2012), 16.

"Hymns and psalms... represent the corporate voice of God's people, over the span of many generations, responding to his Word, to creation, to teaching, to creeds, and to truth."

Paul S. Jones, *Singing and Making Music: Issues in Church Music Today* (Phillipsburg, NJ: P&R Publishing, 2006), 69.

"As Christians, we have the responsibility, indeed the privilege and imperative, of dialoguing constructively with the saints of the past in a way that can help us think clearly in the present."

Carl R. Trueman, *Luther on the Christian Life* (Wheaton, IL: Crossway, 2015), 26.

"A good hymnbook is the repository of the deepest devotion of the saints of the ages. Its treasures are priceless.... Next to the Bible a good hymnbook is a Christian's greatest devotional guide."

Robert G. Rayburn, *O Come, Let Us Worship: Corporate Worship for the Evangelical Church* (Grand Rapids, MI: Baker, 1980), 225-26.

"When you hold a hymnal in your hands, you hold something of your Christian heritage. The physical nature of a hymnal has the effect of embodying a collection of the work of the church triumphant, and in using such a book, you identify with the entire church, and you sing her experience into yours."

Scott Aniol and Ryan J. Martin, preface to *Hymns of the Living God*, ed. Scott Aniol and Ryan J. Martin (Fort Worth, TX: Religious Affections Ministries, 2017), iv.

"What makes a hymnal uniquely compelling is that it is intended to endure. It's filled with a collection of songs that its compilers believe are worthy of typesetting and printing. Such a value judgment is somewhat subjective, admittedly. It's possible that a number of the hymns we sing today may not outlast us. But such a commitment to enduring music is less of a prediction than it is a statement of intent. Hymns are meant to be poured out, offered up, and passed down to future generations."

Dan Kreider, preface to *Sing the Wonders: Hymns and Psalms for the Church*, ed. Dan Kreider (Jupiter, FL: Grace Immanuel Bible Church, 2016).

"Believers have sung their way through history, and in the process have accumulated a body of hymns that express divine truth."

John MacArthur, preface to *Hymns of Grace*, ed. Philip Webb (Los Angeles, CA: The Master's Seminary Press, 2015).

"Modern congregations ignore too many great hymns of the past and shun too many great hymns of the present."

Fred R. Coleman, preface to *Hymns Modern and Ancient*, ed. Fred R. Coleman (Milwaukee, WI: Heart Publications, 2011).

Hymnody "unites us with those who sang this song before us, and may contribute its own small offering to those as yet unborn."

Timothy Dudley-Smith, *A Functional Art: Reflections of a Hymn Writer* (Oxford, UK: Oxford University Press, 2017), 144.

"Hymns can root us firmly in the apostolic Christian tradition, giving continuity, authority, and a sense of permanence: we are not adrift, we are not alone."

Timothy Dudley-Smith, *A Functional Art: Reflections of a Hymn Writer* (Oxford, UK: Oxford University Press, 2017), 146.

"No church or service can be all things to all people. But we do not value stylistic narrowness. We believe there are affections owing to God that different tunes and different texts and different genres may awaken better than others. We will strive to be who we are without exalting our own tastes as the standard of excellence or power. We will see God's guidance in each worship setting to be both indigenous and stretching."

> Bethlehem Baptist Church in Minneapolis, MN, "What Unites Us in Worship." https://bethlehem.church/what-unites-us-in-worship.

"Next to the Bible is your Hymn Book. Enshrined within its pages, beautifully phrased in words and melodies are the songs written by the inspired Saints of yesteryears and the poets and composers of today. Its truths are glorious and priceless, worth more than silver and gold. With glad hearts, we can share and sing the sublime truths of God's eternal goodness, His sovereignty, His will, a Zion to come and the Saviour's mighty love. Herein is a spiritual treasury of devotion, aspiration, comfort and assurance. This is your Hymn Book. Cherish it and cast it not aside lightly and tear not its pages. Rather, hold it with reverent hands. This is the prayerful and humble admonition of The Publishers."

> Earl Smith and John T. Benson, eds., preface to *All-American Church Hymnal* (Nashville, TN: John T. Benson Publishing Company, 1957). I was struck by this simple, almost parental charge that greets readers when they open this hymnal. It's quaint, but I find it moving.

"The Bible's 'sorrowful songs' allow the singer to articulate the very real emotions of life in the fallen creation. But at the same time they never doubt God's sovereignty and justice; and never discount our own responsibility in sin."

> Philip Pervical, *Then Sings My Soul: Rediscovering God's Purposes for Singing in Church* (Sydney, Australia: Matthias Media, 2015), 102.

CHAPTER 10: SING SONGS THAT ARE EMOTIVE

"How greatly did I weep in the hymns and canticles, deeply moved by the voice of thy sweet-speaking Church! The voices flowed into mine ears, and the truth was poured forth into my heart, whence the agitation of my piety overflowed, and my tears ran over, and blessed was I therein."

St. Augustine. Mignel. XXXII, 769; Nicene & Post-Nicene Ser. 1, 1, 134. Cited by Donald P. Hustad, *Jubilate II: Church Music in Worship and Renewal* (Carol Stream, IL: Hope Publishing Company, 1981), 31.

"The sum of the matter is that the overall mood of worship should be celebration in community."

Allen P. Ross, *Recalling the Hope of Glory: Biblical Worship from the Garden to the New Creation* (Grand Rapids: Kregel, 2006), 441.

"Through music and singing God is exalted and glorified in ways that unembellished speech could not do, and in ways that are fitting for his holy and glorious nature."

Allen P. Ross, *Recalling the Hope of Glory: Biblical Worship from the Garden to the New Creation* (Grand Rapids: Kregel, 2006), 261.

"Our God inspires happy, cheerful worship. Those who are fortunate enough to be in His presence are stirred by the inner urge to break forth into singing and jubilant praise. In acclaiming Him as their King the subjects are moved to express themselves in a loud and joyous manner."

Kyle M. Yates, *Preaching from the Psalms* (New York, NY: Harper & Brothers Publishers, 1948), 164.

"Singing expresses God's truth in a way that stirs the soul of the worshipper. True religion is not stoic, leaving worshippers emotionally flat, but it ignites the affections of the heart, especially with joy."

Steven J. Lawson, *Holman Old Testament Commentary: Psalms 76-150*, ed. Max Anders (Nashville, TN: Holman Reference, 2006), 110.

"It is not always easy to unite enthusiasm with reverence, and it is a frequent fault to destroy one of these qualities while straining after the other. The perfection of singing is that which unites joy with gravity, exultation with humility, fervency with sobriety."

Charles Spurgeon, *The Treasury of David* (Peabody, MA: Hendrickson Publishers, 1988), 2, Part 2: 165.

"We should strive for a thinking heart and a feeling mind."

Harold M. Best, *Dumbfounded Praying* (Eugene, OR: Wipf and Stock Publications, 2011), 108.

"Magnifying God's greatness begins with the proclamation of objective, biblical truths about God, but it ends with the expression of deep and holy affection toward God."

Bob Kauflin, *Worship Matters: Leading Others to Encounter the Greatness of God* (Wheaton, IL: Crossway, 2008), 65.

"God made us passionate creatures. The redemptive gift is applicable to every part of being, including emotions. Worship can be fervent, even impassioned, because we have the capacity to love and feel deeply. Christians have experienced God's warmth, understanding, and divine love in the giving of Jesus Christ to be the propitiation for sin, in the record of Christ's dealings with God's people, and in the personal relationship believers have with the Son."

Calvin M. Johansson, *Music & Ministry: A Biblical Counterpoint* (Peabody, MA: Hendrickson Publishers, 1984), 92-93.

"There is something inevitable in true praise. It is an overflow of our joy. You cannot help but praise what you enjoy and delight in."

Tom Ascol, "Songs of Salvation," *The Founders Journal* 90 (Fall 2012), 7.

"When our faith and our worship look away from themselves to Christ, then the sweet and true affections of our faith will be felt. Then we will recognize that the affections reinforce the worship that we offer out of faith. But when emotions are the center of concern and the object of the worshiping experience, only impure and fleeting emotions will result.... The emotions must be properly channeled and directed. They must be governed by the sanctified intellect and will of the Christian. They must be the effect of faith."

W. Robert Godfrey, "Worship and the Emotions" in *Give Praise to God: A Vision for Reforming Worship*, ed. Philip Graham Ryken, Derek W. H. Thomas, and J. Ligon Duncan III (Phillipsburg, NJ: P&R Publishing, 2003), 367.

"Like few others through the ages, Watts gives us both the head and the heart of sung worship; he helps us both think and feel in our singing."

Douglas Bond, *The Poetic Wonder of Isaac Watts* (Orlando, FL: Reformation Trust, 2013), 26. Bond cites Watts as "the perfect combination that everyone in the church ought to be striving to reach: passion and feeling grounded on solid theological foundations."

"We should not be embarrassed at the thought of feeling deeply when we worship. We don't just pursue God with our minds, but also with our hearts. God's Word is meant to work through our emotions, to cause us to feel deeply, to love what we learn about God."

> Matt Boswell, "Reforming the Role of the Worship Leader" in *Doxology and Theology: How the Gospel Forms Worship Leaders*, ed. Matt Boswell (Nashville, TN: B&H Publishing Group, 2013), 11.

"What we need is a range of songs driven by the word of Christ that teach the whole story of the Bible and its theology, that reflect our unity with one another in Christ, and that allow us to respond to the gospel with genuine and right emotion."

> Philip Pervical, *Then Sings My Soul: Rediscovering God's Purposes for Singing in Church* (Sydney, Australia: Matthias Media, 2015), 58.

CHAPTER 11: SING SONGS THAT ARE EXPERIENTIAL

"Worship is the response of all that man is to all that God is and does."

> Warren W. Wiersbe, *Real Worship: It Will Transform Your Life* (Nashville, TN: Oliver Nelson, 1986), 22. In the quotation, Wiersbe is summarizing the view of William Temple, Archbishop of Canterbury.

"The hymnbook is a theological guidebook for meeting the challenges of daily living and the spiritual problems encountered in ordinary human relationships."

> Harry Eskew and Hugh T. McElrath, *Sing with Understanding: An Introduction to Christian Hymnody* (Nashville, TN: Broadman Press, 1980), 60.

"The hymns of the faith, both ancient and modern, offer us a vocabulary for expressing our fears, anxieties, and questions to the One who hears."

Matt Merker, "25 Hymns to Sing in Troubled Times," *9Marks*, March 15, 2020, accessed February 22, 2021. https://www.9marks.org/article/25-hymns-to-sing-in-troubled-times.

"Worship music is not merely a recital of things that happened objectively in history, though it is partly that. It is also a deeply subjective interaction with the God who sees our hearts."

John M. Frame, *Contemporary Worship Music: A Biblical Defense* (Phillipsburg, PA: P&R Publishing, 1997), 92.

"It is not well balanced to lean heavily on doctrinal truth to the exclusion of personal testimony; neither is it wise to lean heavily on testimony to the exclusion of biblical doctrine."

Ron and Shelly Hamilton, Preface to *Rejoice Hymns*, ed. Shelly Hamilton (Greenville, SC: Majesty Music, 2011).

"Singing makes our burdens lighter, soothes our tired and weary souls, drives away the sorrows and heals our broken hearts. It lifts us and gives us new courage."

Martin Luther King Sr., "What Part Should Singing Play in Our Church Worship?", *Georgia Baptist* (March 1, 1936), 1.

"Any man can sing in the day. When the cup is full, man draws inspiration from it; when wealth rolls in abundance around him, any man can sing to the praise of a God who gives a plenteous harvest, or sends home a loaded argosy [large merchant ship]. It is easy enough for an Aeolian harp to whisper music when the winds blow; the difficulty is for music to come when no wind bloweth. It is easy to sing when we can read the notes by daylight; but he is the skillful singer who can sing when there is not a ray of light by which to read,—who sings from his heart, and not from a book that he can see, because he has no means of reading, save from that inward book of his own living spirit, whence notes of gratitude pour forth in songs of praise."

Charles Spurgeon, "Songs in the Night" in *Metropolitan Tabernacle Pulpit*, volume 44.

CHAPTER 12: SING SONGS THAT ARE BEAUTIFUL

"The song of God's people plays a crucial role in the faith formation and doctrinal understanding of the church because the content of worship shapes the worshiper's view of God.... The words and music of corporate worship should reflect the truth of God's beauty."

Jonathan Blackmon, "Scripture, Shekinah, and Sacred Song: How God's Word and God's Presence Should Shape the Song of God's People" in *The Artistic Theologian* 1 (2012), 25.

"If we consider and ask ourselves what sort of music we should wish to hear on entering a church, we should surely, in describing our ideal, say first of all that it must be something different than what is heard elsewhere; that it should be a sacred music, devoted to its purpose, a music whose peace should still passion, whose dignity should strengthen our faith, whose unquestioned beauty should find a home in our hearts, to cheer us in life and death; a music worthy of the fair temples in which we meet, and of the holy words of our liturgy; a music whose expression of the mystery of things unseen never allowed any trifling motive to ruffle the sanctity of its reserve. What power for good such a music would have!"

Robert Bridges, *A Practical Discourse on some Principles of Hymn Singing* (Oxford, UK: B. H. Blackwell, 1901), 43.

"Church music that does not clearly exhibit genuine creativity has no place in church because it dishonors and demeans the *imago Dei*."

Calvin M. Johansson, *Music & Ministry: A Biblical Counterpoint* (Peabody, MA: Hendrickson Publishers, 1984), 31.

"In the service of God's Church, music without devotion, a lovely sound void of heartfelt meaning, is not praise, but profanation. Better omit singing from our service altogether, than have the finest music to the praise and glory, not of God, but of the performers. But when the spirit of praise, the heart and soul of worship, inspires our song, can we be too careful in perfecting its form? There is no spirituality in bad music; no piety in singing praises ignorantly, slovenly, untunefully."

E. R. Conder and W. Clarkson, *The Pulpit Commentary*, ed. H. D. M. Spence and Joseph S. Exell (Peabody, MA: Hendrickson Publishers), VIII:366.

"Another implication of glorifying God as the goal of our worship is that in order to please God we must worship Him with excellence. The God we seek to glorify has created a world in which there are real artistic standards. What kind of music does God like? Excellent music. Our worship music must be appropriate to His character. Thus the excellence of His divine being establishes the criteria for our worship."

Philip Graham Ryken, *City on a Hill: Reclaiming the Biblical Pattern for the Church in the 21ˢᵗ Century* (Chicago, IL: Moody Publishers, 2003), 66.

"Hymns are to be rich in meaning, to be pleasing and sweet, and thus productive of enjoyment for all hearers."

Martin Luther, *The Complete Sermons of Martin Luther*, ed. John Nicholas Lenker, trans. John Nicholas Lenker and others (Grand Rapids, MI: Baker Books, 2000), 4.1, 90.

"The song of God's people plays a crucial role in the faith formation and doctrinal understanding of the church because the content of worship shapes the worshiper's view of God.... The words and music of corporate worship should reflect the truth of God's beauty."

Jonathan Blackmon, "Scripture, Shekinah, and Sacred Song: How God's Word and God's Presence Should Shape the Song of God's People," *The Artistic Theologian* 1 (2012), 25.

"Christians are obligated to excellence because of who God is."

Robert Elmore, "The Place of Music in Christian Life" in *The Christian Imagination: Essays on Literature and the Arts*, ed. Leland Ryken (Grand Rapids, MI: Baker Book House, 1981), 429.

"God is worthy enough for us to consider carefully how we worship."

Scott Aniol, *Worship in Song: A Biblical Approach to Music and Worship* (Winona Lake, IN: BMH Books, 2009), 244.

"Music must be done well, not because it is a performance, but because it is an offering given to God, the best that the worshipping community can do."

> Allen P. Ross, *Recalling the Hope of Glory: Biblical Worship from the Garden to the New Creation* (Grand Rapids: Kregel, 2006), 442.

"Be specific when you write songs about God. Avoid cliché. Avoid convenience. Avoid an obsession with the consumer. Avoid the temptation to make commercial success your central goal. Write with intelligence, employing all the craft, skill, and experience with which God has endowed you."

> Fernando Ortega, "Avoiding Convenience: A Word to Hymn Writers," *The Rabbit Room*, September 20, 2011, accessed February 3, 2021, https://rabbitroom.com/2011/09/avoiding-convenience-a-word-to-hymnwriters.

"It is wretched to hear God praised in a slovenly manner. He deserves the best that we have. Every Christian should endeavour to sing according to the rules of the art, so that he may keep time and tune with the congregation. The sweetest tunes and the sweetest voices, with the sweetest words, are all too little for the Lord our God; let us not offer him limping rhymes, set to harsh tunes, and growled out by discordant voices."

> Charles Spurgeon, *The Treasury of David* (Peabody, MA: Hendrickson Publishers, 1988), 1, Part 2: 105.

Author's note: I appreciate the following quotations from hymnologist and hymn-writer Margaret Clarkston. Note the balance they demonstrate between the composer's head (the techniques listed in the first paragraph) and the composer's heart (the virtues listed in the second). Significantly, they appear on the same page of her fine article.

"Good hymns display preciseness and finesse of poetic technique and expression. Good hymns have a single theme and organic unity. They move from a bold attack in the opening line through a definite progression of thought to a clear and decisive climax. Rhymes and rhythms are interesting, original, and correct."

"Writing a hymn is more than using certain techniques correctly. It is a matter of looking on the face of God; of worshiping in His presence, embracing His will, accepting His cross, living daily under its obedience; then, having learned the disciplines of good writing, of singing God's grace. True hymnwriters have not primarily sought to write hymns, but to know God; knowing Him, they could not but sing."

E. Margaret Clarkston, "Christian Hymnody" in *The Christian Imagination: Essays on Literature and the Arts*, ed. Leland Ryken (Grand Rapids, MI: Baker Book House, 1981), 422.

CHAPTER 13: SING SONGS THAT ARE DOXOLOGICAL

Worship is "pure adoration of God, in which the worshipper is taken up with the glory of what the Lord is."

Alan Cairns, *Dictionary of Theological Terms* (Greenville, SC: Ambassador International, 1998), 529.

"Christians believe that true worship is the highest and noblest activity of which man, by the grace of God, is capable."

John R. W. Stott, *Christ the Controversialist: A Study in Some Essentials of Evangelical Religion* (London: Tyndale, 1970), 160.

"We worship God because He is worthy and not because we as worshipers get something out of it.... We worship God because He is worthy and because He has commanded us to worship Him."

Warren W. Wiersbe, *Real Worship: It Will Transform Your Life* (Nashville, TN: Oliver Nelson, 1986), 29.

"Given the distance between Creator and creature... what makes us think we can possibly fathom what would please God, apart from his telling us what to do in his word?"

J. Ligon Duncan III, "Foundations for Biblically Directed Worship" in *Give Praise to God: A Vision for Reforming Worship*, ed. Philip Graham Ryken, Derek W. H. Thomas, and J. Ligon Duncan III (Phillipsburg, NJ: P&R Publishing, 2003), 54.

"Worship is about recognizing God's primacy in all things.... If God's glory is not magnified in our services, then what occurs is not worship at all.... Nowhere should God be revealed more often or more clearly than in the church's worship."

Paul R. House, "Worship is Not About Us" in *The Southern Baptist Journal of Theology* 2, no. 4 (1998), 2-3.

"Biblical worship is theocentric. It is a creaturely response to the Creator who is at once transcendent and immanent. In accord with the Psalmist's exhortation it ascribes to the Lord 'the glory due His name' (Ps 96:8) by directing to Him prayer, praise, and presents (or offerings) congruous with His nature and character."

Carl F. H. Henry, "The *SBJT* Forum: The Current State of Worship" in *The Southern Baptist Journal of Theology* 2, no. 4 (1998), 58.

"The primary purpose of worship is not evangelism, nor church growth, nor even the edification of believers, though these are all blessings that accompany true worship. But in thinking of how we should worship, we must never lose sight of why we worship. In worship we respond to God's amazing love and sovereign grace. In worship we lift our hearts to heaven to praise and adore the triune God of eternity because He is infinitely worthy of such acclaim and simply because he likes it."

> Timothy George, "The *SBJT* Forum: The Current State of Worship" in *The Southern Baptist Journal of Theology* 2, no. 4 (1998), 59.

"The great hymns of the past, like their predecessors in Scripture, praise God for being God, for being sovereign, for being a saving and keeping God."

> Sinclair B. Ferguson, *Some Pastors and Teachers: Reflecting a Biblical Vision of What Every Minister Is Called to Be* (Carlisle, PA: Banner of Truth, 2017), 772.

"We should sing because of God's attributes and acts in creation and redemption. We should sing because this was the exemplary response of biblical saints. We should sing because God has commanded us to do so. We should sing because it is a Christian and heavenly activity of eternal duration and significance."

> Paul S. Jones, *Singing and Making Music: Issues in Church Music Today* (Phillipsburg, NJ: P&R Publishing, 2006), 128.

TIPS FOR SINGING WITH UNDERSTANDING

1. Does the hymn text quote or allude to the Bible? Which passages? Are the passages used accurately?
2. What is the theme of the hymn?
3. What doctrinal assertions are being made? Are they clear, accurate, and consistent with Scripture?
4. Does the hymn progress from stanza to stanza? How? *(Does it deepen? Look at the theme from different angles? Tell a story? Advance chronologically? Build toward a climax? Would anything be lost if one of the stanzas were omitted?)*
5. What is the purpose of the song's refrain or bridge, if it has one? *(Does it apply the truths of the stanzas? Respond with thanksgiving or commitment? Give the singer a mental break?)*
6. Are there any phrases or word pictures that are especially moving or insightful?
7. Are there any phrases or words that are unfamiliar or confusing?
8. Are there any words or concepts that would be challenging for a new believer or a child?
9. Is the song distinctly Christian? Could an unbeliever agree with its teaching?
10. Is the song distinctly Trinitarian?

11. Does this song remind you of another song on the same theme, perhaps from a different era? What light does each text shed on the other?

12. How does the music fit the text? Is it consistent with the words, musically and emotionally? Does it climax where the text climaxes? Does it add to the song's emotion?

13. How does it seem that the other members of your church are responding to the song? Do they seem to understand it? Do they struggle with it, or do they sing out with confidence?

14. How can the truth of this song influence your life right now? Is there someone you can encourage by sharing this song with them?

TIPS FOR ASPIRING HYMN-WRITERS

PART I: PREPARATION
(BEFORE YOU WRITE A LYRIC...)

1. Be a lover of words—what I call a "word nerd." If you enjoy rhymes, think Scrabble should be an Olympic sport, and just roll words around in your head, you're off to a good start.

2. Read. Widely. Yes, read hymns. But read Scripture. And great poets. And great novels. And devotional works. And theological works. And everything else. Reading widely will make you a better writer. Plus, it's just fun—See first tip.

3. Read Scripture. I know I said this already. But you need to know the Bible exceptionally well, not only as source material, but as your heart's delight. The craft of writing is a lot easier than mastering the Scriptures, but there's no point being great at communicating if you have nothing to say. If the Word of God doesn't thrill you, write something else, not hymns.

4. Write. Write letters. Keep a journal. Start a blog. But find your voice, even if nobody is reading what you're saying. The only way to improve as a writer is to write.

**PART 2: MEDITATION
(THINK...)**

5. Find a big idea that thrills you—from Scripture reading, Christian books, sermons, etc. This is probably the key to writing a compelling hymn: *Have something important to say.* Great hymns are inevitable in one sense. They marinate in the hymn-writer's heart and mind and eventually just have to come out. Remember the order of Colossians 3:16: The Word of Christ dwells richly in you; *then* you pour it out in song.

6. Meditate deeply on the theme that has captured your attention. Don't settle for surface thoughts. Drill down. Think intently on *one worthwhile theme*—regeneration, for example, not every aspect of salvation. Work for depth, not breadth.

7. Understand the doctrine so well that you can express it in fresh terms. The goal of lyric-writing is accuracy, but it's also novelty. You can't invent a doctrine, but you can describe it in an imaginatively accurate way.

8. Be patient. I was once asked how long it took to write "His Robes for Mine." Honestly? It took 15 years from the time I started meditating on justification until the time I completed the lyric—maybe more. I was thrilled by the Zechariah 3 description of justification. I thought and thought and thought on it long before I knew it would be a hymn. Take your time to develop your thoughts—don't rush just to finish.

**PART 3: COMPOSITION
(PEN TO PAPER...)**

9. Start with a "hook"—a concise, beautifully crafted phrase that will be the core of the hymn. Often this will be the first line, as with "In Christ Alone." Laboring for this perfect phrase is the hardest part of writing a hymn, in my experience. Examples of my favorite hooks are "His robes for mine" and "I run to Christ." Once I had those lines,

the hymns came rather easily. Other great hooks: "Be still, my soul," "It is not death to die," and "He will hold me fast." Notice that most of them have four syllables, and not more than six.

10. Settle on a meter. Google it. You must master this part of hymn-writing. I initially did it by ear, going with what sounds right. Notice that it's not enough to get the right number of syllables per line—accentuation has to be right as well. I'm a zealot on this; I don't like it when lyrics "cheat" and insert an extra syllable in one stanza. This is a key part of the craft. Beginners: Borrow a favorite hymn tune. I originally wrote "His Robes for Mine" to the tune for "Abide with Me" and wrote "My Jesus, Fair" to "My Shepherd Will Supply My Need." You'll replace the tune later, but this crutch will help you get the syllables and accents right.

11. Figure out your rhyme scheme: ABAB? AABB? You'll have an ear for it based on hymns you already sing. While rhyming is useful, not all hymns rhyme. Much of "In Christ Alone" doesn't. For my part, I'd rather use "slant rhymes" (like "exchange/rage") than use a forced rhyme. If the line doesn't make great sense or if the reader will think you chose the word *just* to get a rhyme, it's forced. Try again.

12. Get acquainted with thesaurus.com and rhymezone.com. Now, that tip will help you—but it could also hurt you. You're not looking for obscure words that work, and you're certainly not looking for obscure rhymes. Use these resources, but use them with care.

13. Don't waste a single word. No clichés. No filler words that are just there to make the meter work. Demonstrate unity and progress, not only from line to line, but from stanza to stanza. Don't allow your ideas to sprawl. Your content should be a rifle-shot, not a shotgun-blast. Be relentless. You might write a great hymn in thirty minutes... but I doubt it. Don't settle. Become a severe self-editor.

PART 4: CRITIQUE
("FAITHFUL ARE THE WOUNDS OF A FRIEND...")

14. Ask for feedback from fellow "word nerds." Have someone like a pastor or professor check your theology. Have someone else check your artistry. Make it clear that you're looking for ways to improve the lyric, not for *attaboys*, which feel good but don't help you make the hymn better.

15. When you do get feedback, be teachable, not defensive. Treasure the friend who tells you that a line doesn't make sense, doesn't strike the correct tone, and so on. If several people cite the same line as confusing or awkward, change it. Your lyric needs to make sense immediately, without your having to explain it.

16. Determine which advice to take and which advice to set aside. Make sure you're right. You don't have to take every bit of counsel; you're the writer, after all. But if you keep a line "as is" and disregard your friend's (or friends') counsel, at least you'll be doing it on purpose.

PART 5: COMPOSITION / COLLABORATION
("MATCHMAKER, MAKE ME A MATCH...")

17. Find someone to compose a tune that matches the text and pathos of your lyric. Be careful—It's difficult to ask someone to write a tune and then reject it in favor of another.

18. Be willing to give and take suggestions until both of you (or all of you, based on the current trend of hymn-writing-by-committee) are happy. In my experience, the musician often makes my lyrics better, and I often have a suggestion to make his tune better. Collaborate.

Joe Tyrpak describes hymn-writing as "meditation on steroids." Whether or not anyone ever sings your song, you will be spiritually and artistically sharpened by the process.

So write! Best wishes! Break a leg! Enjoy!

TIPS FOR WORSHIP LEADERS, MUSICIANS, AND A/V TECHIES

I noted in chapter 6 that congregational singing should sound like the congregation. The congregation should know that. But those who lead, accompany, and control the volume *must* know that. What you do is so valuable to the church, and we're deeply grateful. Truly! But if you're not careful, you can inadvertently smother congregational singing. Although this isn't primarily a "how-to" book, let's consider a few quick tips for those involved in leading and supporting congregational singing.

HACKS FOR THE SONG LEADER

It's hard to know exactly what to call the person who verbally leads the musical portion of the service. The song leader? The worship leader? The lead worshiper? The emcee? At any rate, the reality is that no one sets the tone for the worship service more than the person who leads the congregation in song. Here are some thoughts for consideration if you're that person.

- Prepare yourself spiritually. This is a sacred task, and you should have a sense of awe that you get to do it. Pray that you'll do it well.
- Prepare yourself musically. You're probably involved in choosing the songs. But even if you're not, know them well. Don't be surprised because you failed to practice and plan ahead.
- Script or at least mentally prepare your introductions, allusions to Scripture, and transitions. Worship isn't performance, but it mustn't be "amateur hour" either. Make brief comments that highlight song lyrics, show coherence between songs, and generally point people Godward. But don't ramble. Less is usually more.
- Lead with confidence, not timidity. Don't make it about you. Be sure that attention is drawn to the Lord—not your wit, your friendliness, or even your sincerity. Be authentic, but don't emotionally bleed-out in front of the congregation, and don't put on a quivering voice that sounds like your life is about to expire. Be conversational. Sound like you, not a whiny deathbed version of you or an artificial "lights, camera, action!" version of you. Try to be a *window* through which people see Christ, not a *portrait* that diverts attention from Him.
- Lead as simply as possible. Most congregations don't need to have a song leader who makes sweeping gestures and gives karate-chop downbeats. People tend to follow your face and voice anyway. Take an obvious breath before entries, perhaps extend your hand at times, but generally just lead in worship by singing in the front—or even from the side.
- As much as possible, direct people to Jesus and stay out of the way. And again, thank you for what you do!

HACKS FOR THE AUDIO-VISUAL TEAM

I love you guys. I'm all too familiar with microphone squawks, late lyric advances, dead batteries, and painful feedback, especially from my church-planting years. I have to confess a guilty pleasure: When I'm at a big church or conference, it makes me feel warm inside when something goes wrong with the sound system. I think, "We're not the only ones!" That probably makes me a terrible person, but there it is. I sincerely appreciate those with the know-how to lead this important part of modern ministry well!

So, some quick thoughts for you.

- Prepare ahead of time. If a mic didn't work last Sunday, don't try to figure it out during this Sunday's service. The church I pastored in Atlanta has a top-shelf A/V guy. As far as I can tell, his three rules are *prepare, prepare*, and *prepare*. Hope is not a strategy.
- Know your equipment. Candidly, I have no idea what all those knobs and slides do. I don't really want to know. I thank God for people who care. But you *do* need to care enough to read the manuals and master the equipment. Ask your church to pay for a training seminar. And ask your church to invest in better equipment when necessary. But you need to know what's what, not guess.
- Get there early. Things are going to go wrong at times, but mistakes are far more likely when you're grabbing a donut five minutes before the service begins. Be conscientious about mic checks, dry runs, and the like.
- If you're advancing slides from the presentation deck, do it just a few seconds before the new lyrics are needed. Waiting too long—or, worse, mentally spacing out and not advancing the slide at all— brings the entire service to a screeching halt.
- Focus. There are people who lose sleep over a minor mistake, and those people need to relax. Tech won't work perfectly until heaven, and maybe not even then. (Kidding!) But honestly, the kind of conscientious concentration that leaves you bothered by mistakes is probably a good thing. Shrugging things off like they don't matter may not be a virtue. The best A/V people are borderline OCD.
- You're the volume controller. It's a big deal—more important even than controlling the TV remote at home. *You have the power.* Listen

to how loud the accompaniment sounds in real life, not just through headphones. Ask for feedback. If you're in a massive space, have moles in different parts of the auditorium who can let you know if the amplified sound is too much. But more than anything, *don't let it be too much.* Err on the side of too soft instead of too loud. It's spiritually important that people hear each other sing, as we discussed in chapter 6.

• Train somebody. Most churches have volunteers on the A/V team, and it's probably best to find more help by approaching the right people rather than just asking for volunteers in an assembly-wide announcement. But however you do it, try to make yourself expendable by training people to do what you do. You're going to need a break, and if you burn out, it's bad for everybody.

• Thank you. You serve the body in a vitally important way. You invest hours in this. More significantly, you often don't sit with your family during worship services because you're attending to this ministry. When you succeed, we don't notice. When you slip, everyone gets irritated. We're sorry for that. But we need you. Thank you. Thank you. Thank you.

HACKS FOR INSTRUMENTALISTS AND PRAISE BANDS

Bob Kauflin insists, "The sound of the musicians shouldn't dominate or overpower the congregation."[272] If the sound of human voices is what we want to hear, the musicians who are leading—from the piano, the organ, the orchestra, or the praise band—need to stay out of the way. William S. Smith gives this simple rule of thumb for volume: "sufficient that people can hear the instruments, not so much that they cannot hear themselves."[273]

I've heard pianos and organs drown out the congregation. I've heard praise bands do the same thing. And I've heard instrumentalists of all

272. Kauflin, *Worship Matters*, 102.
273. William S. Smith, 269.

varieties beautifully support the congregation's voice. But make no mistake: It matters. As we've seen, we lose a great deal when we take music away from the entire assembly and entrust it to a select few. Tim Challies laments that this has already happened in countless churches:

> As congregations have lost their knowledge of their songs, they have lost the ability to sing them well. We tend to compensate for our poorly-sung songs by cranking up the volume of the musical accompaniment. The loss of the voice has given rise to the gain of the amplifier. This leads to our music being dominated by a few instrumentalists and perhaps a pair of miced-up vocalists while the larger congregation plays only a meager role. In fact, it often seems like all we want from the congregation is their enthusiasm.[274]

Gifted accompanists can be an amazing help to congregational singing, but they can also hurt it by being too loud, too complicated, or too showy. Church musicians need to memorize this principle and repeat it like a mantra: *I'm here to serve—not impress—the congregation. I am most effective when I prop up the congregation and foster its enthusiastic singing without being a distraction.*

- Be conscious of your volume, especially when you control it without help from the A/V team. If people can't hear the voices of the worshipers around them, you're playing too loud. On the other hand, if you're not supporting them in a way that gives them the courage to really sing out, your accompaniment is too tentative.
- Embellish, but don't detract from the congregation. If people can't find a downbeat or can't sing parts because you're jamming out or improvising, that might indicate that something is off.

---

274. Tim Challies, "What We Lost When We Lost Our Hymnals," *Challies*, March 29, 2017, accessed February 14, 2021, https://www.challies.com/articles/what-we-lost-whenwe-lost-hymnals.

- Keep your modulations brief. It's awkward to stand silently and wait for a guitar solo or other instrumental embellishment to finish up. My friend Paul Thompson, who wrote grand and glorious orchestrations for Stonebriar Community Church in Frisco, Texas, gave himself four measures to make a modulation. *Four!* For an entire orchestra! And he pulled it off, artfully, time and time again.[275] Don't make people who want to sing wait for you.
- Less is more. I've said this way too much, and I'm sure it sounds unkind, but *don't get in the way.*
- Thank you. Thank you!

One more word on instrumentalists supporting congregational singing. Because healthy church music sounds like the church, let me advocate for more *a cappella* singing. One of my favorite sounds is the unadorned singing of God's people. I love to have the instruments drop out (at strategic times, during familiar songs) so that the congregation can hear and enjoy each other's voices. I often led singing at the end of our services, and the accompanist knew that a simple nod from me meant to drop out. Those who could sing parts, sang parts. Those who couldn't, sang the melody. But all of us enjoyed the sound of the redeemed praising their Redeemer.

A COMMUNION-THEMED RABBIT TRAIL

Let me take a quick rabbit trail on a related topic. If an accompanist needs to avoid being a distraction during congregational singing, those who provide music during the Lord's Table need to be even more careful. I've been greatly blessed by simple, familiar, and reflective hymns about the cross that are played as the bread and cup are passed. Music is such a force for good, and having my attention directed to beautiful hymns, tastefully

---

275. Paul's congregational accompaniments (for piano and organ or for orchestra) for a dozen Church Works Media hymns can be purchased and downloaded from www.churchworks-media.com/product-category/arrangements/.

played, has often helped me in my remembrance of Jesus. But I've also been in a communion service during which the congregation's anxiety over whether the pianist would successfully manage a key change or come out the other side of an improvisation was palpable. If you're playing hymns during the Lord's Table, do everything you can to point people to Christ, not to distract from Him. Keep it soft, simple, and meaningful. Choose *really* familiar songs related to Christ's dying for our sins.

Those planning communion services should consider mixing it up some. Allow for silence as the elements are distributed. Or read Scripture on Christ's saving work. Or sing an appropriate congregational hymn. Or utilize a soloist who can effectively point people to Christ. Go out of your way to avoid being too predictable, as though there were some "magic" process that makes the Lord's Table legitimate.

HACKS FOR VOCALISTS, ENSEMBLES, AND CHOIRS

The choir or other vocalists can be a vital part of leading congregational singing. Especially if they are on the platform or in a choir loft during the congregational songs, they can model joyful engagement, enthusiasm, and earnestness. When not singing, they can show interest by participating in the Scripture reading, by listening to the speaker, and so on. Facial expressions and posture matter. For better or worse, people are watching you. Lead them. Point them to Christ even when you're not singing.

Keith and Kristyn Getty rightly encourage choirs to assist congregational singing, not compete with it:

While we enjoy hearing anthems and special performance music, what we appreciate most (and what we think is the central calling of the church choir) is a choir's ability to help the congregation sing better, as those with strong vocal ability help everyone else sing out familiar tunes and navigate newer ones.[276]

276. Getty and Getty, 124.

I'll close with this compelling illustration from Frank E. Gaebelein:

> A distinguished artist had finished a canvas of the Last Supper. All was done with great skill, and the chalice in particular had been portrayed most beautifully. As one after another of the artist's friends looked at the painting, they said, "What a beautiful cup!" Then the artist realized that he had diverted attention from the Lord. Taking his brush, he painted out the gorgeous chalice and substituted for it a more quietly beautiful but far less obtrusive one. So should it be with music in worship. It should not call attention to itself or monopolize the center of attraction that belongs to the Lord alone.[277]

---

277. Frank E. Gaebelein, "The Christian and Music" in *The Christian Imagination: Essays on Literature and the Arts*, ed. Leland Ryken (Grand Rapids, MI: Baker Book House, 1981), 444-45.

THE HYMNS AND POEMS OF CHRIS ANDERSON

Most of these hymns are available for free download and duplication from churchworksmedia.com. Many are also available as choral pieces, as noted below.

A NEW SONG
Music by Jonathan Hamilton; Choral arrangement by Shelly & Megan Hamilton available from Majesty Music

A TRIUNE PRAYER
Music by Molly Ijames; Choral arrangement by Molly Ijames available from Beckenhorst Press

ALL, AT LAST, IS WELL
Music by Richard Nichols; Choral arrangement by Richard Nichols available from Fred Bock Music

ALMIGHTY SLEPT
Poem, published without musical accompaniment

CALL TO WORSHIP

Music by Richard Nichols; Choral arrangement by Richard Nichols available from SoundForth/Lorenz

CHRIST IS SUFFICIENT

Music by Greg Habegger; Choral arrangement by James Koerts available from The Wilds

COME, LONELY HEART

Music by Greg Habegger; Orchestration by Paul Thompson available from Church Works Media

COME QUICKLY, LORD

Music by Greg Habegger; Orchestration by Paul Thompson available from Church Works Media; Choral arrangement by Mac Lynch available from The Wilds

COME, REJOICE THIS RESURRECTION DAY

Music by Paul Thompson

DEPART IN PEACE

Poem, published without musical accompaniment

DRAW NEAR THROUGH CHRIST

Music by James Koerts; Choral arrangement by James Koerts available from SoundForth/Lorenz

EVERY KNEE SHALL BOW

Music by Molly Ijames; Orchestration by Paul Thompson available from Church Works Media

FOR THE SAKE OF HIS NAME

Music by Greg Habegger; Orchestration by Paul Thompson available from Church Works Media; Choral Arrangement by Greg Habegger available from Church Works Media

FRIENDLY THORNS

Music by Jonathan Hamilton; Choral arrangement by Shelly Hamilton available from Majesty Music

GAZE ON THE CHRIST

Music by Molly Ijames; Orchestration by Paul Thompson available from Church Works Media; Choral arrangement by Mac Lynch available from The Wilds

GIVE HIM GLORY!

Music by Richard Nichols; Choral arrangement by Richard Nichols available from Fred Bock Music

GLORIA DEO!

Music by Joey Hoelscher

GOD HAS SPOKEN

Music by Greg Habegger; Choral arrangement by Richard Nichols available from The Wilds

GOD SUPREME

Music by Paul Keew

GOD'S SUFFICIENT WORD

Music by Peter Anglea; Choral arrangement by Peter Anglea available from The Wilds

HE WAS WOUNDED (ISAIAH 53)

Music by Greg Habegger

HEAR MY PRAYER (PSALM 55)

Music by Dwight Gustafson, arranging a Russian tune

HIS ROBES FOR MINE

*Music by Greg Habegger; Orchestration by Paul Thompson available from
Church Works Media; Choral arrangement by Dan Forrest available
from SoundForth/Lorenz*

HOLY, MIGHTY, WORTHY

*Music by Greg Habegger; Orchestration by Paul Thompson available from
Church Works Media; Choral arrangement by Dan Forrest available
from SoundForth/Lorenz*

HOPE OF GOD

Music by Richard Nichols

HOSANNA TO THE KING!

*Music by Alexander Reinagle; Choral arrangement by Richard Nichols available
from Fred Bock Music*

HOW DARK THE NIGHT

Music by Greg Habegger

I AM WITH YOU

*Music by Greg Habegger; Choral arrangement by Molly Ijames available
from SoundForth/Lorenz*

I LOVE THE CHURCH

Music by Greg Habegger

I RUN TO CHRIST

*Music by Greg Habegger; Orchestration by Paul Thompson available from
Church Works Media; Choral Arrangement by Molly Ijames available
from SoundForth/Lorenz*

JEHOVAH'S BRIDE

*Music by Greg Habegger; Orchestration by Paul Thompson available from Church
Works Media*

LORD, BUILD YOUR CHURCH

Music by Greg Habegger

LORD OF THE STORM

Music by Richard Nichols

LOVE HAS TRIUMPHED!

Music by Richard Nichols

MAN OF SORROWS

*Music by Richard Nichols; Choral arrangement by Richard Nichols available from
Fred Bock Music*

MATCHLESS GOD OF GRACE

*Music by Richard Nichols; Choral arrangement by Richard Nichols available from
Fred Bock Music*

MY JESUS, FAIR

*Music by Greg Habegger; Orchestration by Paul Thompson available from Church
Works Media; Choral Arrangement by Greg Habegger available from Church
Works Media*

MY LORD WAS EMPTIED

Music by Greg Habegger; Lyric collaboration with Chad Phelps

NOT TO US (PSALM 115)
Music by George J. Elvey; Choral arrangement by James Koerts available from The Wilds

PRAISE OUR SAVIOR, JESUS CHRIST
Music by Paul S. Jones; Orchestration by Paul Thompson available from Church Works Media

REFORMATION HYMN
Music by Bob Kauflin; Choral arrangement by Molly Ijames available from Church Works Media

RELENTLESS LOVE
Music by Greg Habegger

SALVATION'S CUP
Music by Molly Ijames

SEE THE CHRIST
Music by Rowland H. Prichard (HYFRYDOL); Choral arrangement by Hart Morris available from Fred Bock Music

THE BIRTH OF CHRIST
Music by Richard Nichols; Choral arrangement by Richard Nichols available from Fred Bock Music

THE FATHER LOOKS ON ME
Music by Rebekah Anderson Holden; Choral arrangement by Shelly Hamilton available from Majesty Music

THE JUST SHALL LIVE BY FAITH
Music by Jonathan Hamilton; Choral arrangement by Benjamin David Knoedler available from Majesty Music

THE LOVE OF CHRIST

Music by Richard Nichols; Choral arrangement by Richard Nichols available from Fred Bock Music

THE RESURRECTION OF CHRIST

Music by Richard Nichols; Choral arrangement by Richard Nichols available from Fred Bock Music

THE SHEPHERD OF MY SOUL

Music by Jonathan Hamilton; Choral arrangement by Shelly Hamilton available from Majesty Music

THE SPIRIT OF CHRIST

Music by Richard Nichols; Choral arrangement by Richard Nichols available from Fred Bock Music

TO LIVE OR DIE

Music by Greg Habegger; Choral arrangement by Richard Nichols available from The Wilds

UNTO YOU I LIFT MY SOUL (PSALM 25)

Music by James Mountain (EVERLASTING LOVE)

WAVES OF PRAISE

Music by Molly Ijames; Choral Arrangement by Molly Ijames available from SoundForth/Lorenz

WE BELIEVE

Music by Dan Forrest; Choral arrangement by Dan Forrest available from Beckenhorst Press

WE REMEMBER

Music by Richard Nichols

WE WILL FOLLOW
Music by Greg Habegger; Choral arrangement by James Koerts available from
The Wilds

YOU ARE ALWAYS GOOD
Music by Jonathan Hamilton; Choral arrangement by Shelly Hamilton available
from Majesty Music

YOU ARE PRECIOUS
Music by Richard Nichols; Choral arrangement by Richard Nichols available from
Fred Bock Music

YOUR BEAUTY FILLS OUR EYES
Music by Greg Habegger; Orchestration by Paul Thompson available from Church
Works Media; Choral arrangement by Mac Lynch available from The Wilds

SAMPLE THEMATIC SERVICE ORDERS

Greg Habegger was my fellow pastor at Killian Hill Baptist Church. He is my long-time friend and my hymn-writing partner at Church Works Media. He is responsible for designing the worship services at Killian Hill, and he does so with great care. After some of my own thoughts about service orders, this appendix includes a few samples that Greg has constructed, demonstrating the thematic worship approach discussed in chapter 9.

Every church has a liturgy or order of service, intentional or not. There are countless ways to arrange a service. This appendix is intended merely to spark some thought in the minds of those coordinating congregations for worship and to give real-life examples of intentional service planning. Here are some considerations and ideas on this subject.

- The goal in planning an order of service ought to be to focus the congregation's attention on a particular theme from Scripture and to unite the various elements of the service—Scripture reading, congregational hymns, solos or choral songs, prayer of adoration, etc.—around that theme. The benefit is an intentional plan which teaches and which allows the congregation to respond to a focused idea for that particular meeting.

- The bedrock of the service order needs to be the reading of God's Word. Worship is our response to divine truth. God speaks first, and we respond. The passage read together, then, is the glue that holds together the entire service. Start here. Choose a passage of the Bible and then add elements which reinforce what those verses say.

- Churches I have been part of generally begin the service with an anthem of praise. We prefer to start our service with singing, and the nature of the song is intentionally Godward, as opposed to a song of lament or testimony to start the service.

- Words of welcome are good to include somewhere early on, after a song or two, but these should be minimal. More important is a brief (two- to three-minute) pastoral word highlighting the theme of the service. I encourage worship leaders to intentionally "connect the dots" between the Scripture reading and the songs, perhaps quoting a few hymn lines and highlighting how they align with the Bible verses which will be the focus.

- With a little effort and time, it is relatively simple to choose congregational songs that match a select theme. Topical song lists in this book give you a starting point, and similar lists are included in the back of many hymnals. A bigger challenge is to connect the "prepared music" to the theme, which requires more forethought and planning for soloists, ensembles, or choirs. But it's worth it!

- A prayer of confession is an important element to include somewhere in the service. In this time, a worship leader or pastor helps the congregation to corporately approach God as sinners, depending on the finished work of Christ as the basis of our access into God's presence.

- A prayer of adoration is a pastoral response in which the minister speaks on behalf of the congregation, again highlighting the service theme and giving praise to God for the truths about which the congregation has been singing. Whereas the worship leader's theme introduction is a teaching moment focused on the church, the prayer of adoration is a corporate response focused primarily on thanksgiving and praise to God. It can often be helpful to give the congregation a few quiet moments to respond to the truths of the theme before praying aloud on the church's behalf, reminding them that this is a corporate prayer, not a private prayer.

- Both public prayers can be helped by a simple introductory comment to the congregation: "Please join me in prayer as we confess our sin to the Lord, acknowledging that we need forgiveness through Jesus Christ today." Or, "Please join me in prayer as I give praise to God on our church's behalf. Agree with me in affirming our Savior's greatness [or some mention of the service theme]."

- I have encouraged service planners (like Greg) to unite the service around a theme within the Scripture reading rather than the sermon. There are practical reasons for this, like a desire to set the themes earlier and to let the sermon be prepared closer to the service date. A separate, Scripture-aligned theme also lets the service themes vary even if the sermons address similar themes for a longer period of time as a result of preaching through a particular book of the Bible, for example.

- Of course, it is often helpful to vary the order of service. The goal isn't novelty but intentionality. The preaching could happen earlier in the service, closing with three or four hymns that respond to the sermon. Consider doing the Lord's Table after the prayer of adoration rather than at the service's conclusion. Perhaps structure the prayer of adoration as a shared corporate response rather than having a single spokesman. Weave extra elements (from membership to baby dedications to baptisms to missions updates) into a holistic service, praying and praising God for these things (perhaps even in a way that connects them to the theme when appropriate), rather than treating them as mundane "announcements."

- One more idea. A final way in which we have trained the congregation to worship attentively is that we email the order of service to them every Friday. This allows private worship on the weekend in preparation for the Sunday service.

With a little extra effort, a coordinated, thematic liturgy or order of service can help your congregation praise the Lord with joyful intentionality rather than mindlessly meandering through "random acts of worship." Godspeed!

SAMPLE SERVICE ORDER #1
GOD'S LOVE FOR US

Congregation "And Can It Be"
Congregation "Here Is Love"
Welcome and Introduction of Service Theme
Scripture Reading 1 John 4:7-12
Prayer of Confession
Special Music "My Shepherd Will Supply My Need"
Choir "O the Deep, Deep Love"
Congregation "How Deep the Father's Love for Us"
Congregation "The Power of the Cross"
Prayer of Adoration
Message
Closing Song "Living Hope"

SAMPLE SERVICE ORDER #2
GOD'S MERCY TOWARD US

Congregation "Come, People of the Risen King"
Prayer of Confession
Choir "Lord, I Need You"
Welcome and Introduction of Service Theme
Congregation "His Mercy Is More"
Scripture Reading Psalm 51:1-12

Congregation "God, Be Merciful to Me"
Congregation "Before the Throne of God Above"
Special Music "Beneath the Cross"
Prayer of Adoration
Sermon
Closing Songs "Come, Ye Sinners, Poor and Needy" and "All I Have Is Christ"

SAMPLE SERVICE ORDER #3
GOD'S TRANSCENDENCE AND IMMANENCE

Congregation "Holy, Holy, Holy"
Congregation "Immortal, Invisible, God Only Wise"
Junior Choir "God Is with Me"
Welcome and Introduction of Service Theme
Scripture Reading Psalm 56
Prayer of Confession
Choir "Father of Light"
Congregation "Yet Not I, But Through Christ in Me"
Congregation "He Will Hold Me Fast"
Prayer of Adoration
Message
Closing Song "How Deep the Father's Love for Us"

ACKNOWLEDGMENTS

A project like this has a lot of fingerprints on it.

Thanks to the early readers of the draft: Dan Totten, Tom Martin, Dan Kreider, Matt Merker, Kevin Moses, Jim Newcomer, Joe Tyrpak, and JoEllen Anderson (Thanks, Mom!). All of you managed to balance words of encouragement with the "faithful wounds" of a friend. The message I heard with drum-like consistency was "shorten it." All I can say is, I tried.

Thanks to Abby Huffstutler, essentially the only copy editor I ever work with. She was dealing with other deadlines, a bout with COVID, and life in general, so she offered to hand the book off to another editor. I waited. Abby knows Scripture, knows English, and knows how I write. As always, you made the book better.

Thanks to Bekah Holden, my lovely daughter, for preparing the three indices. It was tedious work, but I'm certain it will make the book more useful. Love you!

Thanks to Tri-County Bible Church and Killian Hill Baptist Church, where many of these convictions were settled and executed. I've been so blessed to be part of two churches that love to sing praise to God congregationally. I truly enjoyed being your pastor, and I'm grateful for the time the Lord had me serving and worshiping together with you.

Thanks to the team at Church Works Media: Joe Tyrpak, Greg Habegger, and Paul Keew. It's a delight to team with you on *Gospel Meditations* (Joe), hymn-writing (Greg), and the ongoing work of Church Works Media (Paul).

At the end of every CWM project, I'm glad I work with Joe Tyrpak, who has once again delivered. Joe spearheaded the book's artistic direction with excellence, open-mindedness, and perseverance. Special thanks to long-time project partner Jared Miller for designing a cover I immediately fell in love with. Great work! Many thanks to Brannon McAllister for brainstorming with me, commencing the design work, and introducing me to Ryan Leichty. Ryan, it's been a great first adventure working with you. Thank you for doing such an efficient job typesetting this book so that its beautiful look matches the rest of its style. And Paul Keew, thanks for keeping us all on track as we dealt with the minutiae required to finish this project well.

Thanks to The Master's Seminary (Austin Duncan), G3 Ministries (Josh Buice), and Majesty Music (Shelly Hamilton). The Master's Seminary allowed me to use this research as part of my dissertation work, which was a huge blessing. G3 Ministries and Majesty Music both had me give conference workshops on the importance of exceptional hymns, planting the seed for this book.

Finally, thanks to those who have been such an encouragement to me over the years with emails, notes, and conversations. Nearly every week I'm amazed to hear how the Lord has used CWM hymns to encourage fellow Christians around the world. My goal as a hymn-writer has been to point you to Christ, and my goal with this book is the same. May the Lord alone be glorified (Psalm 115:1).

SDG! Now... *Sing!*

BIBLIOGRAPHY

Ahlstrom, Sydney E. *A Religious History of the American People*. New Haven, CT: Yale University Press, 1972.

All-American Church Hymnal. Edited by Earl Smith and John T. Benson. Nashville, TN: John T. Benson Publishing Company, 1957.

Allen, Ronald and Gordon Borror. *Worship: Recovering the Missing Jewel*. Portland, OR: Multnomah Press, 1982.

Anderson, Bernard W. *Out of the Depths: The Psalms Speak for Us Today*. Philadelphia, PA: The Westminster Press, 1974.

Aniol, Scott. *Worship in Song: A Biblical Approach to Music and Worship*. Winona Lake, IN: BMH Books, 2009.

Ascol, Tom. "Singing in the Church." *The Founders Journal* 90 (Fall 2012): 1.

———. "Songs of Salvation." *The Founders Journal* 90 (Fall 2012): 3-13.

Ashton, Mark with C. J. Davis. "Following in Cranmer's Footsteps." In *Worship by the Book*. Edited by D. A. Carson, 64-108. Grand Rapids, MI: Zondervan, 2002.

Bailey, Albert Edward. *The Gospel in Hymns*. New York: Charles Scribner's Sons, 1950.

Barrett, Michael P. V. *The Beauty of Holiness: A Guide to Biblical Worship*. Greenville, SC: Ambassador International, 2006.

———. *Beginning at Moses: A Guide to Finding Christ in the Old Testament*. Grand Rapids, MI: Reformation Heritage Books, 1999.

Baptist Hymnal. Edited by Mike Harland. Nashville, TN: LifeWay Worship, 2008.

Bauder, Kevin. "Why Pastors Should Be Learned in Worship and Music." *The Artistic Theologian* 1 (2012): 3-15.

Begbie, Jeremy S. *Resounding Truth: Christian Wisdom in the World of Music.* Grand Rapids, MI: Baker Academic, 2007.

———. "Through Music: Sound Mix." In *Beholding the Glory: Incarnation through the Arts.* Edited by Jeremy Begbie, 138-54. Grand Rapids, MI: Baker Academic, 2001.

Begg, Alistair. Foreword to Sinclair B. Ferguson, *In Christ Alone: Living the Gospel-Centered Life.* Lake Mary, FL: Reformation Trust, 2007.

Benedict, Bruce. "The Worship Leader and Liturgy." In *Doxology and Theology: How the Gospel Forms Worship Leaders.* Edited by Matt Boswell, 101-18. Nashville, TN: B&H Publishing Group, 2013.

Best, Harold M. "Christian Responsibility in Music." In *The Christian Imagination: Essays on Literature and the Arts.* Edited by Leland Ryken, 401-14. Grand Rapids, MI: Baker Book House, 1981.

———. *Dumbfounded Praying.* Eugene, OR: Wipf and Stock Publications, 2011.

Bethlehem Baptist Church, "What Unites Us in Worship." https://bethlehem.church/what-unites-us-in-worship.

Blackmon, Jonathan. "Scripture, Shekinah, and Sacred Song: How God's Word and God's Presence Should Shape the Song of God's People." *The Artistic Theologian* 1 (2012): 25-39.

Block, Daniel I. *For the Glory of God: Recovering a Biblical Theology of Worship.* Grand Rapids, MI: Baker Academic, 2014.

Boer, Ken. "The Worship Leader and the Gospel." In *Doxology and Theology: How the Gospel Forms Worship Leaders.* Edited by Matt Boswell, 189-205. Nashville, TN: B&H Publishing Group, 2013.

Boice, James Montgomery. "Soli Deo Gloria – Rev. 1:5-7." Preached at Tenth Presbyterian Church. Spring 2000.

———. *Whatever Happened to the Gospel of Grace? Recovering the Doctrines That Shook the World*. Wheaton, IL: Crossway, 2001.

Bond, Douglas. *The Poetic Wonder of Isaac Watts*. Orlando, FL: Reformation Trust, 2013.

Bonhoeffer, Dietrich. *Life Together: The Classic Exploration of Christian Community*. New York: HarperOne, 1954.

Booth, Edwin P. *Martin Luther: Oak of Saxony*. Westwood, NJ: Barbour and Company, Inc., 1988.

Boswell, Matt. "5 Marks of the Worship of the Church." *Lifeway*. July 1, 2013. Accessed October 5, 2021. https://www.lifeway.com/en/articles/music-marks-worship-church-theology-doxology.

———. "Reforming the Role of the Worship Leader." In *Doxology and Theology: How the Gospel Forms Worship Leaders*. Edited by Matt Boswell, 5-22. Nashville, TN: B&H Publishing Group, 2013.

Breed, David R. *The History and Use of Hymns and Hymn-Tunes*. New York: Fleming H. Revell Company, 1903.

Bridges, Robert. *A Practical Discourse on Some Principles of Hymn Singing*. Oxford, UK: B. H. Blackwell, 1901.

Bruce, F. F. *The Epistles to the Colossians, to Philemon, and to the Ephesians*. Grand Rapids, MI: William B. Eerdmans Publishing Company, 1984.

Butterfield, Rosaria Champagne. *The Secret Thoughts of an Unlikely Convert: An English Professor's Journey into Christian Faith, Expanded Edition*. Pittsburgh, PA: Crown & Covenant Publications, 2014.

———. "Why I Sing Psalms." *Challies*. December 21, 2015. Accessed February 18, 2021. https://www.challies.com/sponsored/why-i-sing-psalms.

Buzin, Walter. *Luther on Music*. Saint Paul, MN: North Central, 1958.

Cairns, Alan. *Dictionary of Theological Terms*. Greenville, SC: Ambassador International, 1998.

Calvin, John. *Calvin's Commentaries*. Volume 4. Translated by James Anderson. Grand Rapids: Baker Books, 1999.

———. *Calvin's Commentaries*. Volume 21. Translated by William Pringle and John Pringle. Grand Rapids: Baker Books, 1999.

———. *Calvin's Commentaries*. Volume 22. Translated by John Owen. Grand Rapids: Baker Books, 1999.

———. *Institutes of the Christian Religion*. Vol. 1. Edited by John T. McNeill, translated by Ford Lewis Battles. Philadelphia: The Westminster Press, 1960.

———. Preface to *The Genevan Psalter*, 1542.

———. Preface to *The Genevan Psalter*, 1565.

Carson, D. A. "Worship under the Word." In *Worship by the Book*. Edited by D. A. Carson, 11-63. Grand Rapids, MI: Zondervan, 2002.

Challies, Tim. "What We Lost When We Lost Our Hymnals." *Challies*. March 29, 2017. Accessed February 14, 2021. https://www.challies.com/articles/what-we-lost-whenwe-lost-hymnals.

———. "Why Your Church Should Sing New Songs (Not Only Old Songs)." *Challies*. October 28, 2019. Accessed February 15, 2021. https://www.challies.com/articles/why-your-church-should-sing-new-songs.

Chapell, Bryan. *Christ-Centered Preaching: Redeeming the Expository Sermon*. Grand Rapids, MI: Baker Academic, 2005.

———. *Christ-Centered Worship: Letting the Gospel Shape Our Practice*. Grand Rapids, MI: Baker Academic, 2009.

———. *Ephesians*. Phillipsburg, NJ: P&R Publishing, 2009.

Chrysostom, John. *Old Testament Homilies*. Translated by Robert Charles Hill. Brookline, MA: Holy Cross Orthodox Press, 2003.

Clarkston, E. Margaret. "Christian Hymnody." In *The Christian Imagination: Essays on Literature and the Arts*. Edited by Leland Ryken, 415-28. Grand Rapids, MI: Baker Book House, 1981.

Clowney, Edmund P. *The Church*. Contours of Christian Theology. Edited by Gerald Bray. Downers Grove, IL: InterVarsity Press, 1995.

Collins, C. John. Psalms Notes in the *ESV Study Bible*. Edited by Lane T. Davis and Wayne Grudem. Wheaton, IL: Crossway, 2008.

Conder, E. R. and W. Clarkson. *The Pulpit Commentary*. Volume VIII. Edited by H. D. M. Spence and Joseph S. Exell. Peabody, MA: Hendrickson Publishers.

Cook, Robert A. "That New Religious Music." *Moody Monthly*, April 1977, 40.

Cummings, Tony. "Stuart Townend: The Worship Leader and Hymn Writer." *Cross Rhythms*, 85 (March 2005).

Daniel, James. "The Psalter: Hymnbook of Humanity." *Christianity Today*. April 15, 1966. Accessed February 3, 2021. https://www.christianitytoday.com/ct/1966/april-15/psalter-hymnbook-of-humanity.html.

Davies, Horton. *The Worship of the English Puritans*. Morgan, PA: Soli Deo Gloria Publications, 1990.

Davis, Dale Ralph. Lecture to Doctor of Ministry Students, The Master's Seminary, July 2019.

Dever, Mark and Jamie Dunlop. *The Compelling Community: Where God's Power Makes a Church Attractive*. Wheaton, IL: Crossway, 2015.

Dever, Mark and Paul Alexander. *The Deliberate Church: Building Your Ministry on the Gospel*. Wheaton, IL: Crossway Books, 2005.

DeYoung, Kevin. "Ten Principles for Church Song." *The Founders Journal* 90 (Fall 2012): 14-20.

Doran, David. "Three Qualities of God-Honoring Worship Songs." *Sermon Audio*. July 29, 2007. Accessed February 8, 2021. https://www.sermonaudio.com/sermoninfo.asp?SID=820711246.

Dudley-Smith, Timothy. *A Functional Art: Reflections of a Hymn Writer*. Oxford, UK: Oxford University Press, 2017.

Duncan, J. Ligon III. "Does God Care How We Worship?" In *Give Praise to God: A Vision for Reforming Worship*. Edited by Philip Graham Ryken, Derek W. H. Thomas, and J. Ligon Duncan III, 17-50. Phillipsburg, NJ: P&R Publishing, 2003.

———. Foreword to *Corporate Worship: How the Church Gathers as God's People* by Matt Merker. Wheaton, IL: Crossway, 2021.

———. "Foundations for Biblically Directed Worship." In *Give Praise to God: A Vision for Reforming Worship*. Edited by Philip Graham Ryken, Derek W. H. Thomas, and J. Ligon Duncan III, 51-73. Phillipsburg, NJ: P&R Publishing, 2003.

Edwards, John Harrington. *God and Music*. New York, NY: The Baker & Taylor Co., 1903.

Edwards, Jonathan. *Religious Affections*. Abridged and updated by Ellyn Sanna. Uhrichsville, OH: Barbour Publishing, 1999.

Elmore, Robert. "The Place of Music in Christian Life." In *The Christian Imagination: Essays on Literature and the Arts*. Edited by Leland Ryken, 429-34. Grand Rapids, MI: Baker Book House, 1981.

Eskew, Harry and Hugh T. McElrath. *Sing with Understanding: An Introduction to Christian Hymnody*. Nashville, TN: Broadman Press, 1980.

Evangelical Lutheran Church in America. *Principles for Worship*. (Minneapolis, MN: Augsburg Fortress Press, 2001.

Ferguson, Sinclair B. *In Christ Alone: Living the Gospel-Centered Life*. Lake Mary, FL: Reformation Trust, 2007.

———. *Some Pastors and Teachers: Reflecting a Biblical Vision of What Every Minister Is Called to Be*. Carlisle, PA: Banner of Truth, 2017.

Fisher, Tim. *The Battle for Christian Music*. Greenville, SC: Sacred Music Services, 1992.

Ford, David F. *Self and Salvation: Being Transformed*. Cambridge, UK: Cambridge University Press, 1999.

Forrest, Dan. "The Art of Worship." *Desiring God*. August 16, 2015. Accessed February 4, 2021. https://www.desiringgod.org/articles/the-art-of-worship.

Forsyth, W. *The Pulpit Commentary.* Volume VIII. Edited by H. D. M. Spence and Joseph S. Exell. Peabody, MA: Hendrickson Publishers.

Frame, John M. *Contemporary Worship Music: A Biblical Defense.* Phillipsburg, PA: P&R Publishing, 1997.

———. *Worship in Spirit and Truth: A Refreshing Study of the Principles and Practice of Biblical Worship.* Phillipsburg, PA: P&R Publishing, 1996.

Gaebelein, Arno C. *The Book of Psalms: A Devotional and Prophetic Commentary.* Neptune, NJ: Loizeaux Brothers, 1965.

Gaebelein, Frank E. "The Christian and Music." In *The Christian Imagination: Essays on Literature and the Arts.* Edited by Leland Ryken, 441-48. Grand Rapids, MI: Baker Book House, 1981.

Garlock, Frank and Kurt Woetzel. *Music in the Balance.* Greenville, SC: Majesty Music, 1992.

George, Timothy. "The *SBJT* Forum: The Current State of Worship." *The Southern Baptist Journal of Theology* 2, No. 4 (Winter 1998): 59-60.

Getty, Keith and Kristyn Getty. *Sing!: How Worship Transforms Your Life, Family, and Church.* Nashville, TN: B&H Publishing Group, 2017.

Godfrey, W. Robert. "Worship and the Emotions." In *Give Praise to God: A Vision for Reforming Worship.* Edited by Philip Graham Ryken, Derek W. H. Thomas, and J. Ligon Duncan III, 358-71. Phillipsburg, NJ: P&R Publishing, 2003.

Gordon, T. David. *Why Johnny Can't Sing Hymns: How Pop Culture Rewrote the Hymnal.* Phillipsburg, NJ: P&R Publishing, 2010.

Gregory, Arthur E. *The Hymn-Book of the Modern Church.* London: Charles H. Kelly, 1904.

Guinness, Os. Endorsement for Keith and Kristyn Getty. *Sing!: How Worship Transforms Your Life, Family, and Church.* Nashville, TN: B&H Publishing Group, 2017.

Hansen, Collin. "Keith Getty on What Makes 'In Christ Alone' Accepted and Contested." *The Gospel Coalition.* December 9, 2013. Accessed on February 19, 2021. https://

www.thegospelcoalition.org/article/keith-getty-on-what-makes-in-christ-alone-beloved-and-contested.

Hendriksen, William. *New Testament Commentary: Exposition of Colossians and Philemon.* Grand Rapids, MI: Baker Academic, 1964.

―――. *New Testament Commentary: Exposition of Ephesians.* Grand Rapids, MI: Baker Academic, 1967.

Henry, Carl F. H. "The *SBJT* Forum: The Current State of Worship." *The Southern Baptist Journal of Theology* 2, No. 4 (Winter 1998): 58-59.

Henry, Matthew. *Matthew Henry's Commentary on the Whole Bible: Complete and Unabridged in One Volume.* (Peabody, MA: Hendrickson Publishers, 1991.

Hicks, Zac. "The Worship Leader and the Trinity." In *Doxology and Theology: How the Gospel Forms Worship Leaders.* Edited by Matt Boswell, 39-54. Nashville, TN: B&H Publishing Group, 2013.

Hiestand, Gerald and Todd A. Wilson. *The Pastor Theologian: Resurrecting and Ancient Vision.* Grand Rapids, MI, 2015.

Hindmarsh, D. Bruce. "'Amazing Grace': The History of a Hymn and a Cultural Icon." In *Sing Them Over Again to Me: Hymns and Hymnbooks in America.* Edited by Mark A. Noll and Edith L. Blumhofer, 3-19. Tuscaloosa, AL: The University of Alabama Press, 2006.

Hodge, Charles. *Commentary on the Epistle to the Ephesians.* Grand Rapids, MI: William B. Eerdmans Publishing Company, 1994.

―――. *Systematic Theology.* Vol. 1. Peabody, MA: Hendrickson Publishers, 2001.

House, Paul R. "Worship is Not About Us." *The Southern Baptist Journal of Theology* 2, No. 4 (Winter 1998): 2-3.

Hughes, R. Kent. "Free Church Worship." In *Worship by the Book.* Edited by D. A. Carson, 136-72. Grand Rapids, MI: Zondervan, 2002.

Hustad, Donald P. "Don Hustad, Musician, Composer, and Teacher: On Hymnology." Posted August 11, 2015. Accessed January 28, 2020. https://youtu.be/2viinJrB6Ko.

———. *Jubilate II: Church Music in Worship and Renewal*. Carol Stream, IL: Hope Publishing Company, 1993.

———. "Let's Not Just Praise the Lord." *Christianity Today*. November 6, 1987. Accessed February 9, 2021. https://www.christianitytoday.com/ct/1987/november-6/lets-not-just-praise-lord.html.

Hymns of Grace. Edited by Philip Webb. Los Angeles, CA: The Master's Seminary Press, 2015.

Hymns of Grace and Glory. Edited by Joan J. Pinkston and Sharalynn E. Hicks. Greenville, SC: Ambassador Emerald International, 2002.

Hymns Modern and Ancient. Edited by Fred R. Coleman. Milwaukee, WI: Heart Publications, 2011.

Hymns to the Living God. Edited by Scott Aniol and Ryan J. Martin. Fort Worth, TX: Religious Affections Ministries, 2017.

Isaacson, Walter. *The Innovators: How a Group of Hackers, Geniuses, and Geeks Created the Digital Revolution*. New York: Simon & Schuster, 2014.

Johansson, Calvin M. *Music & Ministry: A Biblical Counterpoint*. Peabody, MA: Hendrickson Publishers, 1984.

Johnson, Samuel. *Lives of the Poets*. London: Oxford University Press, 1977.

Johnson, Terry L. "Restoring Psalm Singing to Our Worship." In *Give Praise to God: A Vision for Reforming Worship*. Edited by Philip Graham Ryken, Derek W. H. Thomas, and J. Ligon Duncan III, 257-88. Phillipsburg, NJ: P&R Publishing, 2003.

Jones, Paul S. "Hymnody in a Post-Hymnody World." In *Give Praise to God: A Vision for Reforming Worship*. Edited by Philip Graham Ryken, Derek W. H. Thomas, and J. Ligon Duncan III, 222-56. Phillipsburg, NJ: P&R Publishing, 2003.

———. *Singing and Making Music: Issues in Church Music Today*. Phillipsburg, NJ: Presbyterian & Reformed, 2006.

Kaiser, Walter C. Jr. *Preaching and Teaching from the Old Testament: A Guide for the Church*. Grand Rapids: Baker Academic, 2003.

Kauflin, Bob. "The Most Important Instrument on Sunday Morning." *Desiring God.* March 8, 2020. Accessed January 14, 2021. https://www.desiringgod.org/articles/the-most-important-instrument-on-sunday-morning.

———. *Worship Matters: Leading Others to Encounter the Greatness of God.* Wheaton, IL: Crossway, 2008.

Keller, Tim. *The Songs of Jesus: A Year of Daily Devotions in the Psalms.* New York: Viking, 2015.

Kent, Charles Foster. *The Songs, Hymns, and Prayers of the Old Testament.* New York: Charles Scribner's Sons, 1914.

Kidner, Derek. *Psalms 1-72: An Introduction and Commentary.* Downers Grove, IL: InterVarsity Press, 1973.

Kilby, Clyde S. "Christianity Imagination." In *The Christian Imagination: Essays on Literature and the Arts.* Edited by Leland Ryken, 37-46. Grand Rapids, MI: Baker Book House, 1981.

King, Charles. "Appendix D: When Music Equals Worship." In *Worship by the Book.* Edited by D. A. Carson, 192. Grand Rapids, MI: Zondervan, 2002.

King, Martin Luther, Sr. "What Part Should Singing Play in Our Church Worship?" *Georgia Baptist*, March 1, 1936.

Kuyper, Abraham. *Our Worship.* Edited by Harry Boonstra. Translated by Harry Boonstra, Henry Baron, Gerrit Sheeres, and Leonard Sweetman. Grand Rapids: Wm. B. Eerdmands Publishing Company, 2009.

Lawson, Steven J. *Holman Old Testament Commentary: Psalms 76-150.* Edited by Max Anders. Nashville, TN: Holman Reference, 2006.

Leaver, Robin A. *The Whole Church Sings: Congregational Singing in Luther's Wittenberg.* Grand Rapids, MI: William B. Eerdmans Publishing Co., 2017.

Letham, Robert. *The Holy Trinity: In Scripture, History, Theology, and Worship.* Phillipsburg, NJ: P&R Publishing, 2019.

———. "The Trinity and Worship." In *The Essential Trinity: New Testament Foundations and Practical Relevance*. Edited by Brandon D. Crowe and Carl R. Trueman, 264-88. Phillipsburg, NJ: P&R Publishing, 2017.

Lewis, C. S. "Christianity and Culture." In *The Christian Imagination: Essays on Literature and the Arts*. Edited by Leland Ryken, 23-36. Grand Rapids, MI: Baker Book House, 1981.

———. *English Literature in the Sixteenth Century excluding Drama* (Oxford, UK: Oxford University Press, 1954.

———. *Surprised by Joy: The Shape of My Early Life*. Orlando, FL: Harcourt, Brace, Jovanovich, 1966.

Lindsley, Art. "C. S. Lewis on Chronological Snobbery." *Knowing and Doing* (Spring 2003). https://www.cslewisinstitute.org/webfm_send/47.

Longman, Tremper III. *How to Read the Psalms*. Downers Grover, IL: IVP Academic, 1988.

Lorenz, Edmund S. *The Singing Church: The Hymns It Wrote and Sang*. Nashville, TN: Cokesbury Press, 1938.

Luther, Martin. *The Complete Sermons of Martin Luther*. Volume 4.1. Edited by John Nicholas Lenker. Translated by John Nicholas Lenker and others. Grand Rapids, MI: Baker Books, 2000.

———. Introduction to the *Baptsche Gesangbuch*. WA, Volumen 35.

———. *Luther's Works*. Volume 15. Edited by Jeroslav Pelikan. Saint Louis, MO: Concordia Publishing.

———. *Luther's Works*. Volume 53. Edited by Ulrich S. Leupold. Philadelphia, PA: Fortress, 1965.

———. *Luther's Works*. Volume 54. Edited by Theodore G. Tappert. Philadelphia, PA: Fortress Press, 1967.

———. *Martin Luther: Selections from His Writing*. Edited by John Dillenberger. New York: Anchor Books, 1962.

———. "Preface to the Burial Hymns." 1542.

MacArthur, John. "Frequently Asked Questions About Expository Preaching." In *Preaching: How to Preach Biblically*. Edited by Richard L. Mayhue and Robert L. Thomas, 273-86. Nashville, TN: Thomas Nelson, 2005.

———. *The MacArthur New Testament Commentary: Colossians & Philemon*. Chicago: Moody Publishers, 1992.

———. *The Master's Plan for the Church*. Chicago: Moody Press, 2008.

———. *Worship: The Ultimate Priority*. Chicago: Moody Press, 2012.

Marks, Harvey B. *The Rise and Growth of English Hymnody*. New York: Fleming H. Revell Company, 1937.

Martin, R. P. *The Worship of God: Some Theological, Pastoral, and Practical Reflections*. Grand Rapids, MI: Eerdmans, 1982.

Mason, Matt. "The Worship Leader and Singing." In *Doxology and Theology: How the Gospel Forms Worship Leaders*. Edited by Matt Boswell, 173-88. Nashville, TN: B&H Publishing Group, 2013.

McCutchan, Robert Guy. *Hymns in the Lives of Men*. New York: Abingdon-Cokesbury Press, 1945.

Merker, Matt. "6 Lessons from Luther on Congregational Singing." *The Gospel Coalition*. October 27, 2017. Accessed February 15, 2021. https://www.thegospelcoalition.org/reviews/the-whole-church-sings.

———. "25 Hymns to Sing in Troubled Times." *9Marks*. March 15, 2020. Accessed February 22, 2021. https://www.9marks.org/article/25-hymns-to-sing-in-troubled-times.

———. *Corporate Worship: How the Church Gathers as God's People*. Wheaton, IL: Crossway, 2021.

———. "Help! I Don't Like the Music at My Church." *Crossway*. February 27, 2001. Accessed March 1, 2021. https://www.crossway.org/articles/help-i-dont-like-the-music-at-my-church.

Mohler, R. Albert Jr. "Satan Cannot Sing: Martin Luther's Celebration of the Gospel in Christian Hymn." *Sermon Audio*. October 30, 2011. Accessed November 27, 2021. https://www.sermonaudio.com/sermoninfo.asp?SID=10301122443110

Morgan, Robert J. *Then Sings My Soul: 150 of the World's Greatest Hymn Stories.* Nashville, TN: Thomas Nelson, 2003.

Motyer, J. Alec. *Look to the Rock: An Old Testament Background to Our Understanding of Christ.* Grand Rapids, MI: Kregel, 2004.

Mungons, Kevin and Douglas Yeo. *Homer Rodeheaver and the Rise of the Gospel Music Industry.* Urbana, IL: University of Illinois Press, 2021.

Naselli, Andy. "On Swimming Elephants." *Andy Naselli.* April 3, 2009. Accessed March 1, 2021. https://andynaselli.com/on-swimming-elephants.

Noll, Mark A. and Edith L. Blumhofer. "'Introduction." In *Sing Them Over Again to Me: Hymns and Hymnbooks in America.* Edited by Mark A. Noll and Edith L. Blumhofer, vii-xvii. Tuscaloosa, AL: The University of Alabama Press, 2006.

O'Donnell, Douglas Sean. *God's Lyrics: Rediscovering Worship through Old Testament Songs.* Phillipsburg, NJ: P&R Publishing, 2010.

Ortega, Fernando. "Avoiding Convenience: A Word to Hymn Writers." *The Rabbit Room.* September 20, 2011. Accessed February 3, 2021. https://rabbitroom.com/2011/09/avoiding-convenience-a-word-to-hymnwriters.

Ortlund, Dane. *Gentle and Lowly: The Heart of Christ for Sinners and Sufferers.* Wheaton, IL: Crossway, 2020.

———. *In the Lord I Take Refuge: 150 Daily Devotions through the Psalms.* Wheaton, IL: Crossway, 2021.

Osbeck, Kenneth W. *Devotional Warm-Ups for the Church Choir: Preparing to Lead Others in Worship.* Grand Rapids, MI: Kregel Ministry, 2016.

Packer, J. I. Foreword to *From Heaven He Came and Sought Her: Definite Atonement in Historical, Biblical, Theological, and Pastoral Perspective,* edited by David Gibson and Jonathan Gibson, 13-16. Wheaton, IL: Crossway, 2013.

———. *Knowing God.* Downers Grove, IL: InterVarsity Press, 1973.

Payne, J. Barton. *The Theology of the Older Testament.* Grand Rapids, MI: Zondervan Publishing House, 1962.

Percival, Philip. *Then Sings My Soul: Rediscovering God's Purposes for Singing in Church.* Sydney, Australia: Matthias Media, 2015.

Peterson, David. *Engaging with God: A Biblical Theology of Worship.* Downers Grove, IL: IVP Academic, 1992.

Peterson, John. *The Praises of Israel.* New York, Scribner's, 1950.

Piper, John. *A God-Entranced Vision of All Things: The Legacy of Jonathan Edwards.* Wheaton, IL: Crossway Books, 2004.

———. *Brothers, We Are Not Professionals: A Plea to Pastors for Radical Ministry.* Nashville, TN: Broadman & Holman, 2002.

———. "Delighting in the Law of God." *Desiring God.* July 21, 1980. Accessed February 15, 2021. https://www.desiringgod.org/messages/delighting-in-the-law-of-god.

———. *Desiring God: Meditations of a Christian Hedonist.* Colorado Springs: Multnomah, 2001.

Platt, David. *Follow Me: A Call to Die. A Call to Live.* Carol Stream, IL: Tyndale House Publishers, Inc., 2013.

Plumer, William S. *Psalms: A Critical and Expository Commentary with Doctrinal and Practical Remarks.* Carlisle, PA: The Banner of Truth Trust, 2016.

Powlison, David. *God's Grace in Your Suffering.* Wheaton, IL: Crossway, 2018.

Price, Carl F. "What Is a Hymn?" *Hymn Society Paper* VI, 1937.

Rayburn, Robert G. *O Come, Let Us Worship: Corporate Worship for the Evangelical Church.* Grand Rapids, MI: Baker, 1980.

Reeves, Michael. *Delighting in the Trinity: An Introduction to the Christian Faith.* Downers Grove, IL: InterVarsity Press, 2012.

———. *Theologians You Should Know: An Introduction: From the Apostolic Fathers to the 21ˢᵗ Century.* Wheaton, IL: Crossway, 2016.

Rejoice Hymns. Edited by Shelly Hamilton. Greenville, SC: Majesty Music, 2011.

Reynolds, William J. *Songs of Glory: Stories of 300 Great Hymns and Gospel Songs*. Grand Rapids, MI: Zondervan Books, 1990.

Rosner, Brian S. "Paul and the Trinity." In *The Essential Trinity*. Edited by Brandon D. Crowe and Carl Trueman, 118-134. Phillipsburg, NJ: P&R Publishing, 2016.

Ross, Allen P. *Recalling the Hope of Glory: Biblical Worship from the Garden to the New Creation*. Grand Rapids: Kregel, 2006.

Routely, Erik. *Christian Hymns Observed: When in Our Music God is Glorified*. Princeton, NJ: Prestige Publications, 1982.

———. *Hymns Today and Tomorrow*. Nashville, TN: Abingdon, 1964.

———. *Music, Sacred and Profane*. London: Independent Press, 1960.

———. *Rejoice in the Lord: A Hymn Companion to the Scriptures*. Grand Rapids, MI: Wm. B. Eerdmans Publishing Company, 1985.

Ross, Allen P. *Recalling the Hope of Glory: Biblical Worship from the Garden to the New Creation*. Grand Rapids: Kregel, 2006.

Rothenbusch, Esther. "The *SBJT* Forum: The Current State of Worship." *The Southern Baptist Journal of Theology* 2, No. 4 (Winter 1998): 60-62.

Russell, Eric. *J. C. Ryle: That Man of Granite with the Heart of a Child*. Fearn, Scotland: Christian Focus, 2001.

Ryken, Leland. *The Christian Imagination: Essays on Literature and the Arts*. Edited by Leland Ryken. Grand Rapids, MI: Baker Book House, 1981.

Ryken, Philip Graham. *City on a Hill: Reclaiming the Biblical Pattern for the Church in the 21st Century*. Chicago, IL: Moody Publishers, 2003.

Saucy, Robert L. *The Church in God's Program*. Chicago, IL: Moody Press, 1972.

Schaeffer, Francis A. *Art and the Bible: Two Essays*. Downers Grove, IL: IVP Books, 1973.

Second London Baptist Confession of 1689, 22.1.

Segler, Franklin M. *Christian Worship: Its Theology and Practice*. Nashville, TN: Broadman Press, 1967.

Shelley, Percy Bysshe. "Music, When Soft Voices Die." 1821.

Sing the Wonders: Hymns and Psalms for the Church. Edited by Dan Kreider. Jupiter, FL: Grace Immanuel Bible Church, 2016.

Smith, Alfred B. *Al Smith's Treasury of Hymn Histories*. Columbia, SC: Al Smith Ministries, 1985.

Smith, William S. *Joyful Noise: A Guide to Music in the Church for Pastors and Musicians*. Franklin, TN: Providence House Publishers, 2007.

Snoeberger, Mark. "Singing the Christian Experience." *Detroit Baptist Theological Seminary*. February 18, 2020. Accessed February 7, 2021. https://dbts.edu/2020/02/18/singing-the-christian-experience.

Spiegel, James S. "Aesthetics and Worship." *The Southern Baptist Journal of Theology* 2, No. 4 (Winter 1998): 40-56.

Spurgeon, Charles. *The Autobiography of Charles H. Spurgeon, Compiled from His Letters, Diaries, and Records by His Wife and Private Secretary*. Cincinnati, OH: Curtis & Jennings, 1900.

———. *Lectures to My Students*. Volume 1. Albany, OR: AGES Software, 1996.

———. "Songs in the Night." In *Metropolitan Tabernacle Pulpit*. Volume 44.

———. *The Treasury of David*. Volume 1. Peabody, MA: Hendrickson Publishers, 1988.

———. *The Treasury of David*. Volume 2. Peabody, MA: Hendrickson Publishers, 1988.

Stevens, Daniel. "Hymns as Pillars for the Church." *The Master's Seminary Blog*. May 18, 2016. Accessed December 12, 2021. https://blog.tms.edu/pillars-for-the-church.

Stott, John R. W. *Christ the Controversialist: A Study in Some Essentials of Evangelical Religion*. London: Tyndale, 1970.

Sweatt, Danny M. *Church Music: Sense and Nonsense*. Greenville, SC: Bob Jones University Press, 1981.

Sweeney, Douglas A. *The American Evangelical Story: A History of the Movement*. Grand Rapids, MI: Baker Academic, 2005.

Swindoll, Charles R. *The Church Awakening: An Urgent Call for Renewal*. (New York: Faith Words, 2010.

Tennyson, Alfred Lord. *In Memoriam A. H. H.*, 1850, Canto 56.

Tennyson, Hallam. *Alfred Lord Tennyson: A Memoir*. Volume 2. New York: The MacMillan Company, 1897.

Tomkins, Stephen. *John Wesley: A Biography*. Grand Rapids, MI: William B. Eerdmans Publishing Company, 2003.

Tozer, A. W. *The Knowledge of the Holy*. New York: HarperCollins, 1961.

———. *Whatever Happened to Worship*. Edited by Gerald B. Smith. Camp Hill, PA: Christian Publications, 1985.

Trinity Hymnal. Philadelphia, PA: Great Commission Publications, 1961.

Trueman, Carl R. *Luther on the Christian Life: Cross and Freedom*. Wheaton, IL: Crossway, 2015.

———. Personal interview on August 31, 2021.

———. "The Trinity and Prayer." In *The Essential Trinity: New Testament Foundations and Practical Relevance*. Edited by Brandon D. Crowe and Carl R. Trueman, 222-40. Phillipsburg, NJ: P&R Publishing, 2017.

———. *The Wages of Spin*. Tain, Scotland: Mentor, 2004.

Tyson, John R. *Assist Me to Proclaim: The Life and Hymns of Charles Wesley*. Grand Rapids, MI: William B. Eerdmans Publishing Company, 2007.

Vajta, Vilmos. *Luther on Worship*. Philadelphia, PA: Muhlenberg Press, 1958.

Ware, Bruce A. *Father, Son, & Holy Spirit: Relationship, Roles, & Relevance*. Wheaton, IL: Crossway Books, 2005.

Watts, Isaac. *The Psalms of David Imitated in the Language of the New Testament and Applied to the Christian State and Worship.*

Wax, Trevin. Endorsement for Keith and Kristyn Getty. *Sing!: How Worship Transforms Your Life, Family, and Church.* Nashville, TN: B&H Publishing Group, 2017.

Wesley, John. "Directions for Singing." In *Select Hymns,* 1761.

Westermeyer, Paul. *Te Deum: The Church and Music.* Minneapolis: Augsburg Fortress, 1998.

Whitney, Donald S. *Spiritual Disciplines for the Christian Life.* Colorado Springs, CO: NavPress, 1991.

Wiersbe, Warren W. *Preaching & Teaching with Imagination: The Quest for Biblical Ministry.* Wheaton, IL: Victor Book, 1994.

———. *Real Worship: It Will Transform Your Life.* Nashville, TN: Oliver Nelson, 1986.

Worship and Service Hymnal. Edited by Donald P. Hustad. Carol Stream, IL: Hope Publishing Company, 1966.

Yates, Kyle M. *Preaching from the Psalms.* New York, NY: Harper & Brothers Publishers, 1948.

SCRIPTURE INDEX

GENESIS

3:18 35

EXODUS

12:5 187
15:1-21 159
15:20 158
15:21 87
20:4-6 209
25-31 189
28:2 189
29:1 187
35:30-35 189

LEVITICUS

22:22 188

NUMBERS

14:18 208

I SAMUEL

7:12 37

2 SAMUEL

6:14 . . . . .158, 159
24:24 188

I KINGS

8:54 159

2 KINGS

19:15 208

I CHRONICLES

15-16 94
15:22 189
16:8-36 127
16:9 . . . . 10, 87
16:23 87

2 CHRONICLES

2-4 189
34:12 189

NEHEMIAH

1:4 159
8:9 159
12:43 159

PSALMS

2:6 174
5:2 174
6 123
6:6 157
8 123

9:11 87
13:6 170
18:1 174
18:2 174
18:18 174
19:14 133,
19:14 174
22:1 127
23 135
23:1 174
27:1 175
28:2 158
32 123
32:1 123
33:1 157
33:3 . . . . 95, 141, 157, 186, 188, 189,
        201, 204
34:6 133
37:23 133
38 123
40:2 197
40:3 . . . . 141, 199
42:1 133
46 . . . . 121, 132
46:1 175
46:7 175
46:11 175
47:1 158
47:6 87
47:7 . . . . 87, 120
51 . . . . 123, 133
51:1-12 288
66 132
66:1 186
66:2 . . . . 123, 186, 188, 204
72 132
81:1 154
86:5 208
86:10 208
86:15 208
90 . . . . .127, 132, 138

92:4 133
95:6 157
96:1 . . . . 2, 141
98 132
98:1 141
100 135
100:4 133
102 123
103 132
103:13 202
104:2 189
104:3 189
110:1 61
111:1 154
115:1 . . . . 96, 292
119:11 48
119:105 133
130 123
133:1 102
139:6 123
143 123
144:9 141
145:3 .188, 206
148:12-13 .112
149:1 . . . . 84, 141
149:3 158
149:4 201

ECCLESIASTES

9:10 191

ISAIAH

1:10-15 181
29:13 181
53 279
55:1-2 27

ZEPHANIAH

3:17 11

ZECHARIAH

3. 266

MALACHI

1:8 188

MATTHEW

1:23 60
2:11 159
3:15 . . . . 60, 63
5:3 27
15:8 181
17:5 73
16:26 27
22:37 167
26:26 27
26:30 127
27:29 35
27:45 36
27:51 . . . . 36, 107
27:52-53 36

LUKE

5:8 159
15:16 27
16:19-31 27
22:53 36
23:34 35
23:44 36
24:44-45 . . . . 127, 129, 131

JOHN

1:14 60
1:18 60
3:30 95
4:10-15 26
4:14 27
6:35 27
6:48 27
6:51 27
7:37 27

7:38-39 27
13:35 104
14:6 . . . . 60, 72
14:7-11 60
14:26 60
15:26 60
16:13-14 60
19:30 36

ACTS

2:25-28 128
2:34 128
2:34-36 61
3:8 160
4:11 128
4:12 60
4:24-26 128
6:1 105
7:46 128
10:26 73
13:22 128
13:33 128
13:35 128
14:15 . . . . 74, 128
14:19 74
15:1-35 105
15:36-41 105
17:11 33
20:19 160
20:27 . . . . 45, 148
20:31 160
20:36 159

ROMANS

4:25 60
8:1 35
8:22 . . . . 144, 146
10:17 58
11:33-36 208
12:10 113

1 CORINTHIANS

1:12-13 104

2:1-5 60

6:7-8 105

12:13 104

12:20 104

14:15 . . . . 37, 40, 48, 167

14:23-25 198

14:26 94

15:3-4 60

2 CORINTHIANS

2:4 160

5:21 . . . . .36, 60

13:14 68

GALATIANS

2:13 35

3:27-28 104

5:15 105

EPHESIANS

1:6 . . . . 81, 207

1:7 27

1:12 . . . . 81, 207

1:14 . . . . 81, 207

1:18 27

1:22 61

2:4 27

2:7 27

2:11-21 106

2:15 104

3:8 27

3:12 60

3:16 27

3:20-21 . . . . .81, 207, 208

4:3 104

4:4-6 104

5:18 . . . . 71, 72, 73, 80, 89, 128

5:19 . . . . . 30, 71, 72, 73, 80, 87, 89, 90,
109, 110, 127, 137, 239

5:20 . . . . 71, 72, 80, 89

5:21 113

PHILIPPIANS

2:3-4 105

2:5-11 61

2:6-11 61

3:8-9 60

4:2 105

4:12 7

COLOSSIANS

1:15-20 61

2:14 35

3:12-15 108

3:16 . . . 24, 28, 29, 30, 31, 32, 33, 43, 57,
58, 71, 72, 73, 80, 87, 89, 90, 108,
109, 126, 128, 137, 212, 217, 266

3:17 . . . . 58, 71, 72, 80, 89

1 THESSALONIANS

5:21 33

1 TIMOTHY

3:16 61

2 TIMOTHY

4:1 61

TITUS

2:13 60

3:10-11 105

HEBREWS

1:3 61

7:25 60

9:14 188

10:19-20 .60, 72

13:15 . . . . 81, 203, 204

JAMES

5:13 .... 87, 127, 128

1 PETER

1:19 188

5:5 105

2 PETER

1:21 72

1 JOHN

1:9 123

2:1-2 60

4:7-8 105

4:7-12 288

4:10 60

4:14 60

JUDE

3 104

24-25 208

REVELATION

1:17 160

3:17 27

4:8 202

4:10 160

4:11 208

5:8 160

5:9 54

5:9-13 61

5:12 208

5:14 160

6:10 160

7:10 160

15:3 136

19:1 160

19:3 160

19:4 160

19:6 .... 160, 208

19:10 74

21-22 .... 61, 146

21:6 27

22:9 74

22:17 27

NAME INDEX

Ahlstrom, Sydney E., 143

Alexander, Paul, 30, 94, 110, 115, 171, 206, 236

Allen, Ronald, 239

Anders, Max, 252

Anderson, Bernard W., 124, 130, 247

Anderson, Fred, 133

Anglea, Peter, 59

Aniol, Scott, 30, 74, 98, 196, 226, 239, 248, 258

Ascol, Tom, 226, 235, 253

Ashton, Mark, 230

Augustine, Saint, 251

Bailey, Albert, 17, 28

Bancroft, Charitie Lees, 197

Baron, Henry, 88

Barrett, Michael, 51, 122, 130, 170, 197

Battles, Ford Lewis, 209

Bauder, Kevin, 121, 229

Begbie, Jeremy S., 10, 79, 191

Begg, Alistair, 17, 235

Benedict, Bruce, 237

Benson, John T., 250

Berg, Jim, 210

Bernard, Saint (of Clairvaux), 140

Best, Harold M., 190, 252

Blackmon, Jonathan, 242, 256, 258

Block, Daniel I., 30, 58, 148, 246

Blumhofer, Edith L., 55

Boer, Ken, 52, 228

Boice, James Montgomery, 13, 42, 219

Bond, Douglas, 17, 130, 165, 195, 218, 253

Bonhoeffer, Dietrich, 241, 244

Boonstra, Harry, 88

Booth, Edwin P., 235

Borror, Gordon, 239

Boswell, Matt, 52, 141, 212, 219, 227, 228, 230, 234, 237, 240, 245, 254

Breed, David R., 31, 32, 33, 214, 225, 238

Bridges, Robert, 188, 257

Bruce, F. F., 237

Butterfield, Rosaria, 125, 126, 156

Buzin, Walter, 84

Cairns, Alan, 260

Calvin, John, 10, 80, 88, 93, 122, 123, 134, 157, 164, 198, 209

Carlill, Adam, 133

Carson, D. A., 19, 54, 95, 230

Challies, Tim, 136, 273

Chapell, Bryan, 61, 233, 240

Chrysostom, John, 227

Clarkson, W., 241, 257

Clarkston, E. Margaret, 197, 210, 259, 260

Clowney, Edmund, 162

Coleman, Fred R., 88, 239, 249

Collins, C. John, 202

Conder, E. R., 241, 257

Cook, Robert, A., 103

Cook, Vikki, 164, 197

Cottrell, Travis, 219

Courtney, Craig, 114

Crosby, Fanny, 143, 179

Crowe, Brandon D., 18, 70, 77

Cushing, William, 178

Davis, C. J., 230

Davis, Dale Ralph, 145

Davis, Lane T., 202

Dever, Mark, 30, 94, 110, 115, 162, 171, 206, 236, 242

DeYoung, Kevin, 215, 232, 247

Dillenberger, John, 122

Doran, David, 33, 167

Dudley-Smith, Timothy, 6, 174, 194, 217, 227, 249

Duncan, J. Ligon, 4, 49, 134, 162, 230, 246, 253, 261

Dunlop, Jamie, 242

Dykes, John B., 79

Edwards, John Harrington, 1

Edwards, Jonathan, 162, 163, 164

Elmore, Robert, 258

Eskew, Harry, 32, 41, 80, 156, 243, 254

Exell, Joseph S., 241, 257

Fee, Gordon, 233

Ferguson, Sinclair B., 17, 43, 57, 236, 262

Fettke, Tom, 99

Fisher, Tim, 246

Ford, David F., 243

Forrest, Dan, 7, 78, 190, 192

Forsyth, W., 241

Frame, John M., 17, 24, 31, 52, 68, 95, 113, 114, 131, 139, 180, 236, 244, 255

Gaebelein, Arno C., 122, 124

Gaebelein, Frank E., 276

Gaither, Bill, 114, 179

Galkin, Will, 7

Garlock, Frank, 171

George, Timothy, 262

Getty, Keith, 5, 7, 14, 35, 40, 44, 56, 59, 86, 89, 107, 114, 148, 177, 196, 199, 218, 219, 238, 242, 243, 275

Getty, Kristyn, 5, 7, 14, 40, 44, 86, 89, 107, 114, 148, 177, 196, 199, 218, 219, 238, 242, 243, 275

Godfrey, W. Robert, 162, 253

Gordon, T. David, 199

Green, Keith, 7

Green, Steve, 7, 45

Gregory, Arthur E., 4

Grudem, Wayne, 202

Guinness, Os, 44

Habegger, Greg, 7, 26, 75, 82, 93, 150, 163, 285

Hamilton, Jonathan, 7

Hamilton, Ron, 255

Hamilton, Shelly, 255

Handel, George F., 44, 92, 143, 191

Harlan, Benjamin, 96

Harris, Margaret J., 75

Hansen, Collin, 59

Harland, Mike, 77, 234

Havergal, Francis Ridley, 179

Hiestand, Gerald, 139

Hendriksen, William, 90, 247

Henry, Carl F. H., 261

Henry, Matthew, 128

Herder, Johann Gottfried von, 121

Hicks, Sharalynn E., 245

Hicks, Zac, 240

Hill, Robert Charles, 227

Hindmarsh, D. Bruce, 55

Hodge, Charles, 74

House, Paul R., 261
Hudson, Ralph E., 144, 197
Hughes, R. Kent, 18, 28, 149, 200
Hus, John, 88, 184
Hustad, Donald P., 132, 141, 143, 173, 179, 229, 238, 243, 251
Ijames, Molly, 7
Isaacson, Walter, 97
James, Daniel, 244
Johansson, Calvin M., 14, 191, 213, 216, 253, 257
Johnson, Terry L., 134, 143
Jones, Paul S., 7, 13, 29, 48, 79, 108, 200, 202, 246, 247, 262
Joy, Edward, 178
Kaiser, Walter C., 125
Kauflin, Bob, 7, 54, 55, 85, 99, 166, 167, 168, 171, 178, 181, 243, 252, 272
Kauflin, Jordan, 140, 163, 178
Keew, Paul, 7, 132
Keller, Tim, 127
Kent, Charles Foster, 128
Kilby, Clyde S., 190, 191
King, Charles, 95
King, Martin Luther, 255
Koerts, James, 7
Kreider, Dan, 133, 233, 249
Kuyper, Abraham, 88, 191
Lawson, Steven J., 206, 213, 252
Leaver, Robin A., 89, 238
Leckebusch, Martin, 133
Lehman, Frederick Martin, 194, 195
Lenker, John Nicholas, 258
Letham, Robert, 70, 77
Leupold, Ulrich S., 231, 244
Lewis, C. S., 139, 151, 191, 193, 198, 199
Lockwood, Don, 161
Longman, Tremper, 128, 130
Lorenz, Edmund S., 58, 132, 171
Lowry, Mark, 216

Luther, Martin, 15, 18, 31, 37, 42, 50, 52, 65, 84, 88, 93, 120, 132, 134, 231, 235, 237, 244, 258
Lynch, Mac, 133
MacArthur, John, 95, 137, 167, 212, 230, 235, 249
Martin, Civilia, 178
Martin, R. P., 29
Martin, Ryan J., 30, 74, 98, 226, 248
Mason, Matt, 136, 245
Mayhue, Richard L., 95
McCutchan, Robert Guy, 16, 166, 186, 239
McElrath, Hugh T., 32, 41, 80, 156, 243, 254
McNeil, John T., 209
Mendelssohn, Felix, 7
Merker, Matt, 45, 89, 92, 102, 109, 114, 115, 129, 219, 228, 255
Miller, Rhea F., 172
Mohler, R. Albert, i–iii, 231–32
Morgan, Robert J., 139–40
Morris, Collin, 6
Motyer, J. Alec, 226
Mungons, Kevin, 97, 145
Newton, John, 55
Nichols, Richard, 7
Niles, John Jacob, 215
Noll, Mark A., 55
O'Donnell, Douglas Sean, 34, 171, 233
Old, Hughes Oliphant, 128
Ortega, Fernando, 99, 259
Ortlund, Dane, 120, 199
Osbeck, Kevin W., 31
Owen, John, 164
Packer, J. I., 40, 68
Papa, Matt, 219
Pelikan, Jeroslav, 84
Percival, Philip, 229, 250, 254
Peterson, Andrew, 140, 146
Peterson, John W., 179

Pettit, Steve, 7

Pinkston, Joan J., 245

Piper, John, 49, 50, 161, 163, 168, 218

Platt, David, 161

Plumer, William S., 121, 207

Powlison, David, 144

Price, Carl F., 194

Rainer, Thom S., 234

Rattenbury, John, 232

Rayburn, Robert G., 228, 248

Reeves, Michael, 2, 71, 83

Rodeheaver, Homer, 145

Rosner, Brian, 70

Ross, Allen P., 12–13, 19, 87, 94, 134, 142, 158, 161, 188, 251, 259

Rothenbusch, Esther, 53

Routley, Eric, 93, 193, 199, 210, 231

Rowe, James, 197

Russell, Eric, 102, 227

Rutter, John, 7, 143

Ryken, Leland, 190, 191, 197, 199, 258, 260, 276

Ryken, Philip Graham, 134, 162, 171, 191, 230, 246, 253, 257–58, 261

Ryle, J. C., 102, 227

Saucy, Robert L., 137, 225

Schaeffer, Francis, 186, 191

Seger, Bob, 139

Segler, Franklin, 84, 91, 103

Sheeres, Gerrit, 88

Smith, Earl, 250

Smith, Howard E., 197

Smith, Walter C., 172

Smith, William S., 42, 88, 96–97, 112, 196, 272

Snoeberger, Mark, 170, 176–77

Sorenson, Heather, 96

Spence, H. D. M., 241, 257

Spiegel, James S., 190

Spurgeon, Charles, 91, 140–41, 150, 151, 154, 252, 255–56, 259

Stevens, Daniel, 233–34

Story, Laura, 143, 179

Stott, John R. W., 260

Strodach, Paul Zeller, 231

Sweatt, Danny M., 24

Sweetman, Leonard, 88

Swindoll, Charles R., 228

Sunday, Billy, 161

Tada, Joni Eareckson, 86

Tennyson, Alfred, 144, 187

Tennyson, Hallam, 187

Thomas, Derek W. H., 134, 162, 230, 246, 253, 261

Thomas, Robert L., 95

Thompson, Paul, 274

Tomkins, Stephen, 165

Townend, Stuart, 7, 35–36, 56, 59

Tozer, A. W., 209, 218

Trueman, Carl, 18, 70, 77, 145, 248

Tyndale, William, 52

Tyrpak, Joe, 131, 132, 268

Tyson, John R., 131, 165, 175, 232

Vajta, Vilmos, 15, 120

Ware, Bruce A., 237

Warren, Rick, 167, 211, 212

Washer, Paul, 161

Watts, Isaac, 7, 28, 51, 76, 129, 130, 131, 132, 165, 171, 176, 195, 196, 197, 212, 213, 216, 218, 253

Wax, Trevin, 241–242

Webb, Philip, 249

Wesley, Charles, 7, 16–17, 35, 129, 140, 143, 165, 171, 175–76, 187, 213, 215, 232

Wesley, John, 15, 16, 81, 111, 154

Westermeyer, Paul, 42

Whitefield, George, 161

Whitney, Donald, 188–89

Wiersbe, Warren W., 145–46, 254, 261

Williams, Clara, 26

Wilson, Hugh, 144
Wilson, Todd, 139
Woetzel, Kurt, 171
Wordsworth, Christopher, 171
Wycliffe, John, 88
Yates, Kyle M., 251
Yeo, Douglas, 97, 145
Zwingli, Ulrich, 88

HYMN INDEX

10,000 Reasons, 58, 96

A Debtor to Mercy Alone, 64

A Mighty Fortress is Our God, 50, 121, 132, 231–232

A New Song, 277

A Tender Heart, 183

A Triune Prayer, 73, 77, 277

Abide with Me, 183, 267

Alas! and Did My Savior Bleed?, 63, 144, 165, 197, 213, 216

All, At Last, Is Well, 277

All Creatures of Our God and King, 79

All Hail the Power of Jesus' Name, 37, 65

All I Have Is Christ, 140, 163, 178, 181, 289

All Praise to Thee, for Thou, O King Divine, 62

All the Way, 182

All Your Anxiety, 147, 178

Almighty Father, 75, 96

Almighty Slept, 277

Amazing Grace, 55, 56

Amazing Grace [My Chains Are Gone], 56

Ancient of Days, 182

And Can It Be, 16, 35, 46, 173, 175, 181, 192, 288

Are We Down-Hearted?, 44

Arise, My Soul, Arise, 16, 51, 64, 79, 140

As the Deer, 133, 182

At the Cross, 144, 197

Be Still, My Soul, 147, 267

Be Strong in the Lord, 182

Be Thou My Vision, 182

Before the Throne of God Above, 13, 51, 64, 159, 164, 173, 197, 289

Before You I Kneel [A Worker's Prayer], 177

Behold Our God, 110, 216

Beneath the Cross, 107, 289

Blessed Assurance, 181

Bow the Knee, 182

Breathe on Me, Breath of God, 76

By Faith, 47

Call to Worship, 278

Cheer Up, Ye Saints of God, 44

Christ Arose, 64

Christ Is Risen, He Is Risen Indeed!, 64

Christ Is Sufficient, 278

Christ Our Hope in Life and Death, 47, 183

Christ Returneth, 47, 65

Christ the Lord Is Risen Today,
64, 148

Come Behold the Wondrous
Mystery, 63

Come, Holy Spirit, Heavenly
Dove, 76

Come, Lonely Heart, 26, 63, 278

Come, My Soul, with Every Care, 147

Come, People of the Risen King, 288

Come Quickly, Lord, 47, 65, 278

Come, Rejoice this Resurrection
Day, 278

Come, Thou Almighty King, 79

Come Thou Fount of Every
Blessing, 37

Come, Thou Long Expected Jesus, 62

Come, Ye Disconsolate, 147

Come, Ye Sinners, Poor and Needy,
183, 289

Complete in Thee, 47, 181

Create in Me a Clean Heart, 133

Crown Him with Many Crowns, 13,
64, 76

Deep and Wide, 53

Depart in Peace, 278

Draw Near through Christ, 278

Eternal Father, Strong to Save, 79

Every Knee Shall Bow, 278

Facing a Task Unfinished, 47

Fairest Lord Jesus, 63, 76

Father of Light, 289

For the Beauty of the Earth, 58, 177

For the Cause, 47

For the Sake of His Name, 47, 279

Friendly Thorns, 279

From the Squalor of a Borrowed
Stable, 62

Gaze on the Christ, 279

Give Him Glory!, 279

Gloria Deo!, 279

God, Be Merciful to Me, 289

God Has Spoken, 46, 279

God Is for Us, 76

God Is So Good, 52

God Is with Me, 289

God Supreme, 279

God's Sufficient Word, 46, 59, 279

Gloria Patri, 69, 70, 74

Grace Greater than Our Sin, 214

Great Is Thy Faithfulness, 58, 177

Hail the Day That Sees Him Rise, 64

Hallelujah, What a Savior, 63

Hark! the Herald Angels Sing, 17, 62

Have Thine Own Way, Lord, 183

He Has Made Me Glad, 133

He Hideth My Soul, 182

He Is Able, More Than Able, 182

He Was Wounded [Isaiah 53], 279

He Will Hold Me Fast, 45, 147, 182,
267, 289

He Will Not Let Go, 179, 180

Hear My Prayer [Psalm 55], 280

Here Is Love, 63, 288

His Eye Is on the Sparrow, 178, 182

His Mercy Is More, 47, 288

His Robes for Mine, 7, 47, 64, 176,
266, 267, 280

Holy, Holy, Holy, 79, 214, 289

Holy, Mighty, Worthy, 77, 82,
214, 280

Holy Spirit, Living Breath of God, 76

Hope of God, 280

Hosanna to the King, 280

How Can I Fear?, 147

How Can I Keep from Singing? 216

How Dark the Night, 280

How Deep the Father's Love for Us,
75, 214, 288, 289

How Firm a Foundation, 46, 144, 147

How Great Thou Art, 65, 177, 214

How Sweet and Awesome Is the
  Place, 46
I Am with You, 77, 280
I Love the Church, 280
I Love You, Lord, 182
I Need Thee Every Hour, 182
I Run to Christ, 7, 64, 147, 177, 178,
  183, 281
I Saw One Hanging on a Tree, 216
I Shall Know Him, 183
I Sing the Mighty Power of God, 58,
  75, 213, 214
I Will Follow, 182
I Will Glory in My Redeemer, 63
I Will Praise Him, 75
I Wonder as I Wander, 215
I'd Rather Have Jesus, 172, 173, 182
Immortal, Invisible, God Only Wise,
  172, 173, 214, 289
In Christ Alone, 37, 56, 57, 59, 65, 76,
  163, 266, 267, 299
Is He Worthy?, 79, 110, 140, 146, 216
It Is Not Death to Die, 183, 267
It Is Well with My Soul, 13, 50, 65, 110,
  147, 182
Jehovah's Bride, 281
Jesus, Draw Me Ever Nearer, 147
Jesus, I Am Resting, Resting, 182
Jesus, Lover of My Soul, 147, 171
Jesus Loves Me, 52
Jesus Paid It All, 47, 173
Jesus Saves, 64
Jesus Shall Reign, 65, 132
Jesus, Strong and Kind, 63, 76
Jesus, Thank You, 47, 63
Jesus, the Very Thought of Thee,
  63, 76
Jesus, Thy Blood and Righteousness,
  46, 52
Joy Has Dawned, 62
Joy to the World, 65, 132, 213

Just As I Am [I Come Broken], 181
Lamb of Glory, 63
Like a River Glorious, 58, 182
Living Hope, 64, 288
Lo, He Comes in Clouds Descending,
  47, 65
Look, Ye Saints! The Sight Is Glori-
  ous, 47, 65
Lord, Build Your Church, 281
Lord, I Need You, 147, 288
Lord of the Storm, 281
Love Divine, All Loves Excelling, 215
Love Has Triumphed! 281
Love Lifted Me, 197
Man of Sorrows, 281
Matchless God of Grace, 281
Mercies Anew, 214
Mercy Tree, 64
My Faith Looks Up to Thee, 183
My Jesus, Fair, 34–35, 64, 267, 281
My Jesus, I Love Thee, 182
My Lord Was Emptied, 281
My Shepherd Will Supply My Need,
  267, 288
My Soul Finds Rest, 147
Not to Us [Psalm 115], 282
Nothing Between, 183
Now I Belong to Jesus, 181
O Church, Arise, 47
O Come, All Ye Faithful, 62
O Come, O Come, Immanuel, 62
O God, My Joy, 183
O God, Our Help in Ages Past, 132
O Great God, 178, 214
O How He Loves You and Me, 182
O Lord, My Rock and My Redeemer,
  64, 147, 182
O For a Thousand Tongues, 16
O Sacred Head, Now Wounded, 63,
  140, 156, 163
O the Deep, Deep Love, 288

O Worship the King, 214
O Zion, Haste, 47
Of the Father's Love Begotten, 62
One Day / Glorious Day, 65
One Day [When We All Get to
    Heaven], 65, 183
Only a Holy God, 76, 214
Our Great Savior, 62, 76
Our Triune God, 80
Praise, My Soul, the King of Heaven,
    58, 75, 132
Praise Our Savior, Jesus Christ,
    65, 282
Praise Ye Jehovah, 76
Praise Ye the Triune God!, 79
Precious Lord, Take My Hand, 44
Reformation Hymn, 7, 47, 282
Rejoice in the Lord, 147
Rejoice, the Lord is King, 65
Relentless Love, 282
Rock of Ages, 46
Salvation's Cup, 282
Satisfied, 26–27, 181
See the Christ, 282
See What a Morning [Resurrection
    Hymn], 64
Shout Out for Joy, 132
Speak, O Lord, 46
Spirit of God, Descend upon My
    Heart, 76
Spirit of the Living God, 76
Soldiers of Christ, Arise, 47
Still, My Soul, Be Still, 147
Stricken, Smitten, and Afflicted, 63
Take My Life, and Let It Be
    Consecrated, 183
Thank You Jesus for the Blood, 47
The Birth of Christ, 282
The Blood of Jesus Speaks for Me,
    64, 183
The Comforter Has Come, 76

The Church's One Foundation, 47
The Doxology, 75, 79, 207
The Father Looks on Me, 76, 282
The Gospel Song, 47
The Just Shall Live by Faith, 282
The Law of the Lord Is Perfect, 133
The Lord's Army, 53
The Lord Is My Salvation, 80
The Love of Christ, 63, 283
The Power of the Cross, 35–36, 63,
    163, 288
The Resurrection of Christ, 283
The Sands of Time Are Sinking, 183
The Shepherd of My Soul, 283
The Solid Rock, 47
The Spirit of Christ, 283
The Steps of a Good Man, 133
There Is a Higher Throne, 47, 65
There Is a Redeemer, 63, 79
This Is My Father's World, 75
This Is the Day, 147
This Poor Man Cried, 133
Thou Whose Almighty Word, 47
Thy Word, 46, 133
To Live or Die, 183, 283
Turn Your Eyes, 63
Turn Your Eyes Upon Jesus, 147, 182
Under His Wings, 178, 182
Unto You I Lift My Soul [Psalm
    25], 283
Waves of Praise, 283
We Are Heirs of God Almighty,
    79, 182
We Believe, 78, 283
We Remember, 283
We Rest on Thee, 147, 184
We Will Follow, 284
When I Survey the Wondrous Cross,
    63, 163, 165, 171, 213
Wonderful Grace of Jesus, 110
Wonderful, Merciful Savior, 214

Yet Not I But through Christ in Me,
    64, 147, 182, 289
You Are Always Good, 7, 147, 284
You Are Precious, 284
You Are the Lord, 80
You Who Were Rich Beyond All
    Splendor, 62
Your Beauty Fills Our Eyes, 284
Zacchaeus, 53

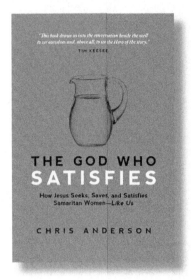

"In this little book, a gifted poet transitions to prose. I have known Chris Anderson for over two decades, first as a student and then as a fellow laborer in the work of the Kingdom. This book's focus on the Samaritan woman is full of Christ and the glorious gospel of grace. Written in an easy-to-read, popular style full of real-life illustrations, the book effectively links helpful background facts and precisely-stated theological truths to experiential application. It is a book that can be used for evangelism as well as for warming the believer's heart to renewed gratitude for what Christ has abundantly supplied."

—**Michael P. V. Barrett**, dean and professor at Puritan Reformed Theological Seminary and author of *Complete in Him*

"Here is a book I would love to put into the hands of young adults in my church so that they see that men and women who have left their mark on the mission field were like us in every way, except in their devotion to the God who called them. We need to get rid of our lackluster Christianity in order to fulfill our individual callings, too. This book might be a brief 31-day journey, but M. R. Conrad has packed it with spiritual dynamite. Read it prayerfully. It might change your life—forever!"

—**Conrad Mbewe**, pastor of Kabwata Baptist Church and Founding Chancellor of the African Christian University in Lusaka, Zambia

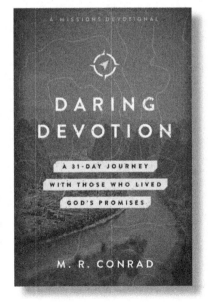

Gospel Meditations for Fathers

"This collection of thirty-one meditations is a must-read for any man striving to fulfill his God-given role as a father. Since each reading is both biblical and practical, it equips the reader to lead family members to greater love to Christ and to God's Word. As parents to four and grandparents to fifteen, Patricia and I recommend this as a fresh resource."

—John MacArthur

Gospel Meditations for Mothers

"In the midst of busy days and sleepless nights, moms need the encouragement that only the gospel can give. *Gospel Meditations for Mothers* offers powerful biblical truth and guidance that reminds moms of the importance of their labors and cheers them on in their daily tasks. Whether you're parenting a toddler or a teen, these gospel-focused reflections will minister to your heart as you care for your children."

—Melissa Kruger

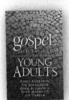

Gospel Meditations for Young Adults

"*Gospel Meditations for Young Adults* is a breath of fresh air for young Christians and for all of us who are raising, discipling, mentoring, or just concerned about them and their spiritual growth and wellbeing. The devotionals are biblical, pastoral, succinct, readable, relevant, and relatable. More importantly, the focus is cross-centered and theological without being forced or trite. This would be a great tool to use in parenting, personal discipleship, group study, or even pastoral counseling."

—Voddie Baucham

Gospel Meditations for Prayer

"Brief and biblical, these meditations are full of sharp edges. They lead us to pray as cross-bearing disciples of Christ. Yet Anderson, Tyrpak, and Trueman comfort us with Christ's perfect grace for fallen people. So *Gospel Meditations for Prayer* is an encouraging book, but one designed to stretch you."

—Joel Beeke

Gospel Meditations for Christmas

"Too often Christmas speeds past us in a blur of busyness and stress, with only the briefest time and the shallowest thoughts given to the Christ that's meant to be at the heart of it all. Give yourself a Christmas to remember by using this profound devotional to pause, ponder, and praise our wonderful Savior."

—David Murray

Gospel Meditations on the Reformation

"Theologically rich, thoughtful, and historically rooted devotionals are a rare treat. This volume, which unfolds the theological commitments and pastoral heart of the Reformers, is a unique and enormously helpful devotional."

—R. Albert Mohler, Jr.

Gospel Meditations for Women

"Wrestling with guilt and frustration, far too many Christian women are living below the privileges of their spiritual inheritance. The solution is not found in any strengthened resolve of duty, but rather in having souls settled in the blessed liberty of Christ through the sweet enjoyment of the gospel. A union of sound doctrine and practical teaching, Gospel Meditations for Women beautifully highlights those unbinding messages of grace that so powerfully ignite joyful passion for Christ and holy living. What an invaluable resource!"

—Holly Stratton

Gospel Meditations for the Church

"We have come to expect meaty, edifying, superbly written devotional entries from Chris Anderson and his team. Here are thirty-one more, and they don't disappoint."

—Phil Johnson

Gospel Meditations for Missions

"Can we do missions without meditating on the gospel? Of course not. Yet, how many well-meaning, mission-minded saints go off into the harvest having failed to prepare their own hearts with due consideration of the good news? Too many I fear. *Gospel Meditations for Missions* helps us slow down to consider what is of first importance that we might hold this treasure more fully in our clay hearts."

—Thabiti Anyabwile

Gospel Meditations for the Hurting

"These meditations are Word-centered prescriptions that blow away the meaningless Christian platitudes often used to mask unanswerable pain. Until that day when Christ Himself wipes away all tears from our eyes, the Scriptures provide strength, help, and hope in this broken world. Let this book guide you to Christ, the only sure and lasting refuge."

—Tim Keesee

Gospel Meditations for Men

"Chris and Joe have co-authored a delightful and helpful little book of daily meditations. This is not one of those trendy Reformed 'the Bible says all men have to act like John Wayne or cavemen with better table manners' kind of productions. Many of the devotions are simply gospel expositions, and those which have a male-specific orientation are on topics like lust, where male psychology is important."

—Carl Trueman

Gospel Meditations on Creation

"Grounded in the truth of Scripture, aimed at the heart, and applied to life, these thirty-one reflections will be sure to strengthen your faith. Pithy, yet profound; brief, yet biblical; these daily insights will draw you closer to Him Who created all things for His own glory."

—Steve Lawson

Made in the USA
Monee, IL
21 May 2022

96854186R00197